Stefan Riedener
Uncertain Values

Ideen & Argumente

Edited by
Wilfried Hinsch and Thomas Schmidt

Stefan Riedener

Uncertain Values

An Axiomatic Approach to Axiological Uncertainty

DE GRUYTER

The open access publication of this book has been published with the support of the Swiss National Science Foundation.

ISBN 978-3-11-127112-5
e-ISBN (PDF) 978-3-11-073619-9
e-ISBN (EPUB) 978-3-11-073622-9
ISSN 1862-1147
DOI https://doi.org/10.1515/9783110736199

Library of Congress Control Number: 2021940410

Bibliographic information published by the Deutsche Nationalbibliothek
The Deutsche Nationalbibliothek lists this publication in the Deutsche Nationalbibliografie; detailed bibliographic data are available on the Internet at http://dnb.dnb.de.

© 2023 Stefan Riedener, published by Walter de Gruyter GmbH, Berlin/Boston. The book is published open access at www.degruyter.com.
This volume is text- and page-identical with the hardback published in 2021.
Cover image: Martin Zech, Bremen
Cover concept: +malsy, Willich
Typesetting: VTeX UAB, Lithuania
Printing and binding: CPI books GmbH, Leck

www.degruyter.com

Meinen Eltern
und meinem Bruder

Philosophy is, today, not a pastime. It is inescapable, because we no longer believe to know what is good. ... [We] are unable to sneak out of the moral point of view, yet there is nobody who tells us what it is.

Ernst Tugendhat, in: Steve Pyke, *Philosophers.*

Acknowledgments

This book is based on my DPhil thesis, which I submitted to the University of Oxford in 2015. Writing my thesis, and this book, would have been impossible without the help I've received. Brian Hedden, Robyn Kath, Lukas Naegeli, Bastian Stern, Christian Tarsney, Teruji Thomas, Aron Vallinder and Silvan Wittwer have generously read parts of the book. They've provided countless invaluable comments on sometimes painfully sketchy drafts. Two anonymous reviewers for De Gruyter have provided extremely thorough and astute comments on the penultimate version of my manuscript, and helped give it its final shape. Nikola Ciganović, Nick Davies, Edi Karni, Robert Nau and David Schwartz have kindly helped me with the formal aspects of my arguments. Samuel Hughes, William Jefferson, Felix Koch, Harvey Lederman, Adam Lovett and Trevor Teitel have been extremely helpful partners in conversation. I'm grateful to them all. I'm also grateful to the audiences at the Ujué Workshop on Topics of Practical Philosophy, the Global Priorities Institute Seminar and the ISUS 2018 Karlsruhe. And I thank the audience at the Oxford DPhil Seminar, and Ralf Bader in particular, for their sharp comments. The Global Priorities Institute has kindly hosted me while I was working on this material, and provided a singularly inspiring environment. The Clarendon Fund and the Swiss Study Foundation have both provided very generous financial support.

I thank Thomas Schmidt and Wilfried Hinsch for including my book in their series. I also thank Marcus Böhm and Mara Weber from De Gruyter for their excellent support in bringing my manuscript to publication. Parts of Chapter 4 are reproduced with permission by Cambridge University Press, from *Utilitas*, 'Constructivism about intertheoretic comparisons', Riedener, S., 31(3):277–290 (2019). Parts of Chapters 1, 2 and 5 are reproduced with permission by Springer, from *Philosophical Studies*, 'An axiomatic approach to axiological uncertainty', Riedener, S., 177(2):483–504 (2020). The open access publication of this book was generously supported by the Swiss National Science Foundation.

I owe a special debt of gratitude to William MacAskill, who introduced me to the topic of this book. Will's characteristic enthusiasm kindled the curiosity I needed to embark on this project. And his questions and objections along the way were indispensable in helping me see what I think. Another special debt of gratitude I owe to my examiners, Christian List and Frank Arntzenius, who made my viva be one of the most interesting philosophical conversations I've ever had.

It's difficult to say how grateful I am to my DPhil supervisors John Broome and Hilary Greaves. They've offered more encouragement and philosophical insights than I could have hoped for. The impact of John's ideas has been profound. But he's taught me much more than ideas. Beyond its rigour and clarity and breathtaking scope, I've always found his writing strangely moving. It's so totally sincere, and somehow animated with a rare kindness and humanity. With all of these qualities, philosophical and otherwise, he has supported me. Hilary has supervised me during the last period of my DPhil. Her brilliant ability at spotting difficulties with my thoughts or ways to take them further sometimes brought me to the point of desperation. But her kind trust and keen philosophical guidance always brought me back. I'll always be very deeply grateful to both.

I thank my friends in Zurich and Oxford for being there for me even after all my absences. The absences during my DPhil have been sadly frequent and long for me. I hope they know how much they've been present during all the days at lonely desks.

I thank my wife, Anna Koim. I'm at home with you, with your warmth and joy. And with the serene autonomy of your questions and the courage of your answers you keep me moving and awake. You make my life grow; you fill it and yet you make it light. How wonderful to have been with you in these years, and to still have everything awaiting us—unheard music and quiet feasts, so many mornings and winters and summers, and the growth of the lights of our lives.

Finally, for that invaluable sense of being unconditionally supported, on which everything ultimately grounds, I thank my parents Sabine Furthmann and Hanspeter Riedener and my brother Lukas.

Contents

1 The problem of axiological uncertainty

1.1 Introduction

We're uncertain about most things. And yet we constantly have to act. So uncertainty is the condition of almost any decision we make. Part of this uncertainty concerns purely descriptive questions. When ordering dinner at a restaurant we're uncertain what precisely we'll get. In starting a relationship we're not certain how it will end. And in fighting climate change we're uncertain about the effects of different measures. This raises the question about what you ought to do if you're uncertain about purely descriptive facts. But often, we're also uncertain about fundamental normative or evaluative questions. In response to climate change, say, we may be uncertain about whether we morally ought to be impartial in weighing different interests, or ought to give more weight to current than to future generations, to acquaintances than to strangers, or to human beings than to non-human animals. And this may not just be because we're uncertain about relevant empirical questions, such as what future generations, strangers or non-human animals desire. It might be, at least partly, because we're uncertain about the fundamental moral principles governing such decisions. So this raises the question about what you ought to do if you're uncertain about fundamental normative or evaluative facts.

   This book is about this latter kind of uncertainty. More precisely, it's about a specific kind of such uncertainty: axiological uncertainty—i. e., uncertainty about fundamental axiological facts, or fundamental facts about moral value. My core question is how you ought to evaluate your options if you're uncertain about which axiology is true. Plausibly, there are fundamental moral facts beyond those of axiology—such as deontic facts about what you *ought* to do. And plausibly, there are fundamental normative or evaluative facts beyond those of morality—such as facts of prudence, rationality or aesthetics. So the question about how you ought to evaluate your options if you're axiologically uncertain is narrower than the general question about what you ought to do if you're uncertain about any fundamental normative or evaluative facts. For reasons that will emerge, this narrower question is simpler. And yet much can be learnt from it about the general problem too. So I'll focus on axiological uncertainty only.[1]

---

1 Most of the relevant literature focuses on the general problems of moral or normative uncertainty. For work on uncertainty concerning deontological morality specifically, see e. g. Tarsney (2018b); for work on uncertainty about the norms of decision theory, see e. g. MacAskill (2016b).

The concept of 'm-value'

Let me clarify my question. In one sense, there's a trivial answer to how you ought to evaluate your options if you're axiologically uncertain. You ought to do so in accordance with the axiology that is *true*. But that's not the answer I'm concerned with. To see that there might be a different one, consider

Purely descriptive uncertainty: Martha is suffering from a mild headache. Raphael has a pill he could give her, but he's uncertain about whether it's a pain reliever or a lethal form of poison. Actually, the pill is a pain reliever.

Is it better for Raphael to give his pill to Martha, or better not to? There's an extensive debate about such cases, mostly concerning the concept of 'ought': about whether there are two distinct senses of 'ought' ('subjective' and 'objective') or just a single one, about which one it would be, or which of the two is more basic or important.[2] I won't go into the details of this debate. It seems undeniable that *something* has to be said, and can be said, in favour of both giving and not giving the pill. On the one hand, we can evaluate Raphael's options on the basis of their actual outcomes, without taking his uncertainty into account. We'll then say giving the pill is better. After all, Raphael will thereby relieve Martha's pain, and nothing else will happen. On the other hand, we can evaluate his options on the basis of the prospects they represent, taking his uncertainty into account. We'll then say not giving the pill is better. After all, Raphael will otherwise risk Martha's death for the sake of a headache. We may be interested in either of these judgments, and both uses of 'good' seem familiar. I'll remain neutral about which of them is more basic or important, or more in line with our common concept of goodness.

A parallel example can be given about axiological uncertainty:

Axiological uncertainty: Raphael has a pill, with which he can either relieve Martha of a mild headache or a donkey, Baldwin, of a much greater pain. He's uncertain between a speciesist and a non-speciesist axiology. According to the speciesist view it would be better to benefit Martha, and according to the non-speciesist view it would be better to benefit Baldwin. Actually, the speciesist view is right.

Here too, we can evaluate Raphael's options on the basis of their actual value, without taking his uncertainty into account. We'll then say it's better for him

---

2 See e. g. Hudson (1989), Jackson (1991), Howard-Synder (1997), Wiland (2005), Feldman (2006), Zimmerman (2008), Bykvist (2009b), Broome (2013, ch. 3) or Kolodny and MacFarlane (ms), among many others.

to benefit Martha. That's what (we're assuming) the true axiology says. However, we can again evaluate Raphael's options on the basis of the prospects they represent—now taking his axiological uncertainty into account. And if we do that, it's an open question which act is better, under his state of uncertainty. By benefiting Martha he risks effecting something comparatively bad. So intuitively, perhaps it's better for him to benefit Baldwin. Judgments of this kind may be less familiar from our ordinary practice, but they're no less distinct than in the purely descriptive case.

I'm concerned with judgments of this latter kind. To distinguish them conceptually, I'll use the term '*meta-value*', or '*m-value*' (or 'm-goodness'), to denote the goodness we refer to by taking into account both your descriptive *and* your axiological uncertainty. I'll use the simple term 'value' (or 'goodness') to denote the goodness we refer to by taking into account your purely descriptive, but not your axiological uncertainty. In the second example, I'll thus say it's better to benefit Martha, but (so far) an open question which of the two options is m-better for Raphael. And that's my core question: which of your options are m-better than which, if you're uncertain about which are better than which? This question has no trivial answer.

The importance of the phenomenon

It's worth reflecting briefly on how widespread axiological uncertainty is, how many of our decisions it affects, and how pressingly it does. Take questions of population ethics. Is a sufficiently large population of people with lives barely worth living better than a smaller population of people living wonderful lives? More basically, is it good to bring people into existence? And are the values of populations with different numbers of people even comparable? Philosophers have wildly contrasting views on these matters, and good arguments on all sides.[3] We shouldn't be certain of any answers. Yet these questions are crucial for very many decisions affecting the number and identity of future people. Those include the largest decisions of humanity—about global poverty, climate change, or (other)

---

3 See e. g. Huemer (2008) for an affirmative answer to the first question, Temkin (2012) or Parfit (1984) for a negative one; Broome (2004, ch. 10) for objections to the intuition that bringing people into existence isn't positively good; Broome (2004, ch. 12) for the claim that there's only some vagueness in the comparisons, Bader (forthcoming) for an argument to the effect that such populations are thoroughly incomparable, and Parfit (ms) for a middle ground. More generally, see e. g. Arrhenius (forthcoming) for impossibility theorems, showing that a number of intuitively plausible principles of population ethics are incompatible.

catastrophic risks like pandemics, artificial intelligence or nuclear wars. They include national policies of public health, security or migration. And they include very personal decisions—such as whether we use our resources to save other people's lives, thereby perhaps enabling them to have long chains of offsprings.[4] In all of these cases, we must make choices under axiological uncertainty. And we must do so now. We can't wait until we're axiologically certain. Or more precisely, even to 'wait' and figure out answers would be a decision, and just raise the question whether *that* would be m-best.[5] So, for very many decisions in the areas just mentioned, it seems vital that we reflect on how to evaluate options under axiological uncertainty.

But population ethics is just one example. Take the theory of welfare. Would it be good for us to experience pleasure artificially stimulated in our brains, have wonderful lives simulated in experience machines, or undergo enhancements through drugs or genetic engineering? Consider discounting. Does the wellbeing of future beings have the same value as that of currently existing ones, from our perspective, or should we discount wellbeing over time? Take environmental axiology. Does biodiversity, the intactness of ecosystems, or the flourishing of plants have value? Consider questions of equality. Is it intrinsically bad if people are unequally well off, through no fault of their own? Or consider animal welfare. Is it bad that non-human animals suffer in the wild, are being eaten by predators or die from starvation? Opinions on these matters diverge, each position has good arguments in its favour,[6] and we can't be certain about them. Yet all of these questions are crucial for momentous decisions we face as humanity and individuals. And there's no way of postponing any decisions until we're certain about them.

Examples can be multiplied with ease. Decision-making under axiological uncertainty is unavoidably widespread. So it seems vital to have a theory of which options are m-better than which in light of such uncertainty.[7]

---

4 For the practical importance of population ethics, see particularly Broome (2004, ch. 1) or Beckstead (2013, ch. 1).

5 See MacAskill (2014, ch. 6) for a discussion of this question; also MacAskill et al. (2020a, ch. 9).

6 See e. g. Nozick (1974, 42 ff.) for a critical stance on pleasure simulations and the experience machine, Ng (1997, 1849 ff.) or Crisp (2006) for a positive one; Broome (2004, ch. 4) for arguments against discounting, and Beckstead (2013) or Bostrom (2003) for the radical implications of this; McShane (2017) for arguments and challenges for the idea that biodiversity has intrinsic value, Callicott (1989) for the view that ecosystems, and Taylor (1986) for the view that plants intrinsically deserve moral consideration; Cohen (1989) for a view on which equality matters, Parfit (1997) for a challenge; McMahan (2010) for the view that wild animal suffering matters.

7 For a further defence of this claim, see e. g. MacAskill et al. (2020a, ch. 1).

1.2 This book

Let me outline what I'll do in this book. My goal is to defend a specific theory of axiological uncertainty—i. e., *Expected Value Maximisation*, or *EVM*. According to EVM, an option is m-better than another if and only if it has the greater expected value—where the expected value of an option is a weighted sum of the values it's assigned by the axiologies, with weights representing the probabilities of these axiologies.

EVM extends the standard theory of decision-making under purely descriptive uncertainty to uncertainty about axiologies. So it's a promising view. But it raises two fundamental questions. The first is the *question of meaning*. It's the question about what EVM should even mean—or what it would *be* for an option to have a higher expected value than another. That's anything but clear. EVM features a number of concepts that have no use in ordinary language and are in need of explanation. One such concept is the quantitative notion of value. Whether an option has a higher expected value than another depends not just on ordinal intratheoretic value comparisons like

(A) according to axiology T_i, outcome x is better than outcome y.

It depends on *cardinal intratheoretic value comparisons*, or facts of the form

(B) according to axiology T_i, the value-difference between outcomes x and y is n times as great as the value-difference between outcomes z and t.

To even understand EVM, we need to know what it is for such facts to hold. But unless more is said, we arguably don't. Suppose you claim that according to your favourite axiology, saving Edward's life is 3.7 times as good as saving Charlotte's—or that the value-difference between the status quo and Edward's death is 3.7 times as great as that between the status quo and Charlotte's death. Unless you explain what you mean by this, we don't understand your assertion. We might think you chose a swaggering way of expressing that according to your axiology, saving Edward is *considerably* better. But we'd think the same if your number was four, or 5.8. What is it for this factor to be 3.7? This isn't to say you can't explain what you mean. You may mean that saving ten people whose lives are exactly like Edward's would be equally good as saving thirty-seven whose lives are exactly like Charlotte's. And this may count as a proper explanation. The point is, you have to give some such explanation, or else your statement remains unclear.

But such intratheoretic comparisons are only one kind of fact that EVM presupposes, and that require explanation. Another, and even more problematic kind are facts about how value-differences compare *across* axiologies. And again, whether an option has a higher expected value than another depends not just on comparisons like

(C) the value-difference between outcomes x and y, according to axiology T_i, is greater than the value-difference between outcomes z and t, according to axiology T_j.

It depends on *cardinal intertheoretic value comparisons*, or facts of the form

(D) the value-difference between outcomes x and y, according to axiology T_i, is n times as great as the value-difference between outcomes z and t, according to axiology T_j.

What it is for such comparisons to hold across axiologies is even less clear. Indeed, many people are sceptical that such comparisons *can* be meaningful. Edward Gracely says that intertheoretic comparisons are 'essentially meaningless' (1996, 330). James Hudson holds that there's generally no 'common measure' between different axiologies and that they therefore '*must* be incomparable' (1989, 224; emphasis added). John Broome similarly contends that for most axiologies 'we cannot take a sensible average' between their different units of value (2012, 185). And many others are similarly sceptic.[8]

And there's a third problematic kind of fact. Whether an option has a higher expected value than another depends not just on qualitative probability facts like

(E) axiology T_i is very plausible.

It depends on *quantitative probability facts*, or facts of the form

(F) the probability of axiology T_i is p_i,

for some $p_i \in [0, 1]$. To understand EVM, we need to know what it is for such a fact to hold. And again, such statements have no use in ordinary language, and are in need of explanation. We understand what you mean in saying the speciesist axiology is implausible. But unless you say more, we don't understand what you mean in claiming it has a probability of 0.05.

So it's anything but clear what it is for an option to have a higher expected value than another. But there's a second question. Even assuming we understand EVM, there's still the *question of truth*. It's the question about whether EVM is indeed the correct theory of m-value. For instance, even if we know what it would be for intertheoretic comparisons to hold, there's a question about whether any

---

8 See e. g. Gustafsson and Torpman (2014), Nissan-Rozen (2015) or Hedden (2016).

of them do indeed hold. Perhaps as a matter of fact no intertheoretic comparison is true. So perhaps under axiological uncertainty, you simply ought to evaluate your options in accordance with the axiology that has the highest probability, as the 'My Favourite Theory'-approach suggests.[9] Or perhaps intertheoretic comparisons hold, but you ought to adopt some less formal meta-deontological or meta-virtue-ethical principles under uncertainty.[10] Or perhaps you ought to be risk-averse about moral value. There are plenty of reasonable alternative views.[11] To endorse EVM, we need an argument to deny them—and preferably a systematic argument that goes beyond brute intuitions about cases.

In this book, I'll adopt an axiomatic approach from standard decision theory to answer the question of meaning and the question of truth about EVM. I'll introduce representation theorems for axiological uncertainty. In decision theory, representation theorems were devised for your preferences. They show that if your preferences satisfy certain axioms, they have an expected utility representation in terms of relevantly unique probability and utility functions. These theorems are conditional and purely mathematical results, implying the existence of certain functions under certain conditions. But they become philosophically significant if two assumptions are added. The first is a conceptual one: that *if* your preferences have an expected utility representation in terms of relevantly unique probability and utility functions, these functions can be taken to represent your credences and values—i. e., you can be interpreted as maximising the expectation of your values relative to your degrees of belief, rather than simply some mathematical measure. The second assumption is a normative one: that your preferences are normatively appropriate in some sense *only if* (or indeed if and only if) they satisfy these axioms. Together with these two assumptions, the formal theorems imply that your preferences are normatively appropriate only if (or if and only if) you maximise the expectation of your values, relative to your credences.[12] And this is a philosophically significant claim.

---

9 See e. g. Gracely (1996) or Gustafsson and Torpman (2014).

10 See e. g. Guerrero (2007) or Williams (2011).

11 For still other views, see e. g. Barry and Tomlin (2016), or (concerning merely ordinal and non-comparable theories) MacAskill (2016a), Tarsney (2019a) or MacAskill et al. (2020a). For a helpful recent survey of the debate, see e. g. Bykvist (2017); also MacAskill et al. (2020a).

12 The biconditional will be true if the second additional assumption is put in terms of a biconditional. That's because the result of the representation theorems, and the first additional assumption, could also be stated as biconditionals: if your preferences have an expected utility representation, they also satisfy the axioms; and if you maximise the expectation of your values relative to your degrees of belief, then your preferences also have an expected utility representation. The three claims, stated as biconditionals, imply that your preferences are normatively appropriate if and only if you maximise the expectation of your values, relative to your credences. Since the two

I'll devise a similar argument for EVM in the context of axiological uncertainty. But instead of your preferences, our theorems will concern the facts about which options are m-better than which, relative to your state of uncertainty. So as I'll understand it, a pertinent representation theorem in our context shows that *if* these m-value facts satisfy certain axioms, they have an expected utility representation in terms of relevantly unique probability and utility functions. I'll provide such theorems, and add two similar assumptions. I'll add the conceptual assumption that *if* the m-value facts have such a representation, the relevant functions can be taken to represent the probabilities and value functions of our axiologies. And I'll add the normative or meta-axiological assumption that (at least for an interestingly large set of underlying axiologies) the m-value facts do indeed satisfy these axioms. Given these two assumptions (and at least for the axiologies under consideration), the theorems imply EVM.

In other words, I'll argue that these representation theorems ground compelling answers to our two questions. First and foremost, they afford us a clear explication of what EVM means. In light of them, we can understand cardinal intertheoretic comparisons, top-down, in terms of m-value facts. For axiologies to compare in a certain way would just be for some such facts to hold. And something equivalent is true for cardinal intratheoretic comparisons and quantitative probability facts. Moreover, once we explicate comparisons and probabilities in this manner, the theorems provide a systematic argument to the effect that EVM is true. If the m-value facts satisfy the relevant conditions, EVM simply follows. Every other view—My Favourite Theory, or meta-deontological principles, or forms of risk-aversion—must be false. So the axiomatic approach can compellingly explicate and vindicate EVM. Or at any rate, it can do so for an interestingly large set of underlying axiologies. Our axioms aren't trivial. There are certain axiologies for which they don't hold. And we arguably can't be certain that these axiologies are false. So the axiomatic approach can't ground EVM as a *fully* general theory of axiological uncertainty. It can ground EVM, at most, as a theory about a certain range of axiologies. But I'll suggest that this range is interestingly large, and that our result thus remains highly significant.

This extension of standard decision theory to the case of axiological uncertainty raises a number of new issues. First, the theorems raise novel formal questions. Axiological uncertainty is structurally different from purely descriptive uncertainty, as commonly understood. Under axiological uncertainty, the propositions you're uncertain about don't determine the outcomes your choices result in.

---

conditionals just mentioned are rather trivial, for simplicity, I'll henceforth state the argument in the form in which I've stated it in the main text.

They determine the utilities or values of these outcomes. This adds complexity. In particular, it raises questions about how to separate probabilities and values—or cases where an axiology has a low probability but an inflated value function from cases where it has a high probability but a deflated value function. Also, in decision theory the standard assumption is that there are only coherence constraints on your preferences, such as the von Neumann-Morgenstern axioms. Under axiological uncertainty, there are arguably further constraints on the m-value facts, on how they relate to the underlying axiologies. So this raises a question about what these constraints plausibly are. All of this requires novel technical machinery. Second, the two extra assumptions raise novel philosophical questions. The meta-axiological assumption raises the question whether the axioms are plausible constraints on m-value—e. g., in light of the problem of intertheoretic comparisons—and on the underlying axiologies, or on moral theories generally. And the conceptual assumption raises the question whether we can interpret the relevant functions as denoting actual axiological probabilities and values. So if I'm right, the results not only compellingly ground a theory of axiological uncertainty, but also provide a cogent substantive extension of decision theory.

In short, EVM raises the questions of meaning and truth. Both require substantive arguments to be resolved. Representation theorems promise to ground such arguments. But it requires novel technical and philosophical work to provide and apply such theorems. This work is the object of this book. Let me spell out in more detail how it will proceed. After this introductory chapter, the book will feature five main chapters, plus an appendix. In the remainder of the present chapter, I'll answer objections against the importance of m-value, and thus clarify why our inquiry is important. In Chapter 2, I'll state the most basic theorem of this book, and the assumptions needed to turn this into a vindication of EVM. This will introduce the argument of the axiomatic approach in its simplest form. In Chapter 3, I'll discuss whether this argument is convincing. I highlight three potential problems for it, specific to the context of axiological uncertainty: the problem of intertheoretic comparisons, the meaning of axiological probabilities, and the existence of incommensurabilities in value.

The remaining three chapters address these problems in turn. In Chapter 4, I'll discuss the problem of intertheoretic comparisons. I argue that existing proposals of such comparisons are unsatisfactory. I provide an argument for why at least some such comparisons must nonetheless hold. And I then introduce a constructivist explanation of why they do, and suggest this account can ground our overall argument. In Chapter 5, I'll focus on the notion of a probability distribution over axiologies. I introduce a more complex representation theorem, which provides a formal separation of credences and values. I then argue against various strands of recent scepticism about such theorems, and suggest they provide the best account of probabilities, at least in our context. This has important implications for the normative structure of EVM. In Chapter 6, I'll relax the least plausible substantive condition of our theorem—the Completeness axiom. I state a representation theorem without this axiom, which allows our theory to cover axiologies that feature intra- or intertheoretic incommensurabilities, and grounds the most comprehensive argument of the book. I end the chapter with a discussion of whether the approach can be extended beyond axiological to moral uncertainty generally, and raise concerns about this extension.

As this indicates, there's a range of issues related to axiological uncertainty that I won't address in this book. Let me flag three of them, just to set them aside. First, I won't address any questions of applied axiological uncertainty: the implications of EVM for population ethics, future discounting, the welfare of non-human animals, or whatever. My discussion remains purely abstract and general.[13] Second, I won't say much more about the normative import of m-value. In particular, I won't discuss the existence of a form of *overall-*(meta-)goodness. Suppose your best option is a, and your m-best option is b. And suppose you're also uncertain about theories of axiological uncertainty, and that according to the true theory of uncertainty about m-value, your m^2-best option (as we might call it) is c. There's a question about whether some option is overall-best, besides being best, m-best, or m^2-best. I think there's no such form of goodness. But I won't enter this debate here.[14] Relatedly, I won't discuss the deontic status of your m-best option. There's a question about whether there are any deontic meta-norms, and if there are, about what they say, and whether they're norms of morality, rationality, or some other source of requirements. I think there's at least a requirement of rationality to the effect that you ought, if one of your options is m-best, *ceteris paribus* choose it.[15] But nothing hinges on this here.[16] I'll just present a theory of m-value. Third, I'll largely set aside metaethical issues underlying the problem of normative uncertainty. My framework presupposes some notion of axiological 'truth', and a notion of an agent's 'credences' in an axiology. There's a question about whether the problem arises, or can be made sense of, within non-cognitivist or

---

13 For implications of normative uncertainty for practical ethics, see e. g. Pfeiffer (1985), Oddie (1994), Guerrero (2007), Moller (2011), Williams (2011), Broome (2012, 183 ff.), Bykvist (2013), Greaves and Ord (2017), Barry and Tomlin (2019), MacAskill (2019), Tarsney (2019b), Koplin and Wilkinson (2019) or MacAskill et al. (2020a, ch. 8).

14 See Sepielli (2013b, 13 ff.) for a defence of a related view.

15 In other words, I think there's a wide-scope requirement of rationality. See e. g. Broome (2013, ch. 7) for the distinction between 'wide-' and 'narrow-scope' requirements.

16 For a helpful survey and discussion of such questions, see Bykvist (2017).

anti-realist views. Some people think non-cognitivists cannot account for the phenomenon of normative uncertainty;[17] others think they can.[18] But in any case, the ability to make sense of normative or evaluative uncertainty is generally treated as a desideratum on metaethical views. If such a view cannot account for such uncertainty, that's standardly seen as a problem for this view, rather than for the project of devising a theory of normative or evaluative uncertainty.[19] I think this is a plausible view of the dialectic. So I'll set general metaethical questions aside.[20]

1.3 Objections

One might think that even if we're uncertain about many axiological questions relevant to many of our decisions, we don't need a theory of m-value. So before I defend such a theory, let me address the three most prominent objections to the importance of that enterprise. This will clarify why it matters.

Fetishism

Some people have argued that we don't need a theory of m-value (or of moral uncertainty more generally) because concern with m-value is *fetishistic*. Suppose you have a choice between a vegan meal and a steak, and are uncertain between a speciesist and a non-speciesist axiology. You find it more plausible that the speciesist view is right, and that it's better to choose the steak. However, you believe that *if* the non-speciesist view is right, killing non-human animals is terrible, and that it's thus m-better to turn vegan. So you do that, because you think it is m-better. Then your vegan diet doesn't spring from a genuine concern for non-human animals, it seems. Rather, you seem to care about m-value *as such*—about whatever turns out to be m-valuable, simply because it's m-valuable. And as Michael Smith pointed out in a similar context, that might seem inappropriate:

---

17 See e. g. Smith (2002), Bykvist and Olson (2009), Bykvist and Olson (2012), Bykvist and Olson (2017) or Björkholm et al. (forthcoming).
18 See e. g. Sepielli (2012), Eriksson and Francén Olinder (2016), Beddor (2020) or Ridge (2020).
19 See e. g. Smith (2002).
20 I'll defend constructivism about intertheoretic comparisons in Chapter 4. But most of my arguments in the other chapters don't hinge on this. And constructivism about intertheoretic comparisons doesn't imply constructivism about axiology or morality more generally. So I'm not committed to any general metaethical view.

Good people care non-derivatively about honesty, the weal and woe of their children and friends, the well-being of their fellows, people getting what they deserve, justice, equality, and the like, not just one thing: doing what they believe to be right, where this is read *de dicto* and not *de re*. Indeed, commonsense tells us that being so motivated is a fetish or moral vice. (1994, 75)

Similar considerations arise for m-value. Concern with m-value might seem inappropriately fetishistic. Brian Weatherson, among others, concluded for this reason (concerning the case just described) that 'it would be perverse for [you] to turn down the steak', or more generally, that 'a mere probability that meat eating is immoral should not change one's actions, or one's evaluations of meat eaters' (2014, 2).[21]

It's not entirely clear what the inappropriateness of being motivated by m-value should consist in. I see three interpretations of this fetishism-worry. On the first interpretation, the inappropriateness of being motivated by m-value is a matter of first-order value. It's *better* to help non-human animals, say, out of unmediated concern with their wellbeing rather than out of a belief that it's m-best. According to the true axiology, concern with m-value is comparatively bad. If this is the idea, I don't deny it. It's a first-order axiological claim, and nothing I say contradicts it. In fact, it can be accommodated in the theory I outline. If an action can be done with different motives, we can treat these motives as different options, on a par with doing something altogether different. So if being motivated by m-value is bad, EVM will imply it's comparatively m-bad. This is perfectly consistent. What I'll defend is a criterion of m-betterness, not a decision procedure, or an account of how to make decisions in practice.[22] So it may well be comparatively m-bad to consciously act on considerations of m-value. Now of course, if it's plausible that *de dicto* concern with m-value is terrible, EVM might become self-effacing.[23] It might imply we should never consciously act on it, or indeed should forget it altogether in practice. And although that would still be consistent, it might raise the question why we should spend much time thinking about it. But it doesn't seem plausible that such concern with m-value is *so* bad as to dominate all other possible badness. And in any case, to find out whether it does, or how it weighs against other forms of disvalue under uncertainty, we need a theory of m-value. So if the inappropriateness is understood as a first-order claim about value, it doesn't establish that we don't need a theory of axiological uncertainty.

---

21 The fetishism objection is also raised in Hedden (2016).

22 For the classic distinction between a criterion of rightness and a decision procedure in utilitarianism, see e. g. Bales (1971), Mill (1861, ch. 2, par.19) or Sidgwick (1907, 413).

23 For the notion and problem of 'self-effacingness', see Parfit (1984, ch. 1).

On a second interpretation, this inappropriateness takes a different form. In the above quote, Smith says that 'good people' are motivated by what's valuable *de re*. Perhaps this doesn't mean that *de dicto* motivation is bad. It might just mean that we aren't ideal moral agents if we're guided by m-value. Moral philosophy doesn't need a theory of m-value because ideal agents aren't motivated by such value. And again, perhaps this is true. Perhaps an ideal agent is motivated *de re* by what's valuable. But the entire project of normative uncertainty is based on the fact that we *aren't* ideal agents. We're inescapably uncertain about what's valuable; and our project is to determine how *we* fallen creatures should evaluate our options. The question about what ideal versions of ourselves would do is simply different from the one we're addressing. And it can't show that *we* don't need a theory of m-value. For all that this second interpretation says, given our human limitations, it still seems m-value is important for us.

Here's a third interpretation. Perhaps the objection is not just that ideal agents aren't motivated by m-value. Perhaps the objection is that even non-ideal agents shouldn't be. Understood thus, the objection isn't that we don't need *any* theory of what to do under normative uncertainty. Instead, it advocates a specific such theory, according to which under uncertainty we should always intuitively follow something we care about *de re*. This claim addresses the question of this book, and contradicts the theory I outline. But it doesn't seem very plausible. To begin with, this theory will often fail to guide us. If we're axiologically uncertain, there will often not *be* anything we unqualifiedly care about *de re*. We'll be torn between different values, both doxastically and emotionally. In such cases, the present theory won't tell us what to do. But more importantly, when it does offer guidance, this guidance often seems rather dubious. As I indicated, we have to make enormously important decisions under uncertainty—about climate change, artificial intelligence, global poverty, and so on. Making a bad decision concerning any of these issues might have enormous ramifications, involving vast numbers of beings until some very far future. It seems very implausible that we should run the risk of incurring such astronomical badness, just to avoid a particular motive.

I can't think of any other plausible interpretation of the fetishism worry. So as far as I see, although being motivated *de re* by the good may in some ways be preferable to being motivated *de dicto* by m-value, this doesn't imply that we don't need a theory of the latter.[24]

---

[24] For other responses to the fetishism objection, see Sepielli (2016), Aboodi (2017), Hicks (2019) or MacAskill et al. (2020a, ch. 2).

Blamelessness

Here's another objection against the importance of m-value, due to Elizabeth Harman (2015).[25] Harman claims that your moral uncertainty is irrelevant for what you subjectively ought to do. In a nutshell, her argument is this:

(G) Suppose your moral uncertainty was relevant to what you subjectively ought to do. Then, if you were certain of a false moral theory and acted in accordance with it, you wouldn't be blameworthy.

(H) However, if you're certain of a false moral theory and act in accordance with it (and objectively morally wrongly), you are blameworthy.

(I) Therefore, your moral uncertainty is irrelevant to what you subjectively ought to do.

Why should we believe these premises? Harman thinks premise (G) follows from a very general fact about blameworthiness and subjective obligation—viz., that

(J) an agent is blameworthy for her behaviour only if she acted as she subjectively ought not have acted. (2015, 56)

Being certain of false moral theory is just a limiting case of being morally uncertain. So given (J), if moral uncertainty was relevant to what you subjectively ought to do, such false certainty would exculpate. To illustrate premise (H), Harman considers a Mafia family member, who's certain they're obliged to kill innocents when necessary for the interests of the family. Harman claims that they're blameworthy if they kill innocents on the basis of their belief. That's because

(K) a person is blameworthy for her wrongful behaviour just in case it resulted from her failure to care *de re* about what is morally important—that is, from her failure to care adequately about the non-moral features of the world that in fact matter morally. (2015, 67)

Clearly, our mafia member doesn't care adequately about the lives of innocents. So they're blameworthy, quite regardless of their beliefs.

However, both of these premises seem dubious. Start with the second. According to (H) and Harman's view of blameworthiness, it's irrelevant how you acquired your false moral beliefs, and how difficult it would have been for you to have correct ones. You're culpable *whenever* you do something objectively wrong, on the basis of false moral beliefs or concerns. There's a large literature on responsibility,

---

25 Hedden (2016) tentatively raises the same objection.

and this isn't the place to discuss it.[26] But suffice it to note that, intuitively, this seems very implausible. It can be extremely difficult for us to have correct moral beliefs. That's in part because we're thoroughly social. It's highly dependent on the society we live in not only which moral arguments and views we encounter, but also what intuitions we have. If everyone around us is convinced of a falsity, it can arguably require outstanding sensitivity to access the truth. So we can end up with wrong beliefs even when, intuitively, we've done all that's required by way of epistemic caution. And in such cases we intuitively aren't blameworthy for our beliefs, or for acting upon them. I take it this can be true even for the conviction that honour can require the killing of innocents.[27] But it seems clearly true for beliefs about more nuanced moral matters like those outlined above—population axiology, the theory of welfare, or future discounting. It seems bizarre to suggest that, regardless of the sincerity and care you devote to your moral inquiry about these difficult questions, you're blameworthy if you end up in the wrong. Whatever the correct theory of responsibility, Harman's uncompromising view of blameworthiness seems false. (H) is wrong.

That's enough to block her argument. But we can also reject premise (G). Harman doesn't argue for her supporting assumption (J). In fact, if I understand her correctly, she simply identifies the relevant subjective 'ought' as the 'ought' for which this assumption holds. So (J) isn't a substantive claim about the subjective 'ought'. It's simply a suggestion about why we should be interested in such an 'ought' in the first place. We're interested in the 'subjective ought' insofar as it's the ought that determines blameworthiness. But that's dubious. Suppose *arguendo* that her view of blameworthiness was right, and that your blameworthiness was fully determined by your non-moral beliefs. Then consider your first-person perspective. If you're morally uncertain, it's singularly unhelpful for you to know you avoid being blameworthy only if you act in accordance with the true moral view. You don't know what that is. So even insofar as you care about blameworthiness, you still face a question—about whether it's reasonable to prefer a low risk of being very blameworthy to a large risk of being only mildly to blame. The answer will pick out a subjective 'ought'. And even if this 'ought' doesn't determine blameworthiness, it's important from your perspective. But more fundamentally, your motivation arguably shouldn't be to avoid blameworthiness in the first place. It should quite simply be to do or try to do *good* (or do the right or the virtuous). And so you

---

26 See particularly Rosen (2003; 2004) or FitzPatrick (2017) for criticism of (H) and (K). For a collection of essays on the epistemic condition for moral responsibility, see Robichaud and Wieland (2017).

27 For a vivid description of a culture with such a code, and of the difficulty of rejecting it if you're born into such a culture, see e. g. Thesiger (2008).

face a more fundamental question—about whether it's reasonable to prefer a low risk of doing something very bad to a large risk of doing something slightly bad. Insofar as you care about doing good, and quite regardless of blame, m-value is important for you. So it's false that we're interested in such an ought just because it determines blameworthiness. At least from the perspective of agents, rather than third-party blamers, it would remain important even if it didn't. By the same token, it's false that the connection between moral uncertainty and blameworthiness expressed in (G) holds. Moral uncertainty would be relevant to the subjective ought even if it didn't determine blameworthiness.

In sum, Harman's view of blameworthiness seems false. And even if true, it can't establish the 'irrelevance of moral [or axiological] uncertainty' (2015, 53). From the first-person perspective, the importance of m-value doesn't hinge on questions of praise and blame at all.[28]

Regress

Here's a third worry. Suppose we say we need a theory of m-value because we aren't in a position to know the true axiology, and thus first-order axiologies aren't action-guiding for us.[29] This claim seems to run into a regress. Just as we're not in a position to know the true theory of value, we're arguably not in a position to know the true theory of m-value. So if axiologies aren't action-guiding, due to our uncertainty, then theories of m-value won't be action-guiding either. So why should we be interested in m-value (or any m^n-value) in the first place?

There's an answer to this worry, even if indeed we aren't in a position to know the true theory of m-value.[30] Note first that, in a standard sense of that term, we can be 'guided' by norms even if we aren't certain about them. Consider the norm that it's best to get 0.8 grams of protein per day and kilogram of body weight. Presumably, we can't be entirely certain about that norm. The best amount of protein might well be 0.7 or 0.9 grams. But the norm seems perfectly action-guiding, in any standard sense of that term. It's not that, without some extra algorithm about how to deal with our uncertainty, we'd be utterly paralysed, or that any deliberate protein consumption would be a random stab in the dark. Presumably, if we act in the face of such uncertainty without explicitly considering meta-norms about doing so, we act on an implicit acceptance of some such higher-order norms. Or

---

28 For other discussions of Harman's worry, see Sepielli (2018) or Geyer (2018).
29 See e. g. Hudson (1989).
30 The main idea behind this answer was sketched in Sepielli (2014).

more precisely, we act on the basis of intuitions about what to do in the face of our uncertainty. We can do that. We have such intuitions, it seems. So similarly, even if we're axiologically uncertain, we needn't be totally dumbstruck by this unless we have a theory of m-value. Our axiologies can still guide us in some sense.

Why then do we need to reflect about m-value? The reason isn't to overcome paralysis or absolute crapshoots. Instead, it's simply to make *better* decisions in light of uncertainty. Reflecting about m-value is a form of gathering evidence about what to do in the face of our uncertainty. And it's, quite simply, almost always better to act on the basis of more evidence.

Or at any rate, that seems plausible. It would take some argument to establish it firmly. In his classic paper 'On the Principle of Total Evidence' (1967) Irving John Good showed that it's always better to act on more evidence. More precisely, he proved that the expected value of the action that has the highest expected value after taking into account more evidence is always greater than that of the action with the highest expected value before we take this evidence into account—if the cost of taking it into account is neglected, and unless the action with the highest expected value would be the same for whatever piece of evidence we gather. So if reflection on m-value is like gathering evidence, then the expected value of acting after reflection about m-value will be greater than that of acting without that reflection, if the cost of the reflection is neglected and unless the action with the highest expected value would be the same for all pieces of evidence. Now our argument can't be so straightforward. Good assumed that whatever evidence we receive, we'll do what maximises expected value, given that evidence. But if we receive good evidence for a theory of m-value that says we *shouldn't* maximise expected value, this assumption is dubious. Moreover, one would clearly have to characterise formally what acting 'without further reflection' would amount to. One would have to argue more fully for the parallel between evidence-gathering and moral reflection. One would ultimately have to take into account the cost of moral reflection too, and thus say something about the efficacy of moral reasoning. And of course, we would also have to argue that EVM is the correct theory of m^2-value. It would take some argument to establish this firmly. But it does seem very plausible that acting after serious reflection about m-value will be m^2-better than acting unreflectedly—just like it seems plausible that acting after reflection about value will be m-better than acting unreflectedly.[31]

Now there's a next worry that the objector might raise. To show that reflecting about m-value is good, we have to assume some form of EVM about m^2-value—or perhaps some other normative theory with the same implication. The proponent

---

[31] This last claim is defended in MacAskill (2014, ch. 7).

of the regress objection might claim that we're begging the question against her: that we aren't entitled to assume EVM, or any other theory, but instead would have to take into account uncertainty about that again, and so on. In other words, she might demand that we show not only that reflection about m-value will plausibly be m^2-better, but also that it's m^3-better, and perhaps m^n-better all the way up. But note what the objector is now demanding. She's in effect asking us to prove beyond any doubt that our project is *ex ante* worth pursuing. I don't see how we could do that. But it seems an unreasonable demand. It would question not only why we should reflect about what's m-valuable, but also why we should reflect about what's *valuable*—or indeed why we should reflect on anything, or do anything else that seems *prima facie* worthwhile. It's a most radical normative scepticism. This may be an interesting philosophical problem. But it's not a problem I can address in this book, and not one I need to answer before moving forward.

So the main motivation for reflection on m-value isn't that we'll always be in a position to know what's m-best, or can't be guided in any ways by norms we're not certain about. It's that it's plausibly *ex ante* better to reflect about m-value and act on that reflection rather than to act in the face of uncertainty without any further reflection. Or at any rate, that's the assumption on which I'll proceed.[32]

---

[32] For other illuminating discussions of (related) regress-problems, see e. g. Sepielli (2013b), Trammell (forthcoming) or Tarsney (ms). For an argument that objective norms aren't action-guiding, see Fox (2019); for a challenge to this, see Barnett (forthcoming).

2 The basic argument

Let me now state the basic argument of the axiomatic approach in detail. To that end, I first outline my formal framework (Section 2.1). I then introduce the most basic representation theorem of this book (Section 2.2), the conceptual assumptions needed to turn this into a philosophically relevant result (Section 2.3), and the argument that this result can ground (Section 2.4). This argument will be interesting in itself. But it will also be helpful for introducing some general features of my approach, and as a starting point for the extensions in subsequent chapters.

2.1 The terminological framework

Background: state-dependent utility theory

Before I introduce my framework, let me provide some background. We'll need novel formal theorems for our arguments. But we don't have to start completely from scratch. We can apply, extend and vary existing results from decision theory, and that's what I'll do throughout. The formal details of this application needn't concern us here. I provide the derivations of my theorems in the appendix. But it's worth introducing the branch of decision theory I'll rely upon, as this will indicate the core formal peculiarity of axiological uncertainty. This branch is best illustrated by how it departed from Leonard Savage's *Foundations of Statistics* (1954). On Savage's framework there's a set of 'states of nature' and a set of 'outcomes'. An 'act' is a mapping from states to outcomes: to each state, it associates an outcome, which that act brings about if this state is actual. An agent is uncertain about which state is actual, and thus about the ultimate outcomes of her acts. Savage provided necessary and sufficient conditions for a preference relation over acts to be representable by a utility function over outcomes and a probability distribution over (sets of[33]) states. To illustrate, suppose one afternoon you must choose between going on a hike and reading at home, and are uncertain whether it'll be rainy or sunny. We can distinguish two states—rain and sunshine—and four outcomes—your reading or hiking, both either while it's rainy or sunny. Your choice is between an act (hiking) which leads either to 'hiking in the rain' or 'hiking while the sun shines', and one (reading) that leads either to 'reading while it rains' or 'reading while the sun shines', depending on the state of nature that is

---

33 In Savage's framework, the set of states is infinite, and the probability distribution thus actually ranges over subsets of it ('events').

actual. If your preferences over these and other acts satisfy Savage's conditions, there'll be utility and probability functions such that you prefer one act to another if and only if it has the greater expected utility according to these functions.

However, there's a problem for Savage's framework. His result required that you have preferences about acts leading to any arbitrary outcome in any state. And note that having distinguished states and outcomes in this way, we can define an 'act' that leads to 'hiking in the rain' under *both* states of nature. So in order for your choices to be representable, you must have a preference between other acts and this one—a hike that's rain-swept even if it's sunny. This is certainly unnatural.[34] And in principle, it seems avoidable. We could distinguish not four outcomes, but only 'hiking' and 'reading'. *These* more coarsely individuated outcomes can take place in any weather. Yet on Savage's framework, this would raise another problem. Savage takes utility to be a function of outcomes alone. But the value of your afternoon doesn't just depend on whether you're 'hiking' or 'reading'. It also depends on the weather. So this individuation would be too coarse to give a proper representation of the value of your options.

This led decision theorists to revise Savage's latter assumption, and develop state-dependent utility theory. That's a framework in which the utility of an outcome can depend on the state in which it arises. So the role of Savage's utility functions is played by state-dependent utility functions: two-place mappings $u(\cdot, \cdot)$, assigning utilities to state-outcome pairs. In such a framework, we can individuate outcomes coarsely, and distinguish $u(\text{rain, hiking})$ from $u(\text{sunshine, hiking})$, as seems natural. So state-dependent utility theory promises to give a more intuitive interpretation of your choice, without requiring you to contemplate a rainy hike in a sunny state of nature.

This development in decision-theory is interesting for the theory of axiological uncertainty. On a natural application of Savage's framework to our problem, the 'states of nature' among which we're uncertain are our axiologies. And instead of the desirability of outcomes, we're concerned with their moral value. But different axiologies assign different values to outcomes. So the 'utility' of an outcome depends on the 'state' in which it arises: its moral value depends on the true axiology. So state-dependent utility theory is a useful tool for the theory of axiological uncertainty. On a natural interpretation, the problem of axiological uncertainty *is* one of state-dependent utility. So this is the branch of decision theory I'll implicitly be relying upon (in a manner made explicit in the appendix).

---

34 See e. g. Joyce (1999, 107 ff.) for a discussion of this problem. For Savage's own unapologetic stance on it, see Drèze (1987, 78).

The framework of this book

Here's our framework. I'll assume all uncertainty is either axiological or purely descriptive.[35] To represent purely descriptive uncertainty, let X be a finite set of basic outcomes—i. e., non-normative, non-evaluative state of affairs that do not feature any probabilities or uncertainty. So an outcome in X may be that a non-human animal suffers, or that a person suffers, or whatever purely descriptive fact. Let $\mathcal{O}$ be the set of prospects over these outcomes. A prospect in $\mathcal{O}$ may be, say, that with probability 1/2 respectively either a non-human animal or a person will suffer. I'll use lower-case letters $a, b, c \ldots$ to refer to such prospects. Formally, they can be represented as the set of probability distributions on X—i. e., $\mathcal{O} = \{a : X \to \mathbb{R}_+ \mid \sum_{x \in X} a(x) = 1\}$, for $\mathbb{R}_+$ being the nonnegative reals. The just-mentioned prospect, say, will thus be represented as the function a in $\mathcal{O}$ that assigns 0.5 to both the fact that the non-human animal suffers and the fact that the person suffers, and 0 to all other outcomes. For any a and b in $\mathcal{O}$, and any $p \in [0,1]$, let $pa + (1-p)b$ in $\mathcal{O}$ be the prospect that leads to a and b with probability p and $(1-p)$ respectively—defined by $(pa + (1-p)b)(x) = pa(x) + (1-p)b(x)$ for all x in X. And let a_x be the prospect that certainly leads to x, with $a_x(x) = 1$.

An *axiology* T_i is a transitive binary relation on $\mathcal{O}$, whose reflexive part is the 'at least as good as' relation. Let '$a \succeq_i b$' denote that a is at least as good as b according to T_i. The relations of strict betterness and equality in goodness are induced as usual: a is better than b on T_i ('$a \succ_i b$') if $a \succeq_i b$ but not $b \succeq_i a$, and a is equally as good as b on T_i ('$a \sim_i b$') if $a \succeq_i b$ and $b \succeq_i a$. Let $\mathcal{T} = \{T_1, T_2, \ldots T_n\}$ be the finite set of axiologies under consideration, and denote its index set by $I = \{1, 2, \ldots n\}$. To refer to specific axiologies in prose, I'll speak of a 'pleasure-theory', a 'human-welfare-theory', a 'virtue/beauty-theory', and so on, to denote axiologies on which only pleasure, or only human welfare, or only virtue and beauty, and so on, have value.

If we're both descriptively *and* axiologically uncertain, we face more complex prospects: prospects that lead to certain theory-outcome *pairs* with particular probabilities—or more intuitively, acts that have certain probabilities of yielding different outcomes, and certain probabilities of being performed under different axiologies. Let $\mathcal{Q}$ be the set of such prospects. Intuitively, a prospect in $\mathcal{Q}$ may be, say, that with probability 1/2 respectively either T_2 or T_3 is true, and that conditional on either theory there's a probability of 1/2 respectively that either a non-human animal or a person will suffer—so that there's a probability of 1/4 of each

---

35 In line with much philosophical literature, I use 'uncertainty' for what economists and formal decision theorists call 'risk'. My formal definitions clarify what I mean.

theory-outcome pair being the case. I'll use bold letters $a, b, c \ldots$ to refer to such prospects. Formally, these prospects can be represented as the set of probability distributions on theory-outcome pairs—i. e., $\mathcal{Q} = \{a : I \times X \to \mathbb{R}_+ \mid \sum_{i \in I, x \in X} a(i, x) = 1\}$. The just-mentioned prospect, say, will thus be represented as the function a in $\mathcal{Q}$ that assigns 0.25 to all four pairs of theories T_2 or T_3 and the facts that the non-human animal or the person suffers, and 0 to all other theory-outcome pairs. The probability assigned to an axiology T_i under a is thus $\sum_{x \in X} a(i, x)$. And again, $pa + (1-p)b$ in $\mathcal{Q}$ is the prospect that leads to a and b with probability p and $(1-p)$ respectively—defined by $(pa + (1-p)b)(i, x) = pa(i, x) + (1-p)b(i, x)$ for all i in I and x in X.

The m-value relation is a transitive binary relation on $\mathcal{Q}$. I'll denote its reflexive part—the 'at least as m-good' relation—by '$\succeq_m$'. The strict m-betterness relation ('$\succ_m$') and the 'equally as m-good' relation ('$\sim_m$') are induced equivalently to the respective value relations.

Another piece of terminology will be helpful. Although prospects in $\mathcal{Q}$ are formally distinct from prospects in $\mathcal{O}$, and I said that axiologies order the latter, I'll sometimes say that a (in $\mathcal{Q}$) *is at least as good as* b (in $\mathcal{Q}$) according to an axiology T_i. By this I'll mean, intuitively, that the prospect represented by a, given T_i, is at least as good according to T_i as the prospect represented by b, given T_i. To define this formally, let $\mathcal{Q}^i \subset \mathcal{Q}$ be the set of prospects in which T_i has a strictly positive probability, i. e. $\mathcal{Q}^i = \{a \in \mathcal{Q} \mid \sum_{x \in X} a(i, x) > 0\}$. For each i in I, define a function $H_i : \mathcal{Q}^i \to \mathcal{O}; a \mapsto H_i(a)$, such that for all x in X,

$$H_i(a)(x) = a(i, x) / \sum_{y \in X} a(i, y). \tag{2.1}$$

The mapping H_i thus turns a prospect a into the prospect that a represents, given T_i (if there is such an prospect, i. e. if the probability of T_i under a is positive). So for some a and b, with a and b in $\mathcal{Q}^i$, I'll say that a is at least as good as b according to T_i if $H_i(a) \succeq_i H_i(b)$—and similarly for 'better' and 'equally good'.

Four features of this framework are noteworthy. First, the assumption that our set of outcomes X and our set of axiologies $\mathcal{T}$ are finite is an unnatural simplification. As a matter of fact, there are infinitely many outcomes, or infinitely many different purely descriptive states of affairs. For instance, if our non-human animal dies one particular day, its final heartbeat could be at 1 pm, or at 2 pm, or at infinitely many points in time in between. Equally, there are infinitely many axiologies. On an extreme speciesist axiology, animal welfare has no value at all. On a somewhat more moderate speciesist axiology, the value of animal welfare is half as great as the value of human welfare. And there are infinitely many scpeciesist axiologies on which the value of animal welfare is somewhere in between. Infinite sets of outcomes or states give rise to certain problems in standard decision theory, such as the St. Petersburg paradox.[36] These problems carry over to the context of axiological uncertainty. However, as far as I see, there aren't any problems *specific* to this latter context, arising with infinite sets of outcomes or theories. My main concern is with the peculiarities of axiological uncertainty, rather than with problems and questions of expected utility theory in general. So for simplicity, I'll just assume that the relevant sets are finite.

Second, our framework presupposes a quantitative notion of probabilities. My very definition of prospects in $\mathcal{O}$ and $\mathcal{Q}$ presupposes that we understand what it is for an outcome to have a particular probability of arising, and for an axiology to have a particular probability of being true. I assume this only for simplicity, to focus on other problems first. I'll provide an explication of axiological probabilities in Chapter 5. These probabilities, and thus the notion of m-value and the main claim of EVM, can be understood in different ways. On a more subjective interpretation of m-value, a prospect is m-better than another if it's better in light of your *credences*. On a more objective interpretation of m-value, a prospect is m-better than another if it's better in light of the credences that your evidence *warrants*. For now, this difference needn't concern us. All I say applies equally to either interpretation. I'll come back to the difference in Chapter 5.

Third, my definition of the set $\mathcal{Q}$ has an implication similar to the one we encountered with Savage. $\mathcal{Q}$ includes *all* probability distributions over theory-outcome pairs. In particular, it includes prospects that lead to different (probability distributions over) outcomes, depending on which axiology is true. That is, for some $\boldsymbol{a}$ in $\mathcal{Q}$, with $\boldsymbol{a}$ in $\mathcal{Q}^i$ and $\mathcal{Q}^j$ for some T_i and T_j, $H_i(\boldsymbol{a}) \neq H_j(\boldsymbol{a})$. These prospects won't represent any natural, practical options. For example, there's no natural act which leads to benefiting a non-human animal if a welfare-theory is true, and ben-

---

36 The St. Petersburg paradox is this. Suppose you're offered a gamble, in which a coin is tossed until it first lands heads. If it lands heads in the first toss, you'll gain £2; if it first lands heads in the second toss, you'll gain £4; if it first lands heads in the third toss, you'll gain £8, and so on. The expected monetary payoff of this game is infinite. So if you ought to maximise the expected monetary payoff of your actions, you ought to pay infinite sums to play this gamble. This seems implausible. For the first published statement of and reply to the paradox, see Bernoulli (1954, 31). For other vexing problems involving infinite sets of outcomes or states, see e. g. Nover and Hájek (2004). There are also problems arising from standard probability distributions over infinite sets of outcomes, or probability zero events. Suppose you throw a point-sized dart at a dartboard. Classical probability theory countenances cases where it has probability 0 of hitting any particular point. So suppose you're offered to win £100 if the dart hits the board at its exact center, and nothing otherwise. If the probability of this is zero, the expected value of the offer is zero. So if you ought to prefer an option if and only if it has the greatest expected value, you ought to be indifferent between accepting and refusing this offer. This seems implausible (see e. g. Skyrms 1980, 74; Briggs 2019, sec. 3.2.3.).

efiting a human being if a human-welfare-theory is true. Such a prospect will be definable in the framework I adopt. And indeed, my results will require that the m-value relation ranges over *all* prospects in $\mathcal{Q}$—such unnatural prospects included. However, unlike (arguably) the ones in Savage's framework, such prospects aren't conceptually impossible. Consider the prospect I just mentioned. Suppose a trust-worthy demon who knows about the true axiology constructed a button for you. It tells you that if you push it, then if the welfare-theory is true, a non-human animal will be benefited, and if the human-welfare-theory is true, a human being will be benefited. On the adequate representation of pushing the button, the probability with which a non-human animal or a person will be benefited by doing so should depend on the true axiology. This story may be unnatural. But since it's concep-tually possible, it seems plausible that m-value facts hold even among such un-usual prospects. So this doesn't seem to be a problem for our framework. On the contrary, since such prospects *are* conceptually possible, it would be a drawback if our theory of m-value didn't apply to them.

Fourth and finally, the framework allows the m-value relation to range over prospects that involve different probability distributions over axiologies. That is, for some prospects $\boldsymbol{a}$ and $\boldsymbol{b}$ in $\mathcal{Q}$, and some theory T_i, $\sum_{x \in X} \boldsymbol{a}(i,x) \neq \sum_{x \in X} \boldsymbol{b}(i,x)$. In-deed, my results will require that the m-value relation ranges over such prospects. And although they may be perfectly natural in themselves, you can't face *choices* between them. For example, you can't face a choice between benefiting a non-human animal if a welfare-theory is true, and doing so if a human-welfare-theory is true. But again, it seems plausible that m-value facts hold even among such prospects. If benefiting a non-human animal is better on the welfare-theory than on the human-welfare-theory, it seems adequate to claim that it has more m-value if the former is certain than if the latter is. So again, this impractical aspect of our framework doesn't seem to be a problem. It would be a drawback if our the-ory didn't apply to such comparisons. In fact, even from a practical point of view, these features of our framework are advantageous. They make it easier to apply our theory in practice. But I can only show this after much further argument. It will have to wait until Section 5.2.

2.2 Three substantive conditions

Within this framework, we can now state the relevant theorem. We want an expected utility representation of the m-value relation in which the utilities cor-respond to our axiologies' value functions. To that end, we need three substan-tive conditions. The first is that the m-value relation $\succeq_m$ satisfies the standard von Neumann-Morgenstern axioms.[37] For a reflexive binary relation $\succeq$ on $\mathcal{Q}$, these are

Transitivity$_\mathcal{Q}$: for all a, b and c in $\mathcal{Q}$, if $a \succeq b$ and $b \succeq c$, then $a \succeq c$;
Completeness$_\mathcal{Q}$: for all a and b in $\mathcal{Q}$, $a \succeq b$ or $b \succeq a$;
Independence$_\mathcal{Q}$: for all a, b and c in $\mathcal{Q}$ and $p \in \,]0, 1[$, if $a \succ b$, then $pa + (1-p)c \succ pb + (1-p)c$; and
Continuity$_\mathcal{Q}$: for all a, b and c in $\mathcal{Q}$, if $a \succ b$ and $b \succ c$, then there exist $p, q \in \,]0, 1[$, such that $pa + (1-p)c \succ b$ and $b \succ qa + (1-q)c$.

If a reflexive relation $\succeq$ on $\mathcal{Q}$ satisfies these conditions, I'll say it's '*vNM-con-formable*'. These conditions are by no means trivial. I'll discuss their plausibility in the next chapter. For now, what matters is that they guarantee a kind of representability. That is, it can be shown[38] that if $\succeq_m$ is vNM-conformable, there's a function $u : I \times X \to \mathbb{R}$, unique up to positive affine transformation,[39] such that for all a and b in $\mathcal{Q}$,

$$a \succeq_m b \quad \text{iff} \quad \sum_{i \in I, x \in X} a(i, x)u(i, x) \geq \sum_{i \in I, x \in X} b(i, x)u(i, x). \tag{2.2}$$

So there's a representation of $\succeq_m$ in terms of state- or theory-dependent utilities. However, (2.2) isn't enough for our purposes. For all we know, the function u might be a random utility function without any relation to our axiologies. We need to ensure that every function $u(i, \cdot)$ in (2.2) represents the underlying axiology T_i. We can do that by adding two further conditions. The first is that all axiologies satisfy the von Neumann-Morgenstern axioms as well. For a reflexive binary relation $\succeq$ on $\mathcal{O}$, these are

Transitivity$_\mathcal{O}$: for all a, b and c in $\mathcal{O}$, if $a \succeq b$ and $b \succeq c$, then $a \succeq c$;
Completeness$_\mathcal{O}$: for all a and b in $\mathcal{O}$, $a \succeq b$ or $b \succeq a$;
Independence$_\mathcal{O}$: for all a, b and c in $\mathcal{O}$ and $p \in \,]0, 1[$, if $a \succ b$, then $pa + (1-p)c \succ pb + (1-p)c$; and
Continuity$_\mathcal{O}$: for all a, b and c in $\mathcal{O}$, if $a \succ b$ and $b \succ c$, then there exist $p, q \in \,]0, 1[$, such that $pa + (1-p)c \succ b$ and $b \succ qa + (1-q)c$.

Since no confusion will arise, I'll often leave out the subscripts '$\mathcal{Q}$' and '$\mathcal{O}$' when referring to these conditions. As with $\mathcal{Q}$, if a reflexive relation $\succeq$ on $\mathcal{O}$ satisfies

---

37 See originally von Neumann and Morgenstern (1944).
38 See Karni and Schmeidler (1980, 8) or Karni (1985, 14). Basically, this result is Fishburn's (1970) Theorem 8.2, applied to state-outcome pairs rather than outcomes.
39 For two functions $u : I \times X \to \mathbb{R}$ and $v : I \times X \to \mathbb{R}$, v is a positive affine transformation of u if there are $s, t \in \mathbb{R}, s > 0$, such that $v(i, x) = su(i, x) + t$ for all i in I and x in X.

these conditions, I'll say it's 'vNM-conformable'. Again, these conditions aren't trivial, and I'll discuss their plausibility in the next chapter. What matters for now is that they guarantee a kind of representability. It can be shown[40] that if a relation $\succeq_i$ on $\mathcal{O}$ is vNM-conformable, there's a function $u_i : X \to \mathbb{R}$, unique up to positive affine transformation,[41] such that for all a and b in $\mathcal{O}$,

$$a \succeq_i b \quad \text{iff} \quad \sum_{x \in X} a(x)u_i(x) \geq \sum_{x \in X} b(x)u_i(x). \tag{2.3}$$

However, even if the m-value relation and all our axiologies are vNM-conformable, this doesn't ensure that each function $u(i, \cdot)$ (from 2.2) represents the underlying axiology T_i, or is a positive affine transformation of the respective function u_i (from 2.3). For all we know, $u(i, \cdot)$ might still have nothing to do with u_i, or might be related to it in some inappropriate way—for instance, by being its negation (such that $u(i, x) = -u_i(x)$ for all x). We need a condition about how the m-value facts relate to the axiologies. What will do is a simple Pareto Condition—to the effect that if two prospects are equally good on all axiologies with nonzero probability, they're equally m-good, and if one of them is at least as good as another on all axiologies with nonzero probability and strictly better on some, it's strictly m-better. To state this formally, define for any probability distribution P on I the set $\mathcal{Q}^P \subset \mathcal{Q}$ of prospects in which P is the underlying probability distribution on I, $\mathcal{Q}^P = \{a \in \mathcal{Q} \mid \sum_{x \in X} a(i, x) = P(i) \; \forall i \in I\}$. For a set of binary relations $\{\succeq_i \mid i \in I\}$ on $\mathcal{O}$ and a binary relation $\succeq$ on $\mathcal{Q}$, define the

Pareto Condition: For any probability distribution P on I, and for all a and b in $\mathcal{Q}^P$, if $H_i(a) \sim_i H_i(b)$ for all i in I with $P(i) > 0$, then $a \sim b$; and if $H_i(a) \succeq_i H_i(b)$ for all i in I with $P(i) > 0$ and $H_j(a) \succ_j H_j(b)$ for some j in I with $P(j) > 0$, then $a \succ b$.

Again, this condition isn't trivial, and I'll discuss its plausibility in the next chapter. For now, what matters is that if $\succeq_m$ and all $\succeq_i$ satisfy these three conditions, they have the kind of representation we need. I'll call this the

Basic Representation Theorem: *Suppose that all our $\succeq_i$ are vNM-conformable. If $\succeq_m$ is vNM-conformable and satisfies the Pareto Condition with respect to our $\succeq_i$,*

---

40 Since $\mathcal{O}$ is equivalent to $\mathcal{Q}$ on the assumption that $|I| = 1$, this follows from the results mentioned in footnote 38 (Karni and Schmeidler 1980, 8; Karni 1985, 14). See also Fishburn's (1970) Theorem 8.2.

41 For two functions $u : X \to \mathbb{R}$ and $v : X \to \mathbb{R}$, v is a positive affine transformation of u if there are $s, t \in \mathbb{R}$, $s > 0$, such that $v(x) = su(x) + t$ for all x in X.

*there's a function u : I × X → ℝ, unique up to positive affine transformation, such that for all **a** and **b** in Q, all a and b in O and all i in I,*

$$\boldsymbol{a} \succeq_m \boldsymbol{b} \quad \text{iff} \quad \sum_{i \in I, x \in X} \boldsymbol{a}(i,x)u(i,x) \geq \sum_{i \in I, x \in X} \boldsymbol{b}(i,x)u(i,x), \quad \text{and} \tag{2.4}$$

$$a \succeq_i b \quad \text{iff} \quad \sum_{x \in X} a(x)u(i,x) \geq \sum_{x \in X} b(x)u(i,x).^{42} \tag{2.5}$$

In other words, if all axiologies are vNM-conformable, and the m-value facts are vNM-conformable and satisfy the Pareto Condition, then there's a theory-dependent utility function, unique up to positive affine transformation, that simultaneously represents all of our axiologies and the m-value facts. This is still a purely mathematical theorem. It says that if the relations $\succeq_i$ and $\succeq_m$ satisfy these conditions, there are mathematical functions that represent these relations. For all we know, these functions might not have any extra-mathematical significance, or stand for actual values. But we can now add the conceptual assumption I mentioned in Chapter 1, and turn this into a philosophically significant result—to the effect that if $\succeq_i$ and $\succeq_m$ satisfy these conditions, *EVM* is true. So let me now state this assumption.

2.3 The prospect-explications

The assumption is twofold. It concerns the meaning of cardinal intra- and intertheoretic comparisons. As I said in Section 1.2, we don't use statements like (B) and (D) (from page 5 f.) in ordinary language. So I take it we can't find out what it *really* is for such comparisons to hold. There isn't anything to discover. Instead, we have to choose *explications* of our pre-theoretic concept of value, and decide what we'll mean by such statements. The following assumptions thus aren't meant to be analyses of existing concepts, but useful explicative definitions.

Intratheoretic comparisons

To state my explication of intratheoretic comparisons, suppose that for some function $u : X → \mathbb{R}$ and some axiology T_i, and for all a and b in O,

$$a \succeq_i b \quad \text{iff} \quad \sum_{x \in X} a(x)u(x) \geq \sum_{x \in X} b(x)u(x). \tag{2.6}$$

---

42 See the appendix (Section A.1) for a proof.

I'll then say that u *represents* $\succeq_i$ *ordinally*. Furthermore, suppose that for some function $u : X \to \mathbb{R}$, and some axiology T_i, the cardinal intratheoretic comparisons between all outcomes, according to T_i, are the same as the ratios among the utility differences between these outcomes according to u—that is, for all x, y, z, t in X and $n \in \mathbb{R}$, the value-difference between outcomes x and y is n times as great as the value-difference between z and t, according to T_i, if and only if $(u(x) - u(y))/(u(z) - u(t)) = n$. I'll then say that u *represents* T_i *cardinally*. The *prospect-explication of intratheoretic comparisons* says that if there's a function $u : X \to \mathbb{R}$, unique up to positive affine transformation, which represents $\succeq_i$ ordinally, then u represents $\succeq_i$ cardinally. Or in other words, for such a utility function to represent $\succeq_i$ cardinally just is for it to be such that it represents $\succeq_i$ ordinally and is unique up to positive affine transformation in doing so.[43]

If a utility function u represents an axiology T_i cardinally, we can represent that axiology with a value function G_i that determines the goodness of outcomes according to T_i quantitatively. As long as we consider that axiology in isolation, we can pick any function v among the family of utility functions that represent T_i cardinally—or among the positive affine transformations of u—and take it to be T_i's value function G_i. Which one we choose is irrelevant. The absolute heights of value-levels or sizes of value-differences don't matter in determining which prospects are better than which according to our theory. All that matters are the ratios of value-differences. And these are the same for all positive affine transformations of u. For instance, for any x and y where y has a greater utility than x, we could pick the utility function v on which $v(x) = 0$ and $v(y) = 1$, and suppose that $G_i = v$. This would amount to picking a particular scale. So in what follows, if an axiology can be represented cardinally by a utility function, I'll often represent it with a value function. And since the choice of a scale would be arbitrary, I'll do that without specifying a scale.

Note what the prospect-explication does. Suppose someone says that according to axiology T_i, the best prospect is the one that maximises the expected square root of the value of outcomes:

$$a \succeq_i b \quad \text{iff} \quad \sum_{x \in X} a(x)\sqrt{G_i(x)} \geq \sum_{x \in X} b(x)\sqrt{G_i(x)}. \tag{2.7}$$

The square root function is concave. So a given increase in the argument of that function will produce a greater increase in the value of the function the lower

---

43 See Broome (2004, 89 ff.) for a similar assumption about 'personal goodness', and a helpful discussion of the nature of this assumption. Other illuminating discussions of the issue of cardinalising goodness are provided in Broome (1991, 142 ff., chs. 10–11) or Greaves (2015; 2017).

the argument is. This will manifest in our axiology. Consider the following three prospects, which all lead to two different outcomes with probability 0.5 (where the numbers in the table refer to the values of these outcomes, according to T_i):

Tab. 2.1: Example to illustrate expected square root of value.

	a	b	c
0.5	1	1	4
0.5	0	1	0

Both b and c differ from a in that one of their outcomes is better than in a. In b, the relevant outcome is 1 unit better than that in a; in c, it's 3 units better. However, since

$$0.5 \cdot \sqrt{1} + 0.5 \cdot \sqrt{1} = 0.5 \cdot \sqrt{4}, \tag{2.8}$$

we have $b \sim_i c$. Hence according to this axiology, the relevant increases in the value of outcomes (by 1 and 3 respectively) *count* the same in determining the value of prospects, even though they *aren't* the same. This is ruled out by the prospect-explication. If a relation $\succeq$ on $\mathcal{O}$ is vNM-conformable, then 'utility' is *defined* as that quantity of which $\succeq$ maximises the expectation, in the sense of (2.6). So by definition, increases in the utility of outcomes always count the same in determining the utility of the prospect. According to the prospect-explication, we can use utility to represent goodness. So the explication assumes that if two differences in value count the same in determining the goodness of prospects, they are the same. It assumes that goodness is expectational, like utility. Thus it rules out views like (2.7).

As I emphasised, we should treat this as an *explication*, not as a substantive assumption or faithful analysis of our pretheoretic notion of value. It's not the only possible explication of cardinal intratheoretic comparisons. According to our explication, goodness acquires its cardinal significance in the context of weighing goods in prospects under uncertainty. That's why I called it the 'prospect-explication'. But there are other possible contexts. For example, we could assume a 'time-explication', on which if two differences in value coming at different times count the same in determining the goodness of the history of the world over time, they necessarily are the same.[44] And there may be still other possibilities. When

---

44 See Broome (2004, ch. 15) for a cardinalisation of personal goodness by time.

we come to precise axiological theorising, we have to choose some explication. The assumption that goodness is expectational is one possibility. It's the one by which we can turn the Basic Representation Theorem into a philosophical result. So it's the one I choose.

Intertheoretic comparisons

I said that if a utility function represents an axiology T_i cardinally, we can simply pick one among the family of utility functions that represent it and take it to be T_i's value function G_i. But that's only true if we consider axiologies in isolation. It's not so when we consider multiple axiologies jointly. Suppose we assume that T_i's value function is G_i. If we then simultaneously represent another axiology T_j by some value function G_j, this implies claims about how values compare intertheoretically among them. For example, if $G_i(x) > G_j(x)$, then the value of x is greater according to T_i than according to T_j.[45] If we consider axiologies jointly, then once we picked a *global scale* for representing axiologies (or once we picked a scale for some T_i) it will not be true that we can arbitrarily pick a scale for some other axiology T_j.

So we also need an explication of intertheoretic comparisons, or of what it is for two axiologies to be jointly representable by value functions. Before I introduce this, a comment is in order. Our question is which prospects are better than which if you're axiologically uncertain. If EVM is correct, then in practice, the answer depends only on intertheoretic *unit* comparisons—or facts like 'the value-difference between x and y, according to T_i, is n times as great as the value-difference between z and t, according to T_j'. It doesn't depend on *level* comparisons—or facts like 'the value of x, according to T_i, is greater than the value of y, according to T_j'. The reason is that in practice we don't face choices between prospects with different underlying probability distributions over axiologies. And if the underlying probability distribution over axiologies is the same for two prospects, then which of them has the higher expected value depends on the sizes of value-differences, but not on the heights of value-levels.[46] In that sense, we wouldn't need to explicate intertheoretic level comparisons. However, the Basic Representation Theorem ranges over prospects with different underlying probability distributions over

---

45 At least, this is how I'll understand it. Of course, one might use the same notation (i. e., represent T_i and T_j simultaneously by G_i and G_j) but assume that the implied intertheoretic comparisons have no significance. I assume they have.

46 Formally, if $\sum_{x \in X} a(i,x) = \sum_{x \in X} b(i,x)$ for all i in I, then for any set of $t_i \in \mathbb{R}$, $\sum_{i \in I, x \in X} a(i,x)[u(i,x) + t_i] \geq \sum_{i \in I, x \in X} b(i,x)[u(i,x) + t_i]$ iff $\sum_{i \in I, x \in X} a(i,x)u(i,x) \geq \sum_{i \in I, x \in X} b(i,x)u(i,x)$.

axiologies. Thus it implies a utility function that's unique up to positive affine transformation, not just unique up to the multiplication with a joint scalar and state-wise addition of a constant $(s \cdot u(i,x) + t_i)$. And thus we can use this theorem to explicate intertheoretic comparisons of value-levels as well. We get level comparisons for free, as it were. So I'll provide an explication covering both unit and level comparisons. More precisely, I'll provide an explication not just for what I called 'cardinal intertheoretic comparisons' on page 6. I'll provide one for *cross-cutting cardinal intertheoretic comparisons*, or facts of the form

(L) the difference between the value of x, according to T_i, and the value of y, according to T_j, is n times as great as the difference between the value of z, according to T_h, and the value of t, according to T_k.

Crosscutting cardinal intertheoretic comparisons combine unit and level comparisons; the latter are limiting cases of the former.

To state my explication of such comparisons, suppose that for some function $u : I \times X \rightarrow \mathbb{R}$, and for all a and b in Q,

$$a \succeq_m b \quad \text{iff} \quad \sum_{i \in I, x \in X} a(i,x)u(i,x) \geq \sum_{i \in I, x \in X} b(i,x)u(i,x). \qquad (2.9)$$

I'll then say that u *represents the m-value relation ordinally*. Suppose that for some utility function $u : I \times X \rightarrow \mathbb{R}$, and for each axiology T_i, the function $u(i, \cdot)$ represents that axiology cardinally. I'll then say that u *represents each axiology cardinally*. Furthermore, suppose that for some function $u : I \times X \rightarrow \mathbb{R}$, the crosscutting cardinal intertheoretic comparisons between all outcomes and all theories are the same as the ratios among the utility differences between these outcomes according to u—that is, for all x, y, z, t in X, all i, j, h, k in I and $n \in \mathbb{R}$, the difference between the value of x, according to T_i, and the value of y, according to T_j, is n times as great as the difference between the value of z, according to T_h, and the value of t, according to T_k, if and only if $(u(i,x) - u(j,y))/(u(h,z) - u(k,t)) = n$. I'll then say that u *jointly represents all axiologies cardinally*. Now the *prospect-explication of intertheoretic comparisons* says that if there's a function $u : I \times X \rightarrow \mathbb{R}$, unique up to positive affine transformation, that represents the m-value relation ordinally *and* represents each axiology cardinally, then u jointly represents all axiologies cardinally. In other words, for such a function to jointly represent all axiologies cardinally just is for it to be such that it represents the m-value relation ordinally and each axiology cardinally, and is unique up to positive affine transformation in doing so. If there's such a function u, the crosscutting cardinal intertheoretic comparisons between our axiologies are the same as the respective intertheoretic utility difference ratios according to u. So we can interpret all utility functions $u(i, \cdot)$, *jointly*, as value functions G_i.

Again, I treat this as an explication, not as a substantive claim. It parallels the prospect-explication of intratheoretic comparisons. The latter assumed that intratheoretic comparisons acquire their cardinal significance in the context of weighing goods under uncertainty. This explication now assumes that interthe-oretic comparisons acquire their cardinal significance in the context of weighing axiologies under axiological uncertainty. It assumes that if two crosscutting intertheoretic value-differences count the same in determining the m-value of prospects, they necessarily are the same. I'll rely on this explication throughout the book. But before discussing it in more detail, let me state the theorem it implies.

2.4 The theorem, the argument and our questions

The argument

The Basic Representation Theorem was a purely mathematical result, to the effect that if the relations $\succeq_i$ and $\succeq_m$ satisfy certain conditions, there's a function $u :$ $I \times X \to \mathbb{R}$ that represents $\succeq_m$ ordinally, such that $u(i, \cdot)$ represents $\succeq_i$ ordinally for all i in I. But given our conceptual assumptions, or the prospect-explications, this implies a philosophically significant theorem. I'll call it the

Expected Value Theorem: *Suppose that all our $\succeq_i$ are vNM-conformable. If $\succeq_m$ is vNM-conformable and satisfies the Pareto Condition with respect to our $\succeq_i$, then for all **a** and **b** in Q,*

$$\textbf{\textit{a}} \succeq_m \textbf{\textit{b}} \quad \text{iff} \quad \sum_{i \in I, x \in X} a(i,x)G_i(x) \geq \sum_{i \in I, x \in X} b(i,x)G_i(x).^{47} \tag{2.10}$$

The functions G_i are value functions. So (2.10) is EVM. Now importantly, this theorem is still a conditional. It says that *if* m-value satisfies the von Neumann-Morgenstern axioms and the Pareto Condition, EVM is true. But we can derive EVM from it by adding the normative or meta-axiological assumption I mentioned. We can assume that (at least if all our axiologies are vNM-conformable) the m-value facts *are indeed* vNM-conformable and satisfy the Pareto Condition with respect to our axiologies. Given this assumption, EVM follows. So the Basic Representation Theorem, together with our conceptual assumptions and this meta-axiological assumption, implies EVM. This is the basic argument of this chapter.

---

47 See the appendix (Section A.1) for the derivation of this theorem from the Basic Representation Theorem and the prospect-explications.

I've pointed out that it parallels arguments in standard decision theory. It has another parallel worth noting, to an argument for utilitarianism based on John Harsanyi's (1955) 'utilitarian cardinal welfare theorem'. Harsanyi showed, roughly, that if in a society, each individual's preferences (or the facts about what's better for them) satisfy a set of decision-theoretic axioms, and if 'social preferences' (or the facts about what's impersonally better) also satisfy these axioms as well as something like a Pareto condition, then there are utility functions representing these preferences such that the social utility function is a weighted sum of the individuals' utility functions. In itself, this is a purely formal result. But suppose utility can be taken to represent welfare. And suppose the relevant preferences *should* (or the relevant facts do) satisfy Harsanyi's axioms. Then his argument implies that a form of weighted utilitarianism must be true. And if we also suppose that no one's welfare is given more weight than anyone else's in determining what's socially best (as Harsanyi takes to be a conceptual matter[48]), his theorem implies utilitarianism. Also, we can then read off inter*personal* comparisons of welfare from the social preference relation, just as, I claimed, we can read off intertheoretic comparisons of value from the m-value facts. My formal framework had to be more complex than Harsanyi's. But structurally our arguments are similar.

Now the Basic Representation Theorem can't be denied. It's a mathematical fact. But one can object to the conceptual and normative assumptions required to make it imply EVM. One can dispute that the prospect-explications are viable explications of value comparisons, or that the m-value facts indeed satisfy our conditions. I'll turn to such worries in the next chapter. But let me elaborate first on how, given our assumptions, the Basic Representation Theorem serves the two purposes I suggested—or answers the questions of meaning and truth about EVM.

The question of meaning

First, the theorem allows us to explain what EVM even says. More precisely, it guarantees that there are conditions under which our explications can be used. These explications were conditionals (*'if* there's a function...'). The Basic Representation Theorem shows that if $\succeq_m$ satisfies our conditions, the antecedents of these conditionals hold, and we can employ them to define cardinal value.

This is particularly significant with respect to cardinal intertheoretic comparisons. Many standard explications of cardinal value seem inadequate for them.

---

48 See Harsanyi (1955, 314 ff.).

Consider time. As mentioned, that's a context for explicating *intra*theoretic comparisons. We can assume that if two differences in value at different times count the same in determining the goodness of the history of the world, they are the same. For intertheoretic comparisons, however, this seems impossible, or at best very unsatisfying. We'd have to imagine that different axiologies are true at different periods of time; and we'd then have to consider how valuable the overall empirical-cum-axiological history is. That may be technically feasible. But the truth of axiologies is (arguably) a timeless matter. So it's dubious that there are any facts about which empirical-cum-axiological histories are better than which. And even if there are, we don't seem to have a very good grasp of them. Similar considerations apply to many other candidate explications. Consider space. That's another context for explicating intratheoretic comparisons. We can assume that if two differences in value at different places count the same in determining the goodness of the world, they are the same. But again, the related explication of intertheoretic comparisons seems inadequate. We'd have to imagine that different axiologies are true at different places in space; and we'd then have to consider how valuable the world overall is. But the truth of axiologies is (arguably) a spatially universal matter. So it's again dubious that there are any facts about which spatially axiologically partitioned worlds are better than which, or that we have a good grasp of them.

In Chapter 4, I'll consider some other possible explications of intertheoretic comparisons. But I'll raise various problems for them. So as far as I see, the prospect-explication is ultimately the best explication of cardinal intertheoretic comparisons. And if this is true, the Basic Representation Theorem is a very important result. It provides us with the best means of even understanding what it is for one prospect to have a greater expected value than another.

The question of truth

Secondly and equally importantly, the Basic Representation Theorem can ground a systematic argument to the effect that EVM is true. Given our assumptions, it rules out all alternative theories of m-value at once. Let's see with some examples how it does that. Take the view that under axiological uncertainty, we ought to be strictly risk-averse about value. To express this view, let p_i^a be the probability of T_i under a, and let V_i^a be the (expected) value of a according to T_i:

$$p_i^a = \sum_{x \in X} a(i, x), \tag{2.11}$$

and

$$V_i^a = \begin{cases} \sum_{x \in X} a(i,x) G_i(x)/p_i^a & \text{if } p_i^a > 0 \\ 0 & \text{if } p_i^a = 0. \end{cases} \tag{2.12}$$

Say that *m-value is risk-averse* if there's an increasing strictly concave function ρ, such that for all a and b in Q,

$$a \succeq_m b \quad \text{iff} \quad \sum_{i \in I} p_i^a \rho(V_i^a) \geq \sum_{i \in I} p_i^b \rho(V_i^b). \tag{2.13}$$

The inputs of ρ are the values of our prospects on given axiologies. Since the function is concave, increases in these values count for more in determining m-value the lower these values are. This is a standard interpretation of risk-aversion.[49] And *prima facie*, this view seems perfectly reasonable. We need an argument to rule it out. And our theorem may provide one. (2.13) is inconsistent with the assumption that $\succeq_m$ is vNM-conformable. In particular, it's inconsistent with the Independence axiom for $\succeq_m$. To see this, let ρ be the square root function, $\rho(x) = \sqrt{x}$, and consider the following example. Suppose there are two outcomes x and y, and two theories T_1 and T_2 with $p_1 = p_2 = 0.5$, and $G_1(x) = G_2(y) = 0$, $G_1(y) = 30$ and $G_2(x) = 31$. Prospect a leads to either x or y with a probability of 0.5 each, while b and c lead to x and y respectively (with certainty):

Tab. 2.2: Example to illustrate risk-aversion.

	a		b		c	
	T_1	T_2	T_1	T_2	T_1	T_2
	$p_1 = 0.5$	$p_2 = 0.5$	$p_1 = 0.5$	$p_2 = 0.5$	$p_1 = 0.5$	$p_2 = 0.5$
0.5	0	31	0	31	30	0
0.5	30	0	0	31	30	0

According to (2.13), $b \succ_m c$. So Independence would require that b (or $\frac{1}{2}b + \frac{1}{2}b$) is m-better than $\frac{1}{2}c + \frac{1}{2}b$—which is equivalent to a. However, since

$$3.9 \approx 0.5 \cdot \sqrt{0.5 \cdot 30} + 0.5 \cdot \sqrt{0.5 \cdot 31} > 0.5 \cdot \sqrt{31} \approx 2.8, \tag{2.14}$$

(2.13) implies that $\frac{1}{2}c + \frac{1}{2}b \succeq_m b$. Similar examples could be given for any other increasing strictly concave ρ. If the conditions of our theorem hold, the utility

---

49 See e. g. Buchak (2013) for a slightly different one.

functions that enter the m-value relation are those that represent our axiologies ordinally. If we assume that goodness is expectational at the level of first-order value, the axioms—and Independence in particular—guarantee that the utility functions that determine m-value represent our axiologies cardinally. They rule out views like (2.13). Now of course, the argument could run both ways: views and examples like this can, and have been, used to cast doubt on Independence.[50] Still, the axiom provides a certain argument against such views. It expresses a thought that undeniably has strong intuitive appeal: if one prospect is m-better than another, then lotteries involving the first prospect are m-better than lotteries involving the second, if they're otherwise exactly the same. If we make apparent how *prima facie* plausible judgments contradict this thought, this casts doubt on these judgments.[51] Whether or not this argument is ultimately successful is a complex matter. I'll say more about it in the next chapter, where I discuss our axioms. But in any case, the intuitive plausibility of our axioms provides an argument against views like (2.13).

Consider next 'My Favourite Theory'—the view that under axiological uncertainty, you simply ought to evaluate prospects in accordance with the theory you find most plausible. On this view, a prospect is at least as m-good as another if and only if it's at least as good according to the axiology with the highest probability (if there is such an axiology; if more than one axiology has maximal probability, there's some rule for breaking ties). Some people have endorsed this view with regards to moral uncertainty generally.[52] It contradicts the Pareto Condition. Suppose the probabilities of T_1 and T_2 are 0.6 and 0.4 respectively, so that T_1 determines $\succeq_m$. And suppose two prospects d and e are equally good according to T_1, but d is strictly better according to T_2. Then, according to My Favourite Theory, d is equally as m-good as e, which violates the Pareto Condition. So this condition can provide an argument against My Favourite Theory.

Our theorem also shows that there's no straightforward way for My Favourite Theory to remedy this flaw (if it's a flaw). In light of the just-mentioned example, one may want to say you ought to evaluate prospects in accordance with the most plausible theory—*except* if two prospects are equally good on that theory, and one is at least as good as the other on all axiologies with nonzero probability and strictly better on some, in which case the former is m-better than the latter.

---

50 The most famous (alleged) counterexamples to Independence may be due to Allais (1953) and Ellsberg (1961).

51 With respect to the example by Allais (1953), this has been done—quite compellingly, I think— e. g. by Savage (1954, 101 ff.) and Raiffa (1968, 80 ff.).

52 See Gracely (1996).

Views along these lines have also been suggested.[53] Yet our theorem shows that if $\succeq_m$ is vNM-conformable, the Pareto Condition implies that m-value is a weighted sum of first-order value. There simply is no consistent intermediate view, on which m-value is vNM-conformable and Paretian, and yet doesn't reduce to a weighted sum of first-order value, somehow retaining the spirit of My Favourite Theory. If $\succeq_m$ is vNM-conformable, the project of making My Favourite Theory satisfy the Pareto Condition is doomed.

Finally, one might worry that EVM isn't ecumenical enough as a view of normative or axiological uncertainty. People sympathetic to virtue ethics, say, may want to deny that m-value is a matter of strict computation, and endorse a non-codifiable meta-virtue-ethical view of m-value. On such a view, under axiological uncertainty, you simply ought to act virtuously—be circumspect but not over-cautious, neither reckless nor overly anxious, and so on. Similarly, some people have suggested meta-deontological principles for how to determine one's m-best prospect.[54] *Prima facie*, such views seem perfectly sensible. We need an argument to deny them. And our theorem provides one. If they're to be distinct theories, these meta-virtue-ethical or -deontological views must deny that m-value satisfies our conditions.[55]

In short, various views that seem reasonable and have been defended in the literature contradict one of the conditions of our theorem. To the extent these conditions are plausible, the theorem provides not only a way of explicating EVM, but also a systematic argument for its truth.

---

53 With regards to moral uncertainty generally, Gustafsson and Torpman (2014, 169 ff.) are at least steering towards such a position. They revise My Favourite Theory so as to make it compatible with a Pareto (or 'Dominance') condition. Unfortunately, they don't discuss the von Neumann-Morgenstern axioms; and they explore uncertainty about theories that 'require' or 'permit' certain options, which may involve disanalogies to our case. But at least within the theory of axiological uncertainty, making My Favourite Theory satisfy the Pareto Condition forces one to deny that $\succeq_m$ is vNM-conformable.

54 E. g., Guerrero (2007, 94) endorses the following principle: 'Don't Know, Don't Destroy: If one knows that one doesn't know whether some entity has moral value, then it's morally blameworthy to destroy that entity, unless one believes that something of substantial moral significance compels one to do so.'

55 For other arguments in defence of EVM—or more generally, expectational reasoning under normative uncertainty—see MacAskill and Ord (2020).

3 Evaluating the argument

Are our two additional assumptions—the meta-axiological assumption that the relevant (m-)value facts satisfy our axioms, and the conceptual assumption constituted by the prospect-explications—plausible? That is, do our axiologies and the m-value facts satisfy the conditions of the Expected Value Theorem? And are the prospect-explications viable definitions of cardinal value comparisons? In this chapter, I'll begin to answer these questions.

A conclusive answer, especially to the first question, is beyond the scope of this book. Each of the theorem's conditions is disputed, at least in standard decision theory and social choice theory. I can't defend any of them conclusively. So what I'll mostly do is compare their plausibility in the context of axiological uncertainty with their plausibility in other contexts—specifically, that of decision theory or first-order axiology, and (in the case of the Pareto Condition) that of social choice theory. I'll start with the Pareto Condition (Section 3.1) and the von Neumann-Morgenstern axioms (Section 3.2), and then discuss the prospect-explications (Section 3.3). I'll end the chapter by highlighting two interesting implications of this discussion for decision theory as a general theory of preferences, and for EVM as a higher-order theory of uncertainty about theories of axiological uncertainty (Section 3.4).

3.1 The Pareto Condition

Recall what the Pareto Condition says: for any two prospects with the same underlying probability distribution over axiologies, if they're equally good on all theories with nonzero probability, they're equally m-good, and if one of them is at least as good as the other on all theories with nonzero probability and strictly better on some, it's strictly m-better. Intuitively, this sounds very plausible. However, it's an *ex ante* Pareto requirement. It's concerned not with the betterness of outcomes, but with the betterness of prospects. For this reason especially, one may have doubts about it. Pareto conditions are rarely discussed in decision theory. But as mentioned (with respect to Harsanyi), there's an analogy between the theory of axiological uncertainty and social choice theory. We're concerned with an overall m-value ordering that depends on the value-orderings of axiologies; social choice theory is concerned with a 'general betterness' ordering that depends on the 'individual betterness' orderings of people.[56] And it's controversial whether,

---

56 Or at any rate, that is one interpretation of it. See particularly Broome (1991).

if one prospect is *ex ante* at least as good for all individuals as another and strictly better for some, it's *ceteris paribus* generally better. So we must be careful to assume such a condition in our context.

The most important argument against the *ex ante* Pareto condition for individual goodness is due to Marc Fleurbaey and Alex Voorhoeve (2013). It shows that this condition is in tension with (*ex post*) egalitarianism, the view that it's good if people fare equally well. Suppose we can either let both Antonio and Leonore end up with 20 units of good (prospect *f*), or conduct a lottery yielding, with equal probability, 31 units of good for Antonio and 10 such units for Leonore or vice versa (prospect *g*):

Tab. 3.1: Example to illustrate *ex ante* Pareto condition for individual goodness.

	f		*g*	
	Antonio	**Leonore**	**Antonio**	**Leonore**
0.5	20	20	10	31
0.5	20	20	31	10

Suppose that individual goodness is expectational. Then *g* is *ex ante* better than *f* for both Antonio and Leonore. So if general goodness satisfies an *ex ante* Pareto condition with respect to personal goodness, *g* is *ex ante* better than *f*. However, according to (a relevant form of) egalitarianism, a state in which both Antonio and Leonore have 20 units of good is better than a state in which one has 31 and the other 10. So if it was certain that *g* would lead to 31 for Antonio and 10 for Leonore, *f* would *ex ante* be better. And if it was certain that *g* would lead to 10 for Antonio and 31 for Leonore, *f* would also be better. In other words, whatever the outcome of *g* will be, if it was certain, *f* would *ex ante* be better. Therefore, Fleurbaey and Voorhoeve claim, *f* is *ex ante* better even if *g*'s outcome is uncertain. This is because of the 'Principle of Full Information' (or basically Savage's 'Sure-Thing Principle'[57]): 'When one knows that, in every state of the world with positive probability, one would rightly rank two alternatives in a particular way, then one should so rank them' (2013, 120).

This may be a good reason to reject the *ex ante* Pareto condition concerning individual goodness. I won't explore this. What matters for our purposes is that there doesn't seem to be a plausible parallel reasoning about m-value. Fleurbaey and Voorhoeve's argument depends on the egalitarian claim that *f* would

---

57 See Savage (1954, 21 ff.).

be better than g if g's outcome was certain. But it's not clear why an analogous premise should hold in the context of axiological uncertainty. Consider the following choice between f and g:

Tab. 3.2: Example to illustrate Pareto Condition.

f		g	
T_1	T_2	T_1	T_2
$p_1 = 0.5$	$p_2 = 0.5$	$p_1 = 0.5$	$p_2 = 0.5$
20	20	31	10

Why should f be m-better? What immediately comes to mind is risk-aversion—the view I expressed as

$$a \succeq_m b \quad \text{iff} \quad \sum_{i \in I} p_i^a \rho(V_i^a) \geq \sum_{i \in I} p_i^b \rho(V_i^b). \tag{3.1}$$

For some suitable increasing, strictly concave function ρ (e. g., $\rho(x) = \sqrt{x}$), this view indeed implies that $f \succeq_m g$. However, we can't use it to argue against the Pareto Condition. As is easily verified, (3.1) actually *satisfies* this condition.

To argue against the Pareto Condition, we'd have to endorse a different form of risk-aversion. Say that m-value is *ex post risk-averse* if there's an increasing strictly concave function ρ, such that

$$a \succeq_m b \quad \text{iff} \quad \sum_{i \in I, x \in X} a(i, x) \rho(G_i(x)) \geq \sum_{i \in I, x \in X} b(i, x) \rho(G_i(x)). \tag{3.2}$$

In (3.2), ρ is applied not to the *prospects* that our options represent on given axiologies, but to *outcomes*. If m-value is *ex post* risk-averse, it doesn't violate Independence, as the theory defined in (3.1) does. On the other hand, as is again easily verified, it does violate the Pareto Condition, and imply that $f \succeq_m g$ (for some ρ). So (3.2) might be used in an argument against the Pareto Condition. However, it's a very dubious view. Note what it implies if you're certain of one theory. Suppose you're certain of T_1, and face k and l: k leads to an outcome of value 20 (according to T_1), and l with equal probability either to an outcome of value 10, or to one of value 31 (according to T_1). Since you're certain of T_1, if goodness is expectational at the level of axiologies, you're certain that l is better than k. Yet, (for the relevant ρ) (3.2) implies that k is m-better. So it says that a prospect can be m-better than another, even if it's certainly worse. This is very implausible. Surely, if we're certain that one axiology is true, we ought to rank prospects in accordance with it.

Perhaps there are other reasons, apart from these forms of risk-aversion, for believing that f is m-better than g, and for denying the Pareto Condition on that basis. But I can't think of any plausible candidate. So I tentatively conclude there's no analogue to Fleurbaey and Voorhoeve's objection in the context of axiological uncertainty. As far as their objection is concerned, the condition seems plausible for m-value. Similarly, perhaps there are other kinds of objections to our Pareto Condition, other than reasons that parallel the egalitarian objection. But I can't see any I find remotely convincing.[58] So as far as I see, in our context the *ex ante* Pareto Condition is indeed very plausible. It's a major drawback for a theory to violate it.

3.2 vNM-conformability

The von Neumann-Morgenstern axioms as conditions on value

Let's turn to the other part of our (meta-)axiological assumption, the von Neumann-Morgenstern axioms. There are two levels at which these appear in our theorem: as conditions on our axiologies, and as conditions on m-value. Consider first the assumption that all axiologies are vNM-conformable. Is this plausible? As a claim about all possible axiologies, or even all axiologies we should have *some* nonzero credence in, it's clearly false. There are non-vNM-conformable axiologies, and in some of them we should have at least some nonzero credence. However, this doesn't undermine the relevance of our theorem altogether. We should

---

58 There's a second standard objection against *ex ante* Pareto conditions in social choice theory. Some authors find *ex ante* Pareto improvements problematic when they depend on differences in people's *beliefs* (see e. g. Gilboa et al. 2014 or Mongin and D'Aspremont 1998, 442). Suppose Leonore and Antonio have an apple and an orange each, but Leonore doesn't like apples at all, and Antonio doesn't like oranges at all. In this case, there's a Pareto superior state in which Leonore gets both oranges and Antonio gets both apples. This state is possible because the two have different tastes, and it seems clearly preferable from the point of view of general goodness. But now suppose Felix is certain that it will rain tomorrow, and Mariane is certain that it will snow, and they both own £100 (which they cherish). Relative to their beliefs, it's *ex ante* better for both of them to agree to the bet in which Felix will receive Mariane's £100 if it rains, and Mariane will receive Felix's £100 if it snows. However, since one of them clearly has false beliefs, there's something problematic about that agreement. That's especially true, say, if one of them was intentionally deceived. However, this objection doesn't carry over to our context either. I do allow that the probability distribution over outcomes in a prospect in Q may differ from theory to theory. But that's not because axiologies themselves somehow assign different probabilities to outcomes. I'm simply stipulating these probabilities. So whatever exactly we find problematic about belief-relative Pareto improvements, this won't apply to our condition.

simply see this condition as restricting its scope. Our result isn't a fully general theorem of axiological uncertainty. It's a theorem concerning uncertainty about vNM-conformable axiologies only. That's why I haven't stated this as part of the main conditional of the theorem, but as an antecedent supposition ('Suppose that all our $\succeq_i$ are vNM-conformable'). It's not surprising that our theorem isn't fully general. The biconditional (2.10) is a theory of both axiological and descriptive uncertainty. It says you should maximise expected value across axiologies and descriptive states of nature, in a vNM-conformable manner. But that's implausible if one of our axiologies isn't vNM-conformable. If you were certain of such an axiology, you should arguably judge a prospect m-better than another if and only if it's better according to that axiology. So if that axiology isn't vNM-conformable, the m-value relation isn't vNM-conformable either.[59] As a general theory of both axiological and descriptive uncertainty, a vNM-conformable theory of m-value is plausible at best for vNM-conformable axiologies.

How significant a restriction is this, or how common and plausible are non-vNM-conformable axiologies? For three of our four axioms, the relevant restrictions don't seem all too serious. It's been disputed that the betterness relation even satisfies Transitivity.[60] I won't enter this debate here. But I think it's an analytic fact that 'better than' and 'at least as good as' are transitive. 'Better' is the comparative of 'good', and all comparatives are transitive.[61] So I've been assuming as a matter of definition that an axiology is a *transitive* binary relation.

I take it that there are axiologies that strictly violate Independence. For instance, some views are risk-averse in a way that's strictly inconsistent with this axiom. And plausibly, we should have some nonzero credence in some such axiologies.[62] So the assumption that all axiologies satisfy this axiom is a nontrivial restriction of our framework. Also, it's an essential aspect of it. There are alternative frameworks allowing for other risk-attitudes, potentially grounding theories other than Expected Value Maximisation, and certainly well worth exploring.[63] But Independence is key for the framework and argument in this book.

---

59 In fact, given a suitable Pareto condition, $\succeq_m$ then can't be vNM-conformable. The Pareto Condition on page 26 is slightly too weak to guarantee this. It doesn't rule out that the m-value relation may represent a complete *sharpening* of an underlying axiology that is incomplete. But a slightly stronger condition (like the one on page 115) would do.

60 See most prominently Temkin (2012); also Rachels (1998).

61 This view is defended in Broome (2004, ch. 4); see e. g. Binmore and Voorhoeve (2003) or Voorhoeve (2013) for further defences of the transitivity of betterness.

62 See e. g. Buchak (2013) for a defence of risk-sensitivity in decision theory.

63 See most prominently Buchak (2013); also Dietrich and Jabarian (2018; 2021) for the theory of normative uncertainty.

However, my sense is that axiologies that *strictly* violate Independence are comparatively implausible. That's for two reasons. First, as indicated in Section 2.4 (on page 36), Independence seems to express a compelling thought. If one prospect is better than another, then lotteries involving the former are better than lotteries involving the latter, if they're otherwise exactly the same. Alleged counterexamples to this axiom can be presented in a manner that makes apparent how the relevant judgments contradict this thought. And this often reduces the intuitive plausibility of these judgments significantly.[64] Second, there's a general strategy to render axiologies that *prima facie* violate Independence consistent with this axiom. Standard *prima facie* violations of Independence arise when the value of some state of affairs depends on modal facts—such as facts about what could have happened, or about the probability with which something happened. If this is so, we can take these modal facts to be part of our outcomes. And once we do so, Independence is standardly no longer violated. In other words, we can individuate outcomes in a more fine-grained manner, and thus make axiologies that *prima facie* violate Independence consistent with this axiom.[65] This isn't the place to elaborate on this strategy. I'll discuss it in some depth in Section 6.2. There, I mention an important problem for the strategy when we apply it to standard *deontic* (especially deontological) moral theories. But I argue that this isn't a problem when we apply it to axiologies. As far as I see, the strategy is indeed convincing for standard axiologies.[66] This isn't to say it works for all possible axiologies. As I'll point out, there are possible axiologies that violate Independence, but not because on these axiologies, the value of outcomes depends on any relevant fine-grained features of states of affairs. And our strategy won't work for these theories. But my sense is that these axiologies are comparatively rare and implausible. So in sum, I think there are axiologies that strictly violate Independence, and to which we should assign some nonzero credence. Hence the axiom is a nontrivial restriction of our framework, or of the plausibility of (2.10) as a general theory of axiological uncertainty. However, since these axiologies are rare and implausible, Independence doesn't seem to diminish the relevance of our argument all too much. Even though it rules out axiologies that strictly violate Independence, the argument still applies to an interestingly large class of theories.

---

64 As indicated in footnote 51, this has been done e. g. by Savage (1954, 101 ff.) and Raiffa (1968, 80 ff.) with respect to the example by Allais (1953).

65 For famous applications and defences of this strategy, with respect to the example by Allais (1953), see e. g. Weirich (1986) and Broome (1991, ch. 5).

66 For recent contributions to the debate about the Independence axiom in decision theory and first-order value, see e. g. McClennen (2009), Temkin (2012, 237 ff.) or Buchak (2013, 157 ff.).

In a similar manner, there are axiologies that strictly violate Continuity. If a theory assigns infinite value to some outcome and finite values to others it will violate Continuity. If we don't put any restrictions on the set of outcomes X, then many plausible axiologies are of this form. Take the welfare-theory. On this view, a world that contains beings whose lives are worth living, and only such beings, for an infinite stretch of time, will be infinitely valuable. But there are other ways in which axiologies violate Continuity. An axiology may say that one kind of value lexically dominates another. Consider an axiology on which the value of wellbeing lexically dominates that of beauty—in that a prospect is better than another whenever it expectably leads to more wellbeing, but *ceteris paribus* better if it expectably leads to more beauty. This welfare/beauty-theory doesn't satisfy Continuity.[67] More straightforwardly, an axiology may imply a discontinuous behaviour of value with respect to probabilities. Consider an axiology on which, for some $p_0 \in]0, 1[$, outcomes that arise with a probability of less than p_0 are irrelevant for the evaluation of prospects. This axiology will not be continuous. Again, plausibly, we should have some nonzero credence in such axiologies. So the assumption that all axiologies are continuous is a nontrivial restriction. And again, it's an essential aspect of the argument in this book.

But here too, my sense is that at least for finite worlds, axiologies that *strictly* violate Continuity are comparatively implausible. That's for the same two reasons as with Independence. First, at least for finite worlds, Continuity expresses a very compelling thought. Nothing is infinitely better than anything else; and betterness strictly is a graded and continuous matter. This in itself casts doubt on axiologies that violate this axiom. Second, the strategy of reindividuating outcomes again helps to render standard axiologies that *prima facie* violate Continuity consistent with it. So again, I think this is a restriction that doesn't diminish the relevance of our argument all too much.

The most problematic axiom is Completeness. And Completeness is problematic indeed. To assume that the value facts are complete is to assume that all prospects are *fully commensurable*—i.e., that their values are representable by a single value function. But on many axiologies, there's some intratheoretic incommensurability. Some prospects aren't fully commensurable, but compare only roughly. On these axiologies, there are prospects a and b, where a isn't determinately at least as good as b, and b isn't determinately at least as good as a. Indeed, many such axiologies are plausible, and have been prominently defended

---

67 See e. g. Vallentyne (1993) for a view with this structure. Temkin (2012, 245 ff.) also mentions that some outcomes may be 'good enough', or very significantly better than others, so that Continuity fails. I'm not sure whether he'd regard those as instances of the kind of 'lexical betterness' I mentioned.

by philosophers.[68] To take a classic example,[69] suppose that welfare has value, and consider lives of successful musicians and of successful lawyers. It's plausible that for some such pair of lives, it's neither true that the life of the musician is determinately better than that of the lawyer, nor that it's determinately worse, nor that they're precisely equally good. The standard argument for this is the 'small improvement argument'.[70] Consider some such pair of lives, where it's plausible that neither is determinately better than the other. Now add a small improvement to the life of the musician—an additional successful serenade in place of a bored evening with migraine, say. This new life of the musician is determinately (slightly) better than the former life of the musician. But plausibly, it still needn't be determinately better than the life of the lawyer. So our original lives aren't exactly equally good either. No 'at least as good as'-relation determinately holds between them.

I don't think that Completeness somehow expresses a thought that's independently compelling. And with this axiom, the strategy of reindividuating outcomes won't help. So Completeness at the level of axiologies is a major restriction of the argument from Chapter 2. Fortunately, however, it's a restriction we can overcome within the axiomatic approach, and the broader idea of Expected Value Maximisation. Completeness isn't essential for our main argument. There are representation theorems without the Completeness axiom. These theorems allow our argument to cover axiologies featuring incommensurability. So the plausibility of such axiologies is one major reason to explore such theorems. I'll turn to this in Chapter 6.

The von Neumann-Morgenstern axioms as conditions on m-value

Consider the assumption that the m-value facts are vNM-conformable. Is this plausible, given the presupposition that all axiologies are vNM-conformable? In many respects, the von Neumann-Morgenstern axioms seem just as plausible with respect to m-value as with respect to first-order value. Some people may question whether $\succeq_m$ is even transitive. But since I take m-betterness to be a form of betterness, I again think the transitivity of $\succeq_m$ is analytic. In principle, m-value may also violate Independence, even if all axiologies are vNM-conformable. In particular, it's possible that m-value is risk-neutral with respect to purely descriptive uncertainty, but risk-sensitive with respect to axiological uncertainty. But as far as I see,

---

68 See e. g. Raz (1986, ch. 13) or Broome (1997).
69 See Raz (1986, ch. 13).
70 For early instances of the argument, see e. g. Sinnott-Armstrong (1985) or Raz (1986, ch. 13).

there's no reason why that should be the case—at least none that's somehow specific to the problem of axiological uncertainty. So I think Independence is a plausible axiom about m-value. As with ordinary value, m-value would violate Continuity if it displayed a discontinuous behaviour with respect to probabilities—if there were probability thresholds $p_0 \in]0,1[$ below which an axiology became irrelevant for determining m-value, say. This could be true even if all axiologies are vNM-conformable. But such thresholds seem implausible, in the context of axiological as in that of purely descriptive uncertainty. So in this regard, Continuity seems plausible too.

However, there's at least one specific reason for why the m-value relation may not be vNM-conformable, even if all axiologies are. That's facts about intertheoretic comparisons. The most problematic assumption in this regard is again Completeness. To assume that $\succeq_m$ is complete is to assume that all axiologies are *fully commensurable*—i. e., that they're all jointly representable by single value functions. But as with intratheoretic comparisons, and even if all axiologies themselves are complete, it might be that there's some intertheoretic incommensurability. It might be that some axiologies aren't fully commensurable, but compare only roughly. If so, there are prospects *a* and *b*, where *a* isn't determinately at least as m-good as *b*, and *b* isn't determinately at least as m-good as *a*. And indeed, this again seems plausible. Suppose that T_i is a beauty-theory, and T_j a welfare-theory. Even if both T_i and T_j are complete with respect to $\mathcal{O}$, intuitively, it seems plausible that the value of beauty, according to T_i, isn't fully commensurable to the value of wellbeing, according to T_j. For some increase in beauty and some increase in welfare, the value of the former, according to T_i, is neither determinately greater than that of the latter, according to T_j, nor determinately smaller, nor precisely equally great. A small improvement argument again seems pertinent. It's implausible that any slight additional beauty, say, would have to tip the balance. No positive 'at least as m-good as'-relation may hold between prospects leading to value-beauty-tradeoffs, in light of uncertainty about these theories. So the plausibility of such intertheoretic incommensurability is another major reason to explore theorems without the Completeness axiom. Such theorems allow our argument to cover axiologies that aren't fully intertheoretically commensurable.

However, here the problem runs even deeper than with Completeness about axiologies. At the level of first-order value, some prospects on some axiologies may not be *fully* commensurable. But there doesn't seem to be anything metaphysically problematic about value comparisons, *per se*. At least some intratheoretic comparisons plausibly do in fact hold. It's not that all plausible axiologies are radically incomplete—or such that *a* is at least as good as *b*, according to them, only if it's in *no* respect worse. That's different at the level of m-value. Intertheoretic comparisons seem metaphysically problematic. One might think that *no* such comparisons hold—that there just aren't any facts, say, about how good certain outcomes *would* be if some axiologies were true which actually are false. The universe may contain nontrivial value facts about which purely descriptive prospects are better than which. But it just doesn't contain any nontrivial *m*-value facts, or nontrivial facts about which outcomes on which theories are better than which outcomes on which *other* theories, say. So one might endorse radical scepticism about intertheoretic comparisons, or hold that the m-value relation is *radically incomplete*—that *a* is at least as m-good as *b* only when it's at least as good on all axiologies with nonzero probability. If this is true, the prospect-explication might tell us what it *would* be for an intertheoretic comparison to be the case. But as a matter of fact, no such comparison holds. Some people have defended this. If they're right, it's little use to have representation theorems allowing for *some* incompleteness. The idea of Expected Value Maximisation is more fundamentally flawed. The only positive m-value facts are trivial cases, where all axiologies agree. So we need to address the problem of intertheoretic comparisons: provide a positive reason to think that some such comparisons actually hold, and a story about what could ground them. I'll turn to this in the next chapter. To anticipate: I'll argue that intertheoretic comparisons are possible, or that $\succeq_m$ isn't radically incomplete. But it isn't fully complete either, even if all axiologies are. Some plausible axiologies are indeed less than fully commensurable.

The problem of intertheoretic comparisons affects the Continuity axiom as well. One might hold that there are axiologies that compare in a lexical way—axiologies T_i and T_j such that any positive value-difference between prospects according to T_i is greater than any positive value-difference between prospects according to T_j. This may be so, one might hold, because although there are grounds for intertheoretic comparisons, they're somehow special, or peculiar, and give rise to lexical intertheoretic comparisons. And if two theories compare in this manner, the m-value facts won't satisfy Continuity with respect to them. So to assess Continuity about m-value, again, we have to address the problem of intertheoretic comparisons. To anticipate: on the view of intertheoretic comparisons for which I'll argue, it's implausible that two axiologies compare in a lexical way. So I think (at least for finite worlds) Continuity is a plausible assumption about m-value.

3.3 The prospect-explications

Consider our conceptual assumption, the prospect-explications. Are these viable explications of cardinal value? Start with the most fundamental concern. One might think the prospect-explication of intertheoretic comparisons makes the argument from our representation theorem to EVM *circular*. One might think the explication simply *defines* quantities of value in a way that renders EVM true: that in assuming that intertheoretic comparisons acquire their cardinal significance in the context of axiological uncertainty, I must already *assume* that EVM is correct.[71]

But this suspicion is misguided. To see this, it may help to distinguish two assumptions involved in the explication. The first assumption is that if there's a theory-dependent utility function, unique up to positive affine transformation, which represents the m-value relation ordinally and each axiology cardinally— and in particular, if $\succeq_m$ thus satisfies Completeness—all axiologies are *somehow* fully commensurable, and can somehow jointly be represented by single value functions. This claim doesn't say anything about which value functions jointly represent our theories, or how they compare. It merely says that axiologies are somehow fully commensurable. The second assumption is that the *specific* value functions that can figure in a representation are then determined by the m-value facts. In my explication, I've joined those two assumptions together. I could have stated them separately. Doing so makes more vivid how weak a presupposition the prospect-explication of intertheoretic comparisons really is.

Consider the first assumption first. This is simply a claim about what (perhaps among else) it means that two theories are comparable. And though it is necessary for EVM, it certainly doesn't *presuppose* EVM. Moreover, the assumption doesn't seem very problematic. If there's a theory-dependent utility function, unique up to positive affine transformation, which represents m-value ordinally and each axiology cardinally, there's a unique way in which axiologies weigh against each other to determine complete m-value facts. In any sense that's relevant for the problem of axiological uncertainty, this means all axiologies are 'comparable' in some way. So grant this first assumption. Then, if there is such a function, the respective state-wise utility functions must be positive affine transformations of the value functions of our theories. That is, if G_i are our value functions, there must be s_i and $t_i \in \mathbb{R}$, $s_i > 0$, such that for all prospects $\boldsymbol{a}$ and $\boldsymbol{b}$,

$$\boldsymbol{a} \succeq_m \boldsymbol{b} \quad \text{iff} \quad \sum_{i \in I, x \in X} \boldsymbol{a}(i,x)[s_i G_i(x) + t_i] \geq \sum_{i \in I, x \in X} \boldsymbol{b}(i,x)[s_i G_i(x) + t_i]. \tag{3.3}$$

Hence the only alternative way in which our value functions could determine the m-value relation would be if, apart from their probabilities, one theory had systematically and constantly more weight in determining m-value than another (in

---

71 This objection seems to be raised by Andrew Sepielli (2009, 27): 'The main problem with [the prospect-explication of intertheoretic comparisons] is that it simply assumes the rationality of maximizing [expected value] under normative uncertainty. But this is a position that should be argued for independently of one's solution to the [problem of intertheoretic comparisons], not merely assumed as a means to solving the problem.'

that $t_i \neq t_j$ or $s_i \neq s_j$ for some i and j). So the second assumption—that intertheoretic comparisons acquire their *specific* cardinal significance in the context of axiological uncertainty—doesn't rule out risk-aversion, or the quasi-deontological or virtue-ethical accounts sketched in Section 2.4. It only rules out such constant unequal weighing. And although EVM presupposes that m-value isn't determined by such unequal weighing, to turn this final step into a matter of definition is again by no means to assume EVM. What may be questioned is whether there *is* a utility function that represents $\succeq_m$ in the relevant way—i. e., whether $\succeq_m$ satisfies the conditions of our theorem, and particularly Completeness. These conditions are doing the main work guaranteeing intertheoretic comparability. Once they're in place, the explication of intertheoretic comparisons doesn't add much, and certainly not enough to warrant a charge of circularity.

Here's a second objection against our explications. I suggested in Section 1.2 that we don't use cardinal comparisons in ordinary language, that we thus can't *find out* what they really mean, or that there's no uniquely privileged definition of them. Instead, we should pick a useful explication. One might object to this. One might claim that there is a privileged derivation of cardinal comparisons. In particular, one might say we have a pretheoretic understanding of (ordinal) comparisons of *value-differences*, or facts like

(M) according to T_i, the value-difference between x and y is *greater than* the value-difference between z and t.

Now a comparative ranking of value-differences among a set X of outcomes doesn't always entail a cardinal concept of value. Suppose X has only three members, and that according to T_i, the difference between the best and the second best outcome is greater than the difference between the second best and the third. Clearly, this isn't enough to determine cardinally how much greater the first difference is than the second.[72] However, under some conditions, difference comparability is enough to imply cardinal measurability: if X is rich enough, facts like (M) determine a utility function unique up to positive affine transformation representing T_i. For instance, on one condition introduced by Kaushik Basu (1983, 197), intuitively, if you're able to compare value-differences in a set as rich as the rational numbers, then such ordinal comparability of value-differences implies cardinal measurability.[73] So then an understanding of value-difference

---

72 See e. g. Bossert (1991, 212) for such an example.

73 More precisely, Basu (1983, 197) proved the following. Let X be a set of outcomes, u a real-valued utility function on X, and Ω a set of real-valued functions on $u(X)$. Think of functions in Ω as permissible transformations of u—transformations, say, that also represent the relevant

comparisons is enough to provide a cardinal concept of value. And since facts like (M) must be accepted by everyone as primitives (the objection goes) *this* is the privileged explication of cardinal value.[74]

I'm not convinced by this proposal. For one thing, it seems dubious that we understand statements like (M). They might be unproblematic as long as value-differences count the same no matter in what time and place, and in what prospect they appear. Then these contexts help us understand them. But they become problematic when these contexts vanish. Suppose you say that for you the *ex post* value of money increases linearly: that the value-difference between £n and £$(n + 100)$ is the same for any $n \in \mathbb{N}$. And suppose you say you are risk-averse about this value: that a certain prospect of £n is always better than a 50 % chance of getting £$2n$ or nothing. Then you arguably need to tell us *in what sense* you value money linearly, *ex post*, instead of assigning it diminishing marginal value. Our grasp of value-difference comparisons isn't robust enough to make this clear. Or in short, we don't just lack an unmediated understanding of cardinal comparisons like (B) (from page 5). We also lack an unmediated understanding of facts like (M).

But we can even grant that we understand *intra*theoretic value-difference comparisons. This still doesn't get us very far. Whether a prospect has a higher expected value than another also depends on *inter*theoretic value-difference comparisons, or facts like

(N) the value-difference between x and y, according to T_i, is greater than the value-difference between z and t, according to T_j.

And it seems uncontroversial that we have no direct grasp of *such* facts. So primitivism about (M) will anyway be insufficient to formulate EVM. In the next chapter, as a possible solution to the problem of intertheoretic comparisons, I'll introduce fitting attitude accounts of value. I'll consider whether an ordering of the strength of *attitudes* corresponding to value-differences might provide a cardinally significant concept of value. But I'll argue that (at least with respect to intertheoretic

---

ordering of X that u represents. Say that $(u|\Omega)$ has *cardinality* if for all f in Ω there are s and $t \in \mathbb{R}$, $s > 0$, such that for all a in $u(X)$, $f(a) = sa + t$. In other words, $(u|\Omega)$ has cardinality if only positive affine transformations are permissible transformations of u. Say that $(u|\Omega)$ has *difference comparability* if for all f in Ω and for all a, b, c and d in $u(X)$, $a - b \geq c - d \Leftrightarrow f(a) - f(b) \geq f(c) - f(d)$. In other words, $(u|\Omega)$ has difference comparability if only transformations that preserve ordinal difference-comparisons are permissible transformations of u. Now if $u(X)$ is dense in a connected subset of $\mathbb{R}$, $(u|\Omega)$ has cardinality if and only if it has difference comparability. (The connected subsets of $\mathbb{R}$ are just the intervals on $\mathbb{R}$, and $\mathbb{Q}$ is dense on $\mathbb{R}$. Thus the intuitive formulation above approximates this result.) See e. g. Bossert and Stehling (1994) for another condition; e. g. Bossert (1991), Bossert and Weymark (2004, 1126 ff.) or Bossert et al. (2005, 34 f.) for a general discussion.
74 I thank Ralf Bader for mentioning this worry to me.

comparisons) that's ultimately dubious. So ultimately, I don't think we can find any better—let alone a uniquely privileged and 'correct'—explication of cardinal value in terms of value-differences.

There's a third worry about the prospect-explications. One might think these explications get the *order of explanation* wrong. Consider intratheoretic comparisons, and take two prospects *a* and *b*, where (according to the true axiology) *a* is better than *b*. Intuitively, it's not that outcomes compare in a certain way *because*, as a brute matter of fact, *a* is better than *b*. Rather, *a* is better than *b* precisely *because* outcomes compare in some way. So my explication seems to put the cart before the horse. It explains comparisons in terms of betterness facts, whereas actually such facts seem explained by comparisons. And the same worry arises in the intertheoretic case. Intuitively, it's not that axiologies compare in a certain way because certain m-value facts hold. Rather, such facts hold *because* axiologies compare in that way.[75]

Let me say three things in reply to this objection. For simplicity, I'll only discuss the intratheoretic case. But what I say applies *mutatis mutandis* to intertheoretic comparisons. First, a point of clarification. The prospect-explication doesn't entail that cardinal comparisons are grounded in value facts, or that it's value facts that explain these comparisons. It assumes that for a cardinal comparison to hold *just is* for a certain value fact to be the case. It assumes an identity rather than a grounding relation between comparisons and value facts. So to the extent that one finds the alleged grounding relation objectionable, the worry simply misses our explication.

Second, nothing in the prospect-explication implies that the value facts themselves must be fundamental, or not grounded in anything. They may well have grounds. Suppose according to the true axiology, both natural beauty and well-being have value, that prospect *a* leads to the destruction of some natural beauty with a probability of 0.4, and to some benefits for Antonio with a probability of 0.6, and that prospect *b* represents the status quo:

Tab. 3.3: Example to illustrate prospect-explications.

	a	*b*
0.4	destruction of natural beauty	status quo
0.6	benefits for Antonio	status quo

---

75 This objection is made in MacAskill (2014, 146); it's often raised against similar explications in slightly different contexts (see e. g. Eriksson and Hájek 2007, 207).

Now suppose that a and b are equally good. This fact needn't be brute. It may have grounds. What these are will depend partly on the correct metaethics. Perhaps the fact that a and b are equally good is grounded (in the manner of something like a divine command theory) in the fact that God would be indifferent between them. Or perhaps it's grounded (in a constructivist way) in the fact that the best systematisation of our axiological intuitions implies that a is equally as good as b. Or perhaps this fact is simply grounded (in a realist manner) in the fact that a, while having a good probability of leading to something mind-independently intrinsically valuable, also has a decent probability of destroying something mind-independently intrinsically valuable. And so on. What the explication rules out is only that our comparison is grounded in the *cardinal* fact that the value of benefiting Antonio is 2/3 of the disvalue of destroying that natural beauty. And that's, again, because it assumes an identity relation between value relations and cardinal comparisons. Something similar holds for intertheoretic comparisons. The prospect-explications don't presuppose that the m-value facts are brute. It's compatible with their having grounds, as long as these grounds aren't themselves cardinal comparisons. To show that there are such grounds, or what they can be, we'll have to address the problem of intertheoretic comparisons. But it's important to note that the explication itself is neutral on this.

Thirdly and most importantly, the objector's claim that value facts are explained by *cardinal* value comparisons presupposes an independent cardinal notion of value. So if her objection is to get off the ground, she needs an alternative understanding of cardinal value comparisons. And if my reply to the previous objection is sound, this understanding is only to be had via some alternative explication. There are alternative explications. The objector could assume, say, that value acquires its cardinal significance in the context of weighing goods over time. But presumably, *all* these explications will stipulate an identity where the objector wants to see a grounding relation. On the time-explication, say, the fact that two value-differences coming at different times count the same in determining the goodness of the history of the world isn't explained by the fact that these differences are the same. Rather, for the former fact to hold *just is* for the latter to do so. And to the objector's ear this will presumably sound as objectionable as our equivalent claim about prospects. So by her own lights, nothing is gained with the move from one explication to the other. But this *tu quoque*-response doesn't imply that the entire project of getting a cardinal concept of value is doomed. It reveals that the alleged order of explanation that the objector stipulates is deceptive. It's just not true that there are primitive cardinal comparison facts that ground value facts concerning prospects or times.

If all of this is right, there doesn't seem to be anything wrong with the general approach embodied in the prospect-explications.[76] But there's a final worry, internal to this approach. It doesn't challenge the very idea of explicating value comparisons in terms of m-value facts. But it suggests the specific explications I've given still leave important questions unanswered. For one thing, even if they're viable as far as they go, they only explicate what precise comparisons mean. But if it's right that many plausible axiologies allow for intratheoretic incommensurability, we also need an explication of what rough intratheoretic comparisons mean. And if it's right that many axiologies give rise to intertheoretic incommensurability, we need an explication of what rough intertheoretic comparisons mean. For another thing, these explications don't yet tell us the meaning of axiological probabilities. As indicated, these probabilities require explication as well. And the problem of explicating probabilities isn't separate from that of explicating comparisons. If we don't take probabilities as primitives (as I've done), we need to separate probabilities and values—or cases where an axiology has a low probability but an inflated value function from cases where it has a high probability but a deflated value function. If we can't get this separation, we ultimately can't get a viable explication of either probabilities or interthereotic comparisons. So we have to refine these explications further.

I think these are important worries. They show that the Basic Representation Theorem is still too simple. It must be extended to allow for an explication of probabilities, and for one of incommensurabilities. I'll turn to this in Chapters 5 and 6 respectively.

3.4 Conclusion: decision theory and m^2-value

In sum, there are three issues we need to address to validate the argument from the Basic Representation Theorem. First and most fundamentally, we need to show that intertheoretic comparisons aren't metaphysically dubious—that there can be facts that ground such comparisons, or that such comparisons can hold.

---

[76] Ittay Nissan-Rozen (2015) raised a specific objection related to the axiomatic approach. He suggests that if we adopt the decision-theoretic explication of *intra*theoretic comparisons for our orderings $\succeq_i$, we're forced to conclude that intertheoretic comparisons are impossible—because the utility functions representing our theories will be unique only up to positive affine transformation, and so *inter*theoretic comparisons aren't fixed. But that's simply false. Nissan-Rozen is right insofar as an ordering $\succeq_i$ *in itself* can't provide the information for intertheoretic comparisons. But this doesn't rule out the possibility that *other* facts could provide it—e. g., facts about how this theory weighs against other theories under axiological uncertainty.

This is to confirm that the m-value relation isn't *radically* incomplete, and the idea of EVM not fundamentally flawed. And it's to underpin that the prospect-explications don't presuppose a dubious order of explanation, or fundamentality of the m-value facts. Second, we need to provide a representation theorem that doesn't take axiological probabilities as primitives. This is to show that we can explicate the equally problematic notion of quantitative probabilities, and separate probabilities and values effectively. Third, we need to devise a representation theorem without the Completeness axiom, either at the level of $\succeq_i$ or $\succeq_m$. That's to allow for axiologies that feature some intratheoretic incommensurability, and for axiologies that yield some intertheoretic incommensurability. And it's to extend our definitions to explicate rough comparisons too. In the remainder of the book—Chapters 4, 5 and 6 respectively—I'll address these three issues in turn.

To end this chapter, let me note two negative upshots of our discussion for the project of extending EVM beyond a theory of uncertainty about vNM-conformable axiologies. Both of them follow from the fact that if one of our axiologies isn't vNM-conformable, our m-value facts arguably aren't vNM-conformable either— or more generally, from the fact that if one of our normative assumptions isn't vNM-conformable, the meta-facts about what you ought to do under uncertainty about it arguably aren't so either. First, this has an implication for how plausible the axioms are as axioms of decision theory, or the theory of rational preferences. If m-value isn't generally vNM-conformable, but is so only when restricted to vNM-conformable axiologies, then your preferences arguably needn't be generally vNM-conformable either. You can care about m-value in your preferences. So the von Neumann-Morgenstern axioms aren't fully general constraints on your preferences. Indeed, I suggested that it's reasonable to have nonzero credences in some non-vNM-conformable axiologies. So it's reasonable to violate the von Neumann-Morgenstern axioms in your preferences. We can generalise this gloomy upshot beyond axiological uncertainty. Any uncertainty about the axioms at the level of *first*-order value or preferences implies that they're false as general, or *higher*-order constraints on decision-making in the face of uncertainty. Their mere doubtfulness implies their strict falsity. This may be the most straightforward way to criticise the axioms of decision theory. It's enough to show we can't be certain about them. And this seems almost indisputable.[77]

Second, the abovementioned fact has an implication for how general the axiomatic argument for EVM can be. As mentioned in Chapter 1, we might not be

---

[77] For an interesting general exploration of 'uncertain preferences' (though not of the specific problem I mention), see e. g. Schulz (2020).

certain about the true theory of axiological uncertainty. So we might need a theory of uncertainty about theories of axiological uncertainty—a theory of m^2-value, and so on. Now one might think if EVM is a plausible theory of m-value, it's also a plausible theory of m^2-value. And one might think the axiomatic argument I've provided for EVM as a theory of m-value can straightforwardly be extended to EVM as a theory of m^2-value—using theories of axiological uncertainty instead of axiologies, and the m^2-value relation instead of the m-value relation. Unfortunately, however, this is true only to a very restricted extent. The Basic Representation Theorem presupposes that all first-order theories are vNM-conformable. And it shows that in this case EVM is the only meta-theory that's vNM-conformable and satisfies the Pareto Condition. Accordingly, on the level of m^2-value, a similar argument will presuppose that all theories of m-value are vNM-conformable. But as the theorem itself shows, apart from theories that violate the Pareto Condition, EVM is the *only* theory of this kind. And we saw that the Pareto Condition is very plausible. So the set of theories of m-value that are vNM-conformable but violate the Pareto Condition is not a very interesting set. The more interesting set of theories are those that aren't vNM-conformable. And to those the argument doesn't apply. It follows that my argument, applied to m^2-value instead of m-value, is extremely severely limited. More generally, we can't simply assume that the same kind of argument will in principle be available, and of the same importance, on each level of value. If representation theorems are as important as I'm arguing in this book— not only in defending, but in even *defining* our views—then higher-order problems of uncertainty may be even more serious than it might have seemed. We may not even be able, in any interesting sense, to *define* our views of uncertainty about theories of axiological uncertainty.

4 The problem of intertheoretic comparisons

Let's start to address the issues that our argument from Chapter 2 raised. The most important such issue was the problem of intertheoretic comparisons—the question whether value can be compared across axiologies. Many people are sceptical about this. Edward Gracely considers a form of person-affecting utilitarianism and total utilitarianism. He asks:

> is a small loss of utility as seen by a [person-affecting utilitarian] more or less important under that theory than a large loss of utility (involving lives not created) under total utilitarianism? I don't quite see how this question could be answered. (I'll refrain from saying that it is like comparing apples and oranges, but it is!) [...] There is no abstract scale of "wrongness" outside of the rank provided *within* a theory. (1996, 331)

Similarly, John Broome is concerned with the fact that total and average utilitarianism have different 'units of value' (2012, 185): wellbeing, and wellbeing per person respectively. He says:

> We cannot take a sensible average of some amount of well-being and some amount of well-being per person. It would be like trying to take an average of a distance, whose unit is kilometres, and a speed, whose unit is kilometres per hour. Most theories of value will be incomparable in this way. (2012, 185)

And in a similar vein, James Hudson imagines a person who has some credence in the pleasure-theory (its units being 'hedons') and in the self-realization-theory (its units being 'reals'). He argues:

> What is the common measure between hedons and reals? Note that the agent, for all her uncertainty, believes with complete confidence that there's *no* common measure: she is sure that one or the other—pleasure or self-realization—is intrinsically worthless. Under the circumstances, the two units must be incomparable by the agent, and so there can be no way for her uncertainty to be taken into account in a reasonable decision procedure. (1989, 224)

Other people have expressed similar doubts.[78] In this chapter, I'll address these sceptics.

Let's recapitulate what the problem of intertheoretic comparisons is. In Chapter 1, I defined ordinal and cardinal intertheoretic comparisons respectively as facts of the form

---

78 See Gustafsson and Torpman (2014) or Hedden (2016).

(C) the value-difference between outcomes x and y, according to axiology T_i, is greater than the value-difference between outcomes z and t, according to axiology T_j; and

(D) the value-difference between outcomes x and y, according to axiology T_i, is n times as great as the value-difference between outcomes z and t, according to axiology T_j.

For most of what I'll say in this chapter, the difference between these kinds of facts doesn't matter. So to have a general term, let an *intertheoretic comparison* be a fact of either form. The problem of intertheoretic comparisons comprises three questions about these facts. First, there's a question about the *meaning* or criterion of identification of intertheoretic comparisons: what *is it*—or what would it be—for an intertheoretic comparison to hold? I've emphasised that this is unclear, both with respect to cardinal and ordinal comparisons. We might understand what it is for the value of a certain increase in wellbeing to be greater than the value of a certain increase in beauty, according to a welfare/beauty-theory. But unless more is said, it seems unclear what such comparisons across theories amount to. Yet suppose we know what it would be for intertheoretic comparisons to hold. There's then a second, object-level question about the actual *intertheoretic comparison facts*: do any intertheoretic comparisons hold; and if so, which of them do? Is the value of enjoying a bottle of Château Mouton Rothschild, according to a welfare-theory, say, as great as the value of a certain Paul Klee sketch, according to a beauty-theory—or as great as the value of a mediocre child painting, or of Leonardo's *Lady with an Ermine*? It seems unclear which such comparisons hold, or indeed whether any of them do. Yet suppose we know that some intertheoretic comparisons *do* hold, perhaps in some simple cases. There's then a third question about the *grounds* of these facts: what is it that grounds intertheoretic comparisons? It seems that axiologies themselves don't say how valuable certain things would be if certain other theories were true. So one might wonder what the basis of such comparisons can be.[79]

The sceptical challenge is to answer all of these questions. I've given an answer to the first question. I've provided an explication about what it would be for intertheoretic comparisons to hold. For such facts to hold would just be for certain m-value facts to be the case. We arguably understand what it is for m-value facts to be the case. And as the Basic Representation Theorem shows, given certain conditions, we can explicate cardinal comparisons in this manner. So this provides an answer to the question about meaning or identification.

---

79 I thank Adam Lovett for helping me see these three questions.

However, for one thing, there are other accounts of intertheoretic comparisons. So before we can know that the prospect-explication provides the best reply to the question about what it is for intertheoretic comparisons to hold, we need to discuss these proposals. For another thing, even if the explication provides a sufficient answer to this particular question, the worries about truth and grounding still remain. They now simply arise for the m-value facts. A sceptic might agree that comparisons between the welfare- and the beauty-theory could in principle be understood in terms of m-value facts. But *are* there any nontrivial facts about which prospects are m-better than which in light of uncertainty about these theories? Or is the m-value relation radically incomplete, and *a* is at least as m-good as *b* only in the trivial case when it's at least as good on all axiologies with nonzero probability? And if there are nontrivial m-value facts, what are they? If there are no m-value facts, then no intertheoretic comparisons actually hold. And if we don't know which m-value facts hold, we don't know which intertheoretic comparisons do. So the prospect-explication only defers the questions about the truth of intertheoretic comparisons. Similarly, a sceptic might even concede that some m-value facts seem plausible. But what is it that grounds them? If we don't know what grounds the m-value facts, we don't know what ultimately grounds intertheoretic comparisons. The prospect-explication only defers the questions about the grounds of such comparisons. In order to have a more complete reply to scepticism, we must say more than the simple explication of such comparisons in terms of m-value facts.

So in the remainder of the chapter, I'll first discuss existing accounts of intertheoretic comparisons (Section 4.1). I'll argue that they're all unsatisfactory in one way or another, and that this corroborates the importance of the prospect-explication as an account of the meaning of intertheoretic comparisons. I then provide a minimal argument for the truth of some such comparisons (Section 4.2). This argument doesn't tell us which intertheoretic comparisons hold, or why they do. But if sound, it establishes that at least some such comparisons are true. I'll then introduce a novel account about what grounds these truths: constructivism about intertheoretic comparisons (Section 4.3). I argue that this view provides a compelling answer to the truth and grounding problems, or more generally to scepticism about intertheoretic comparisons. I'll end the chapter by discussing the implications of constructivism for the framework of this book (Section 4.4).

4.1 Existing proposals

Here are some existing proposals about intertheoretic comparisons. These accounts weren't explicitly proposed as theories of how *axiologies* compare. They were intended to account for comparisons between moral theories generally. But we can apply them to axiologies.

Subjectivism

Consider first a proposal that may seem particularly congenial to the decision-theoretic approach of this book. We may call it 'subjectivism'. According to subjectivism, there are no objective facts about which prospects are m-better than which when you're axiologically uncertain. Rather, it all depends on you. *You* must have beliefs not only about the plausibility of axiological orderings, but also about the possible relative sizes of value-differences. You might have credence in the view that the pleasure-theory is true and that pleasure is comparatively valuable—i. e., that you ought to give a lot of weight to the pleasure- vis-à-vis the beauty-theory under uncertainty. Or you might have credence in the view that the pleasure-theory is true and that pleasure is of comparatively little value—i. e., that you ought to give little weight to the pleasure- vis-à-vis the beauty-theory. We might say you must believe in one or another version of the pleasure-theory, relative to the beauty-theory. If you have no such beliefs, there are no facts about which of your prospects are m-best relative to your state of uncertainty. And if you have such beliefs, these beliefs will ground your m-value facts. For example, if you have credence in the view that the pleasure-theory is true and that pleasure is comparatively valuable, then you ought to give the pleasure-theory a lot of weight vis-à-vis the beauty-theory in light of your uncertainty. So which of your prospects is m-best depends, radically, on which prospects you believe are m-best. If I understand her correctly, this is roughly the line that Amelia Hicks (2018) is taking. She says: 'there's no meaningful way of determining the "expected moral value" of an action. [...] However, [...] the *decision-maker* can still ordinally rank lotteries [...] and can assign utilities to the possible outcomes of their choice. It's *those* utilities—*not* the evaluations of actions provided by the competing moral theories—that determine which action has the highest expected utility for the decision-maker.' (2018, 172) As far as I see, she understands the utilities 'assigned [...] by the decision-maker' as thoroughly subjective.

What's nice about subjectivism is that it parallels a standard, Humean interpretation of decision theory. A standard assumption in decision theory is that there are no substantive constraints on your preferences. You may prefer apples to oranges, pushpin to poetry, the destruction of the world to the scratching of your finger. Your preferences are fully rational as long as they satisfy the axioms. And plausibly, there's something to some extent parallel to this in the theory of axiological uncertainty. When we ask which of your prospects is 'm-best', we might be interested in (at least) two things. We might ask how you ought to evaluate your prospects given the credences your evidence *warrants*, and the intertheoretic comparisons that are in fact *correct*. Thus understood, EVM would figure as a substantive constraint on what credences you ought to have in which theories, how you ought to compare them, and how you ought to evaluate your prospects on the basis of these credences and comparisons. However, we might also ask how you ought to evaluate your prospects given the credences you happen to have, and the intertheoretic comparisons you personally make. Thus understood, EVM would be something like a coherence constraint on you. Both of these questions are interesting in distinct ways, as I'll elaborate in the next chapter.

What matters for now is that subjectivism can't be the *whole* story about intertheoretic comparisons. We may be interested in your beliefs about such comparisons. But there must also be an objectivist story about which of these beliefs are correct, or which comparisons actually hold. Most fundamentally, if there are no objective standards to distinguish reasonable m-value beliefs from unreasonable ones, we arguably can't speak of 'beliefs' in the first place. Belief presupposes a standard of correctness. So if subjectivism is the whole story, this reduces the question of intertheoretic comparisons to something like arational personal preference. The fact of an intertheoretic comparison holding between your theories would be a merely psychological fact about you. This would imply that if you have no such preference, the theory of axiological uncertainty can't possibly be action-guiding for you. And it would also imply that you could permissibly assume out of pure caprice that the value of pleasure would be 113.27 times greater if beauty also had value (i. e., that if you have 50 % credence in the pleasure- and the pleasure/beauty-theories, you ought to 'judge' it equally m-good to bring about a certain pleasure while the pluralist theory is true and to bring about 113.27 pleasures of the same sort while the monistic theory is true). Indeed, it would mean that whenever you can permissibly have *some* nonzero credence in a theory on which one of your prospects is best, there's no basis for criticising you if you coherently 'judge' it to be m-best in light of your uncertainty. If you may have *some nonzero* credence in the Nietzschean view that you're an Übermensch for whom it's best to do what they please, there are no grounds for criticising your coherent 'judgment' that it's m-best for you to do what you please. But these are surely unfortunate results. We may ultimately be interested in your subjective credences and comparisons, and in whether you satisfy coherence constraints given them. But to assume that there *aren't any* objective criteria for evaluating your credences and comparisons seems very unsatisfying. We need a ground for saying that some intertheoretic comparisons are more reasonable than others.

Structural accounts

So what objective criteria can there be for rendering some of your beliefs about intertheoretic comparisons plausible or true, and others implausible or false? Consider 'structural accounts'. According to these proposals, intertheoretic comparisons are grounded in general principles of rationality about how to normalize axiologies for evaluating prospects under axiological uncertainty. And these principles take into account only *structural* features of the theories—i. e., features of the theories' (ordinal or cardinal) betterness-ranking. Various principles of this kind have been proposed. For instance, Ted Lockhart (2000, 84) suggested the 'Principle of Equity among Moral Theories', according to which, in every choice-situation, the value-difference between the best and the worst prospect should be considered equally large according to all theories. Andrew Sepielli (2013a, 588) discussed (but didn't endorse) a variation of this principle, according to which the difference between the best and the worst *conceivable* prospect should be considered equally large according to all theories. Will MacAskill (2014, 89 ff.; also MacAskill et al. 2020a, ch. 4) suggested that the *variance* of theories should be considered equal, where the variance of a theory is a measure of how value is spread out over different prospects—viz., the average of the squared value-differences from the mean value of prospects. And infinitely many other structural proposals can be imagined beyond these.

If a structural comparison principle holds, your beliefs about intertheoretic comparisons can be false. They're false if they contradict the relevant principle. What's nice about these accounts is that they're metaphysically parsimonious. They ground intertheoretic comparisons fully in principles of rationality, and don't assume that there's an antecedent fact of the matter about how axiologies compare. Certainly, all of the above proposals have their specific problems. A problem of Lockhart's principle is that in making comparisons relative to choice-situations, it can rank a prospect as best even if it's worse than some available alternative on every axiology in which you have credence.[80] A problem for Sepielli's proposal (as he notes) is that on many axiologies there *are* no best and worst conceivable prospects. And variance-normalisation faces some technical challenges in order to be well-defined.[81] So it remains to be seen what the most plausible principle would be.

---

80 See Sepielli (2013a).
81 See e. g. MacAskill (2014, 104, fn. 94) for an indication of a challenge, and MacAskill (2014, 76 ff.) or MacAskill et al. (2020b) for a suggestion about how to address it.

However, these accounts also face a general problem (at least if they're understood as fully general accounts of intertheoretic comparisons[82]). Insofar as
we have intuitions about intertheoretic comparisons, they're sensitive to the *content* of axiologies. Suppose you're certain that pleasure has value, but uncertain
whether beauty also has value, and that this is the only axiological uncertainty
you have. We can then describe you as being uncertain between two axiologies,
a monistic pleasure-theory and a pluralist pleasure/beauty-theory. Intuitively, it
seems reasonable to compare your two theories in such a way that the value of
pleasure is the same on both theories. After all, you're not uncertain about *that*
value. You're only uncertain about the additional value of beauty. Purely structuralist accounts can't capture this content-based intuition. More specifically, the
guiding idea of standard structural principles is that the axiological stakes should
somehow be considered equal according to all theories. But insofar as we have
intuitions about intertheoretic comparisons, it seems the stakes may be higher
on some theories than on others. For instance, it seems that if *both* pleasure and
beauty have value, the axiological stakes (overall, or in some choice-situations)
are higher than if only pleasure has value. Again, purely structuralist accounts
can't capture this intuition.[83] So the cost of their parsimony, it seems, is that they
have implausible implications. Other things equal, we should prefer accounts on
which intertheoretic comparisons are content-sensitive.

Metaphysical accounts

A range of accounts that *are* content-sensitive is what I'll call 'metaphysical accounts'. On these accounts, intertheoretic comparisons are *not* grounded in any
facts about axiologically uncertain agents—i. e., in criteria of rationality for evaluation under uncertainty, or in epistemic principles, or actual beliefs of such
agents. Rather, they're grounded in facts about values themselves, and are in this
sense 'metaphysical facts' out there. The most explicit such account has been defended by Christian Tarsney (2017; 2018a). So let me consider his version. Tarsney
starts from the comparison between the pleasure- and the pleasure/beauty-theory

---

82 MacAskill (2014) and MacAskill et al. (2020a) understand variance normalisation as applying
only to a restricted class of theories, and hold that there are other grounds for intertheoretic comparisons besides this structural principle. I'll discuss such a hybrid approach in the context of
'metaphysical accounts' below. For now I'm considering whether structural accounts are plausible as general accounts of intertheoretic comparisons.
83 The same has been argued by MacAskill (2014, 134 ff.).

I've just considered. To account for the intuitive intertheoretic comparisons between these theories, he suggests there are facts like

Value-Independence: the degree of value borne by a given unit of hedonic experience is independent of whether aesthetic goods are non-derivative value-bearers. (2017, 312)

Put more simply, Value-Independence says that the value of pleasure is independent of whether beauty also has value. Tarsney understands this as holding independently of any facts about morally uncertain agents. As he understands it, it's a fact about value, quite like the fact that pleasure is valuable (if this is a fact). It's simply a *counterfactual* axiological fact, about how valuable pleasure would be if beauty also had value.[84] I'll call a statement of this kind a *value-counterfactual*.

If such counterfactuals hold, they straightforwardly ground intertheoretic comparisons, and can thus render your beliefs about such comparisons false. This proposal can also straightforwardly account for our content-based intuitions. Value-Independence implies that the value of pleasure is the same on the pleasure- and the pleasure/beauty-theories. However, Tarsney's proposal also faces problems. To begin with, it seems unclear what value-counterfactuals should mean. Suppose the pleasure-theory is correct. What should it *mean*, say, that if beauty had value, the value of pleasure would be less than it actually is? And what should it mean, for that matter, that if beauty had value, the value of pleasure would still be exactly the same? Intuitively, we don't understand these counterfactual claims unless some further explication is given for them. And that's especially true concerning cardinal intertheoretic comparisons. We certainly have no unmediated understanding of the claim that if beauty had value, the value of pleasure would be *half* as great as it actually is, say. So it seems that the sceptical challenge of explaining what intertheoretic comparisons amount to really still remains—or has now simply been pushed back to the facts that allegedly ground them.

But suppose we have a sufficient intuitive grasp, or some helpful explication, of what statements like Value-Independence mean. There are then still worries about the object-level facts and their grounds. It's controversial that the universe contains *any* mind-independent axiological facts. But it seems quite an ontological burden to assume it should contain such *counterfactuals*. Suppose again that the pleasure-theory is true. Why should there be any fact of the matter about how the values implied by a *false* axiology compare to actual values? Why should the fabric of the universe contain not just standard axiological facts, but also counter-

---

84 See Tarsney (2017, 338 ff.).

factuals about how valuable certain things *would* be if they were valuable—when in fact they aren't?

Tarsney gives an argument for the case of Value-Independence. He points out that even in expectational reasoning under purely descriptive uncertainty, we're commonly assuming that the value of certain facts is independent of certain other facts. To use his own example (2017, 314): suppose you can press a button, and are uncertain about whether doing so will save five people or kill ten, but certain that the only valuable thing is pleasure. If you decide *not* to press this button, this will be because you assume the value of pleasure doesn't depend on whether the button saves five or kills ten. You'll assume something like 'the value of pleasure is independent of whether the button will save five or kill ten'. And this latter proposition seems true. And Tarsney says 'there's no reason to expect that whatever story we tell about the truth of these propositions [in the context of purely descriptive uncertainty] will not extend straightforwardly' to value-counterfactuals (2017, 338). However, there is a story about these propositions that doesn't extend to value-counterfactuals. It's a standard story about value. Suppose the pleasure-theory is true, and that the value of an instance of pleasure depends only on its intensity and duration. And suppose these are necessary truths. Then the value of pleasure will be the same in all worlds in which the button will save five or kill ten. So the propositions relevant for empirical uncertainty can simply be grounded in standard first-order axiological facts. But this story doesn't even begin to explain why the value of pleasure would be equally strong in worlds in which beauty also had value. This is simply a different type of fact, which requires a different story about grounding.[85]

But let's even grant the truth of some value-counterfactuals like Value-Independence—counterfactuals to the effect that the value of certain things wouldn't change if other things beyond them were valuable too. These are only the simplest counterfactuals, grounding comparisons between theories that share a common range of values, like our monistic and pluralist views. The existence of counterfactuals seems less and less plausible in more complex cases, or for axiologies that are more distinct. Take the comparison between the pleasure-theory, and a quasi-deontological theory on which there's value and disvalue only in

---

[85] Tarsney might counter that there must be something that grounds the first-order axiological fact that the value of a certain instance of pleasure depends only on its intensity and duration, and that *this* will in turn also ground the value-counterfactual. But this needn't be so. This fact about pleasure might be a fundamental fact with no further grounds. Or it might be ultimately grounded in a fact that doesn't also ground value-counterfactuals—such as the fact that all sentient beings are morally equal. Again, objective mind-independent value-counterfactuals are a peculiar kind of fact, and require a distinct story about grounding.

the following and contradicting of deontological reasons respectively—value in promises being kept or acts of beneficence being done, and disvalue in killings and robberies and lies. Suppose the pleasure-theory is correct. And consider a fact like 'if the quasi-deontological theory was true, the disvalue of breaking this promise would be as great as the actual disvalue of 25 hangnails'. The assumption that the world is populated by such more complex mind-independent counterfactuals quite definitely comes at considerable cost. And unless we have a positive story about what could ground them, or why we should assume them, we're now basically just asserting what the sceptics deny.

Tarsney acknowledges this last difficulty. He defends his metaphysical account only for theories with 'common content' (2018a, 327) or 'shared assumptions' (2018a, 332). So he concedes that 'comparability classes of normative theories may turn out to be few, small, and far between' (2018a, 336). But if this is the most we can hope for in terms of value-counterfactuals, metaphysical accounts are at best rather weak. They only explain intertheoretic comparisons for a relatively small subset of theories. To remedy this shortcoming, proponents of such an account might combine their approach with other methods of comparisons or alternative theories of uncertainty. They might hold that where metaphysical grounds are lacking, you ought to use a structural normalisation principle, or that in such cases you simply ought to evaluate your prospects in accordance with your favourite theory.[86] But these extensions seem *ad hoc*. Suppose some intertheoretic comparisons are grounded in value-counterfactuals. Then, when no such counterfactuals hold, the theories are in an important sense incomparable. And this should arguably mean that no nontrivial m-value facts hold between prospects involving these theories. Why should we ignore this fundamental incomparability, and compare the theories through some convenient normalisation principle in decision-making? Or why should EVM then fail to apply, and My Favourite Theory suddenly come to be correct? Such claims don't seem to have any independent plausibility. They seem *ad hoc* manoeuvres, just designed to avoid the resulting widespread incommensurabilities suggested by metaphysical accounts of comparisons. Other things equal, we should prefer an account that delivers intertheoretic comparisons for a broader range of theories.

Absolutist accounts

Here's a fourth approach. I'll refer to proposals of this kind as 'absolutist accounts'. On these accounts, axiologies make statements about the *absolute* sizes

---

86 See Tarsney (2017, 338 ff.) or MacAskill et al. (2020a).

of value-differences or heights of value-levels, and intertheoretic comparisons are grounded in these claims. The most prominent version of this idea employs fitting attitudes. On this proposal, there's an attitude or set of attitudes such that the fact that x is better than y means it's fitting to have these attitudes. For instance, it might mean it's fitting to be disappointed if you chose y. Furthermore, these attitudes come in degrees, and the greater the value-difference between x and y, the stronger the attitudes that are fitting. A complete axiology must tell us not only which prospects are better than which, but also what absolute degrees of such attitudes are fitting. So it must tell you not only that x is better than y, say, but also whether you ought to be slightly, or quite, or extremely disappointed, if you chose y. Consequently, there are infinitely many versions of any axiological ordering. There's the Keyed Up Pleasure-Theory, say, according to which only pleasure is valuable, and you ought to be extremely disappointed if you made someone suffer a hangnail. And there's the Calmed Down Pleasure-Theory, according to which only pleasure is valuable, but you ought to be only mildly disenchanted if you caused masses of people to be tortured. In this sense, axiologies make statements about the absolute sizes of value-differences or heights of value-levels. This has been suggested by Jacob Ross, who said: 'The scale of a value function can matter [...] quite apart from issues raised by evaluative uncertainty. [...] Two linearly evaluative theories can disagree [...] concerning the degree of disappointment that is warranted.' (2006, 765)[87] If all of this is true, intertheoretic comparisons can be grounded in axiologies' claims about attitudes. So for it to be the case that the value-difference between x and y, according to T_i, is greater than the value-difference between z and t, according to T_j, is for the attitude it would be fitting to have towards x and y if T_i is true to be stronger than the attitude it would be fitting to have towards z and t if T_j is true. And whether or not this is so will depend on the theories we consider.

If absolutism is true, your m-value judgments can also be unreasonable. They're unreasonable if you have credences in implausible versions of axiologies. Moreover, absolutism might be able to ground a cardinal concept of value. As mentioned in Section 3.3 (on page 49), if X is rich enough, an ordinal ranking of value-differences among outcomes in X is enough to determine a utility function unique up to positive affine transformation representing that ordering.[88] So suppose our set of outcomes X is relevantly rich. And suppose we understand what it is for one attitude about the value-difference between x and y to be stronger than

---

87 Sepielli (2010, 181 ff.) discusses a related view.
88 See e. g. footnote 73.

another about the difference between z and t, for all outcomes in X. Then these rankings of attitudes imply a cardinal concept of value.

What's nice about absolutism is that it doesn't presuppose any extra facts, like value-counterfactuals, beyond the facts implied by our theories. It's facts implied by the axiologies themselves that ground comparisons. However, the account faces problems as well. To begin with, there's a general question about whether fitting attitude accounts of value are plausible—or whether it's plausible that for x to be better than y just is for a certain attitude to be fitting. There are worries about this. For instance, there's the 'wrong kinds of reasons' problem—the problem of demarcating the facts that render an attitude fitting from facts that perhaps speak in favour of having it, but don't render it *fitting* (such as a millionaire's offering you £100 for being pleased about a cup of mud).[89] There's the 'circularity problem'—the problem of finding a relevant set of attitudes that are indeed fitting to have towards what's valuable, and that aren't themselves evaluative judgments (on pain of circularity).[90] And there's what we may call the 'fetishism problem'— the worry that normative ethics and value theory should primarily be about what we ought to *do*, rather than about when we ought to be saddened or pleased, as the fitting attitude account suggests.[91] The jury is still open on whether these problems can be solved.

But even if a fitting attitude account of value is plausible in general, there's a specific problem with the absolutist proposal, I think. To me at least, the core absolutist assumption seems dubious. There don't seem to be any facts about fitting absolute degrees of attitudes. If you're certain that the pleasure-theory provides the correct ordering, say, it seems meaningless to wonder whether *everything* is (linearly) more, or less, valuable than you thought, or whether it would be fitting for you to care (proportionally) more, or less, about *everything*. Suppose one person has Keyed Up Pleasure-Theory-attitudes and another has Calmed Down Pleasure-Theory-attitudes. They agree on all the kinds and *relative* strengths of attitudes. So whenever one of them is disappointed about x rather than y happening, then so is the other, and whenever one of them is five times as disappointed about this than about z rather than t happening, so is the other. But all of the first person's attitudes are stronger in absolute terms. On the absolutist proposal, at least one of them must be making a mistake, and misjudge the value of everything. But this seems implausible to me. It seems that the first person is more emotional than the second. And that's that.

---

89 This example is due to Crisp (2000, 459); see also D'Arms and Jacobson (2000).

90 See Bykvist (2009a) for this objection.

91 John Broome raised this objection in conversation.

This isn't to say people's attitudes aren't criticisable. Usually, if you're devastated about someone's suffering a hangnail or feel only a slight disenchantment about an earthquake with 100'000 casualties, your attitudes are unfitting. But this is only because you'll usually have other attitudes that show you're getting the axiological ranking of outcomes wrong—considering a hangnail as on a par with a death, or a huge earthquake as on a par with a mosquito bite. If you had one of these attitudes, but had proportionally strong or weak attitudes about everything else, you wouldn't be misjudging anything. You'd be an exceptionally impassionate or equanimous person. And since your life might be better if you cooled down or warmed up, you might have prudential reasons to work on your mental states. But you wouldn't be getting any *fact* wrong. Or so it seems to me.[92]

4.2 The Minimal Argument

In short, none of these existing proposals seems to offer a convincing general answer to the problem of intertheoretic comparisons—or the questions about what intertheoretic comparisons mean, whether any of them are true or which of them are, and what grounds them.[93] So let's turn back to the prospect-explication. Again, the prospect-explication (unlike arguably metaphysical accounts) provides a satisfying answer to the question of what it would be for an intertheoretic comparison to hold. But it doesn't yet tell us whether any such comparisons do in fact hold or which of them do, or what grounds them. So much of the challenge still remains: are there any nontrivial facts to the effect that some prospects are m-better than others? And what could ground these facts? I'll start with the first question (about truth) in the present section, and will turn to the second (about grounding) in the next.

Are there any nontrivial m-value facts? There's an analogue in social choice theory to the problem of intertheoretic comparisons—the problem of interpersonal comparisons of wellbeing. That's the question whether, or how, the wellbeing of one person compares to that of another. It's not a trivial question what the basis for such comparisons is, or what precisely they mean. But it's helpful to begin discussions in social choice theory with the observation that in everyday life we frequently make such comparisons. We say that healthy Silva is better off than sick Alba, that our money would benefit the latter more than the former, and

---

92 For a more thorough defence of this, and a more detailed exploration of the importance of things and of the limitations you face and the liberties you enjoy in adopting fitting attitudes towards everything, see e. g. Lovett and Riedener (2019).
93 For a further existing proposal, see e. g. Carr (forthcoming).

so on. And in everyday contexts, such claims seem perfectly unproblematic.[94] This doesn't *prove* that interpersonal comparisons are possible, nor does it tell us which comparisons hold, or what their basis is. But it strongly suggests something has gone awry if we deny their possibility altogether. It's helpful to begin a discussion of intertheoretic comparisons with a similar observation. It's very plausible that some nontrivial m-value facts, and intertheoretic comparisons, hold. Let's spell this out more precisely.

I've argued in the last chapter that (given our axiologies are vNM-conformable) m-value plausibly satisfies Transitivity, Independence and the Pareto Condition. I mentioned that Continuity is false if some axiologies compare in a lexical way. But if there are such axiologies, then intertheoretic comparisons are in any case possible. And barring such axiologies, Continuity seemed plausible too. So for present purposes, let's assume that the m-value facts satisfy Transitivity, Independence, Continuity and the Pareto Condition. If they do, we can give the *Minimal Argument*:

(O) The m-value facts aren't radically incomplete;
(P) if the m-value facts aren't radically incomplete (and satisfy Transitivity, Independence, Continuity and the Pareto Condition), some intertheoretic comparisons hold; therefore
(Q) some intertheoretic comparisons hold.

Here's what I mean by this. Say that two prospects a and b in $\mathcal{Q}$ are *in the same possibility-space* if they assign non-zero probability to the same axiologies, i. e., if for all i in I, a is in $\mathcal{Q}^i$ if and only if b is in $\mathcal{Q}^i$. And say that a binary relation $\succeq$ on $\mathcal{Q}$ is *radically incomplete* if for all a and b in the same possibility space,

$$a \succeq b \quad \text{only if} \quad H_i(a) \succeq_i H_i(b) \quad \text{for all } i \text{ in } I \text{ with } a \text{ and } b \text{ in } \mathcal{Q}^i. \quad (4.1)$$

Intuitively, if the m-value relation is radically incomplete, then whenever there's one theory with nonzero probability according to which b is better than a, a isn't at least as m-good as b. (O) says this is not so. It says that sometimes a prospect a is at least as m-good as another prospect b even if, according to some axiology with nonzero probability, it's worse.

This is very plausible. First of all, it simply seems highly intuitive. Take a standard welfare-theory, and a human-welfare-theory, according to which one prospect is better than another if and only if it leads to more human wellbeing, while the wellbeing of non-human animals is irrelevant. Suppose the anthropocentrism of the latter theory makes it very implausible, or that these theories

---

94 This is observed e. g. by List (2003, 229).

have probabilities of 99 % and 1 % respectively. And consider two prospects that differ in terms of the welfare of a million non-human mammals and one human being:

a all the non-human mammals live very long, happy and painless lives but the person suffers from a hangnail; and

b all the non-human mammals live very long lives full of torture and agony, but the person doesn't suffer from the hangnail (and lives otherwise as in *a*).[95]

The welfare-theory says that *a* is better than *b*; the human-welfare-theory says the opposite. Intuitively, *a* is clearly m-better than *b*. If you faced these options, under the abovementioned state of uncertainty, surely you'd judge it m-better to choose *a* in light of your uncertainty. But if *a* is m-better than *b*, that's enough to establish that the m-value facts aren't radically incomplete. Similar intuitions hold also for less closely related views. Take the pleasure-theory and the beauty-theory. Suppose the aestheticism of the latter makes it very implausible, or that these theories have probabilities of 99 % and 1 % respectively. Now consider two prospects that differ in terms of the welfare of a million human beings and the existence of a little Paul Klee sketch:

c all the people live very long, happy and painless lives but the Klee sketch is destroyed; and

d all the people live very long lives full of torture and agony, but the sketch isn't destroyed.

The pleasure-theory says that *c* is better than *d*; the beauty-theory says the opposite. Again, intuitively *c* is clearly m-better than *d*. Denying (O), or holding that even in such extreme cases no positive m-value fact holds, seems very counterintuitive.

But it's not just that. Accepting radical incompleteness would arguably involve a considerable theoretical cost. In Chapter 1 I've argued that m-value is practically very important. Basically all of our decisions are decisions in the face of axiological uncertainty. If according to the correct theory of m-value, the m-value facts are radically incomplete, this suggests that in few of our decisions it's better to do one thing rather than another in light of our uncertainty. Denying (O) amounts to a very radical normative or evaluative scepticism in practice. Consequently, it's in fact something that even many sceptics want to avoid. Few sceptics simply concede that the m-value relation is radically incomplete. Instead, they

---

95 I thank William MacAskill for suggesting this example to me.

generally endorse alternative theories of m-value that satisfy Completeness—such as My Favourite Theory.[96] A denial of (O) seemed unattractive even to sceptics.

What these sceptics may want to deny is (P). The general idea behind this premise is that intertheoretic incomparability should give rise to incompleteness in the m-value relation. The just-mentioned sceptics deny this. They think that if no intertheoretic comparisons hold, the m-value relation might still be complete—e. g. as according to My Favourite Theory. This inference from scepticism to My Favourite Theory is in fact questionable. When we determine the value of a prospect, absent any incomparability, it's very implausible that we can focus on probabilities only and ignore the values of outcomes. Both probabilities *and* values determine the goodness of prospects. That's the basic tenet of decision theory, in its simplest form. So if there *is* incomparability in values, there's no reason why we could ignore *that*, and just focus on probabilities. My Favourite Theory seems like an *ad hoc* solution for sceptics to avoid the radical incompleteness of $\succeq_m$. That's another drawback of this view.

However, for present purposes, we needn't rely on this general argument. I've presupposed that the m-value facts satisfy Transitivity, Independence, Continuity and the Pareto Condition. And at least if that is true, (P) can plausibly be treated as a matter of explication, parallel to the prospect-explications of the last chapter. If these conditions hold, and the m-value facts aren't radically incomplete, there are relevantly unique *sets* of utility functions representing our axiologies, such that a prospect is m-better than another if and only it has a greater expected utility according to all functions in this set. So again, our axiologies will weigh in a particular way against each other to determine the m-value facts. And in the sense that's relevant for us, this means they are comparable. We can say that the value-difference between x and y, according to T_i, is at least n times as great as the value-difference between z and t, according to T_j, if that is true on all utility functions in our set. The technical details of this needn't concern us now. I'll explore them in Chapter 6. What matters for now is that, given the other axioms, the weak and mundane fact that the m-value relation isn't radically incomplete already implies that our axiologies weigh in a particular constant way against each other to determine m-value. It means some intertheoretic comparisons hold.

So, at least given Transitivity, Independence, Continuity and the Pareto Condition, the Minimal Argument seems sound. Again, it establishes a very weak conclusion. The argument doesn't say which comparisons hold, or why they do. Nor does it imply that all or even most axiologies are comparable. (Q) only says that

---

96 See e. g. Gracely (1996) or Gustafsson and Torpman (2014); also Tarsney (2018a, 338 ff.).

some intertheoretic comparisons hold. Or as in the social choice context, it suggest that something has gone wrong if we deny their possibility altogether. Let's see where we get from here.

4.3 Constructivism

In principle, the prospect-explications, and the axiomatic approach of this book, are compatible with different stories about the grounds of m-value facts. My overall argument doesn't depend on the specific view I'll now outline. But I think the following story is plausible. If some nontrivial m-value facts hold, they must either be brute fundamental facts, or there must be a more fundamental kind of facts that grounds them. And m-value facts don't seem to be brute. Plausibly, there are some fundamental normative facts, such as that we're all morally equal, or that pain is bad. But facts about how you ought to evaluate your prospects under uncertainty are highly complex. It seems implausible that *they* should be fundamental.[97] More plausibly, there's a more fundamental set of facts that grounds them. Or in short, the Minimal Argument suggests that there must be a class of facts that grounds intertheoretic comparisons. So what can this be, if intertheoretic comparisons aren't entirely subjective, and if there's no structural normalisation principle, no independent metaphysical fact, or no absolutist value facts that makes certain comparisons correct? Here's the proposal I find most attractive.

The core idea

The key idea is that intertheoretic comparisons are grounded in *epistemic norms*. There are epistemic norms that are plausible independently of the problem of intertheoretic comparisons. We can understand them as holding prior to such comparisons, and grounding them in a constructivist manner.

To illustrate what I mean, let me give some examples of the kind of norms I have in mind, and of how they can be constraining. One type of norm might be synchronic norms concerning your credence distribution at any time. A good candidate of this kind is

Simplicity: *ceteris paribus*, you should favour simpler credence distributions over more complex ones.[98]

---

97 See Tarsney (2018a, 327) for a related thought.
98 I thank Christian Tarsney for suggesting this principle to me.

It's difficult to spell out precisely what 'simple' means. But we arguably have an intuitive understanding of it. So suppose Simplicity holds. Then it constrains the intertheoretic comparisons you can reasonably make. The credence distribution on which the value of pleasure is equally great on the pleasure- and the pleasure/beauty-theory is arguably simpler than that on which their ratio is 113.27, or anything other than 1. So if Simplicity is true, and if you have no reason to believe anything else, you should favour this simple comparison. More generally, you should *ceteris paribus* believe that the values shared by overlapping theories are equally great on both. You should make m-value judgments that imply intertheoretic comparisons of this form.

Other candidate norms are diachronic ones concerning the evolution of your credences over time. Consider epistemic conservatism, the idea that you shouldn't change your beliefs in the absence of any reason to do so.[99] An implication of this idea for how to deal with new evidence might be put as

Conservatism: if you encounter new evidence, then of the possible changes to your credences that accommodate this evidence you should *ceteris paribus* favour less radical over more radical ones.

This norm too constrains your intertheoretic comparisons. Suppose you've so far believed in the pleasure-theory, but now encounter some evidence for the value of beauty. The least radical way to accommodate this evidence is to adopt some positive credence in the value of beauty, but to leave your beliefs about pleasure unchanged. Any comparison on which the value of pleasure is greater, or smaller, on the pluralist theory than on the monist one would suggest you may so far have misjudged that value. It would mean you'd have to change your mind about the value of pleasure if you came to accept the value of beauty besides it. But epistemic conservatism says there's a presumption in favour of not changing your mind, or believing you were wrong, absent any positive grounds. So if Conservatism is correct, and if you have no positive countervailing reason, you should believe that the value of pleasure is equally great on both theories. More generally, you should *ceteris paribus* not change your beliefs about some given values in the face of evidence for additional values besides them.

As a third candidate norm, consider

Coherence: *ceteris paribus*, you should favour more coherent credence distributions over less coherent ones,

---

99 See e. g. Chisholm (1980), Kvanvig (1989) or McCain (2008) for versions of this view.

where coherence is understood roughly as the degree to which your beliefs are mutually supportive. Such a norm can also constrain your intertheoretic comparisons. It can do so, for instance, if you have an error theory about why you might have been mistaken about value. Suppose again you've so far believed in the pleasure-theory, but now encounter some evidence for the value of beauty. And suppose you have a belief, conditional on the pluralist theory, about why you've long missed its truth. For example, you believe that if beauty also had value, you'd simply have been insensitive to its particular worth. This explanation suggests that even if the pluralist theory is true, you've never made any mistake with respect to the value of pleasure. So it arguably coheres best with the intertheoretic comparisons on which the value of pleasure is the same on both theories. Any alternative credence distribution would suggest that you haven't just overlooked the value of beauty, but also misjudged the value of pleasure. And this wouldn't square well with your own simple error theory.

These norms are only examples. Roughly, they suggest that absent any explanation, you shouldn't assume that you've always systematically and radically misjudged the magnitude of everyday paradigm values. And they imply you should more readily assume you may have misjudged some values if you have an explanation for why and how you may have done so, or if these values are less mundane and pervasive. I take it that this is plausible. But Simplicity, Conservatism and Coherence might be false,[100] or not quite correct as I've stated them, or there might be other and more important norms besides them. And there are of course questions about how to best understand even these principles, and further work to do to prove that they'll successfully constrain our judgments.[101] My aim is not to argue for these precise norms. I'm happy if it's plausible that *some* such epis-

---

[100] For instance, Simplicity resembles common principles of Objective Bayesianism, such as the Principle of Indifference or the Principle of Maximum Entropy (see e. g. Keynes 1921, ch. 4; Jaynes 1957a, 1957b; Williamson 2010). These principles face well-known challenges (e. g., representation dependency; see e. g. von Kries 1886, or Keynes 1921, ch. 4). Simplicity might face similar challenges. See e. g. Foley (1983), Christensen (1994) or Vahid (2004) for objections to epistemic conservatism.

[101] One question will be whether agents following these principles will converge on specific judgments, rather than end up in an infinite process of ever-changing judgments, or oscillation between different equilibria. The discussion here might benefit from the existing literature on convergence in Bayesianism (see e. g. the theorem by Doob 1971). More generally, and as already indicated in footnote 100, there's a somewhat parallel debate about the most plausible principles of Objective Bayesianism (see e. g. Williamson 2010). There's also a debate about how to best understand the method of reflective equilibrium (see e. g. Elgin 1996). Important progress on our present questions might be made by building on these debates.

temic norms hold that can successfully constrain the intertheoretic comparisons or m-value judgments you can reasonably make.

If that's so, we can invoke a form of constructivism to ground intertheoretic comparisons, or judge some of your subjective beliefs about them as false. We can understand truth about intertheoretic comparisons as the outcome of ideally reasonable deliberation—in terms of principles like the above—about which of your prospects are m-best in light of your axiological uncertainty. By comparison, consider the view that truth in first-order moral theory is simply the result of an ideal process of systematising our pre-theoretic moral beliefs.[102] On this view, it's not that there's some independent Platonic realm of moral facts, and that norms of simplicity and coherence are best at guiding us towards it. Rather, the principles are first, and 'truth' is simply the outcome of the principles. We can invoke a similar kind of constructivism about intertheoretic comparisons. On this view, principles like Simplicity, Conservatism and Coherence are not justified in virtue of their guiding us towards an independent realm of m-value facts or intertheoretic comparisons. Rather, they help constitute this realm. So this provides an answer to why some m-value facts or intertheoretic comparisons hold. It's *not* because of mind-independent metaphysical facts about how theories compare, or how great certain values would be if they existed. It's simply because of facts about how to respond reasonably to axiological evidence or have reasonable axiological beliefs. Ultimately, we might say, it's because of facts about *us*—about why we might have been wrong about axiology, and by how much and in what way, and so on.

Applications, clarifications, and worries

The case of the pleasure- and the pleasure/beauty-theories was exceptionally simple. So let's see how these epistemic principles could be applied in more complex cases. Suppose you've long believed in the pleasure-theory. But you have recently come to doubt it, and now slightly prefer the above-mentioned quasideontological theory on which there's value and disvalue only in the following or contradicting of deontological reasons respectively. What intertheoretic comparisons (or m-value judgments) would it be most reasonable for you to make?

Simplicity might tell you to look at prospects or outcomes that both of these theories deem good or bad. That might be acts of beneficence, say, which both lead to pleasure and to the following of some deontological reason. So Simplicity might

---

[102] For classic (though more specific) versions of this view, see e. g. Rawls (1980), Korsgaard (1996) or Scanlon (1998).

favour a credence distribution on which the value of such acts of beneficence is the same on both views.

But these values might be comparatively inconsequential within the quasi-deontological theory. That theory might say it's *much* worse to lie or steal or break promises, say, than to omit acts of supererogatory beneficence. So this simple comparison might imply that the relevant *other* values of this theory are massively greater than the value of standard acts of beneficence on the pleasure-theory. It thus constitutes a radical departure from your original beliefs. You've so far believed that there are no such extra quasi-deontological values. But on this comparison, there might be extremely great values of this kind. So the comparison suggests you might have misjudged massively the disvalues of promise-breaking, stealing or lying. Conservatism might thus favour a credence distribution on which the value of beneficence is greater on the pleasure-theory than on the quasi-deontological axiology. Such a comparison suggests you might have misjudged the value of beneficence, as well as the other quasi-deontological values. But it doesn't imply that you might have been so horrendously wrong about the latter. So the overall extent to which you represent yourself as possibly having misjudged values might be smaller on this latter comparison than on the former. And these implications of Conservatism might have to be balanced against those of Simplicity.

But suppose you also have some pertinent non-normative beliefs. According to standard deontology, it's *ceteris paribus* more important not to harm people than to positively benefit them. So on the quasi-deontological axiology we're considering, the disvalue of harming someone is greater than the value of proportionally benefiting them. And if this theory is true, there must arguably be some explanation for why you always got this wrong, believing as you did in the pleasure-theory. Suppose you have a belief about that. Suppose you believe that conditional on the quasi-deontological theory, you always mistook these quasi-deontological values and disvalues for deontic constraints against harming that have nothing to do with axiological values. This suggest you always greatly underestimated the disvalue of harming. Thus Coherence might favour intertheoretic comparisons on which you always knew the value of beneficence—or on which your two theories agree on this—but on which it's of comparatively great disvalue to harm if the quasi-deontological theory is true. But you might have some other explanation. Suppose you believe that conditional on the quasi-deontological theory, it was because you never received much beneficence in your childhood that you turned beneficence into a sort of idol. This suggest you always greatly overestimated the value of beneficence. So in this case, Coherence might favour comparisons on which you always knew the disvalue of harming—or on which your two theories agree on *that*—but on which it's of comparatively little value to benefit if the quasi-deontological theory holds. And whatever explanation you prefer, the implications of Coherence might again have to be balanced against those of Simplicity and Conservatism.

All of this is only a rough sketch of how norms like Simplicity, Conservatism and Coherence could operate in more complex cases. But it suffices to indicate that applying these norms can be fruitful. In particular, they seem to give us more resources to make intertheoretic comparisons than metaphysical accounts allow. Our norms have non-trivial implications for the comparison between the pleasure- and the quasi-deontological theory in light of our prior beliefs, say, or our beliefs about our beliefs in the form of an error theory. These resources don't seem available for metaphysical accounts. Indeed, as I've suggested, it's unclear what a mind-independent basis for intertheoretic comparisons between such theories could be. So there's reason to be more optimistic, I think, that at least some intertheoretic comparisons hold not only for 'few and far between' theories.

One feature of the above principles is worth noting. In light of Simplicity, Conservatism and Coherence, the relevant m-value facts might be different from person to person. Most notably, it depends on your priors which intertheoretic comparisons effect the least radical changes in your credences. So in this sense, if the above principles hold, there won't be a *universal* truth of the form 'the value-difference between outcomes x and y, according to the pleasure-theory, is greater than the value-difference between outcomes z and t, according to the quasi-deontological theory'. Whether or not this statement is true will be different from person to person.

One might be worried about this, for at least three reasons. First, one might think it implies that the truth of certain propositions—i. e., intertheoretic comparisons—can be relative to individuals. And one might find such alethic relativism dubious. However, our constructivism doesn't imply such relativism. Recall that on the prospect-explication, the fact that certain intertheoretic comparisons hold among your theories only means that certain prospects are m-better than others in light of your uncertainty. So if different m-value facts hold for different people who are uncertain about the same axiological orderings, we needn't understand this as meaning that one and the same proposition—about how two specific theories actually compare—is true for one person but false for another. We can understand it as meaning that it's reasonable for these people to believe in different versions of these orderings. Talk of 'different versions' of the pleasure-theory, say, doesn't presuppose absolutism. We can assume (*pace* Ross 2006, 765) that the versions differ in nothing 'apart from issues raised by evaluative uncertainty'. On this assumption, the only difference between the pleasure-theory$_1$ and the pleasure-theory$_2$, say, concerns which prospects are m-better than which in light of uncertainty about them. So their difference will only be apparent *relative* to some fixed version of the pleasure/beauty-theory, say. And two people who have the same credences in the same orderings and for whom the same m-value facts hold cannot be further distinguished—as they can on absolutism, where all of one person's theories might be keyed up versions of the theories of the other. But all of this seems plausible. Different m-value facts can be true relative to different people, insofar as it may be reasonable for them to believe in what are, in this thin sense, different versions of their theories. There's nothing dubious or problematic about that. Or at any rate, it certainly doesn't imply alethic relativism.

By the same token, the constructivism we're invoking is less radical than it might sound. The epistemic norms ultimately determine what's m-best for you in light of your uncertainty, say, between the pleasure-theory and the quasi-deontological view. And in this sense they determine how your axiologies compare. But they needn't imply a *unique* truth about this comparison. So again, we might say they just determine what 'versions' of your theories you should have credence in. And that's to say, they function like we all think epistemic norms function—determining what propositions or theories you should believe. When they imply you should have credence, say, in versions of these theories on which the value of beneficence is equally great on both, this isn't because this value really *is* equally great. And it doesn't imply it is equally great in some Platonic realm independent of axiologically uncertain agents. It simply means beliefs in such versions is most reasonable in light of your evidence and priors.

Second, one might worry that such prior-dependency renders constructivism overly subjectivist. Suppose you started with sufficiently crazy priors—e. g., certainty in the Nietzschean axiology on which it's best if you do what you please. Couldn't this still mean that it will eventually be m-best if you do as you please? And isn't this still very unfortunate, meaning the correctness of your m-value judgments remains highly sensitive to your personal doxastic quirks?

There's a number of points in reply to this. To begin with, the present theory is nowhere nearly as subjectivist as the subjectivism considered in Section 4.1. On that theory, there were no constraints whatsoever on your comparisons. This meant that if you permissibly have *some nonzero* credence in the Nietzschean axiology there are no grounds for criticising your coherent 'judgment' that it's m-best for you to do as you please. Indeed, it meant that this couldn't even be regarded as a judgment. On constructivism, as far as I've said, there may be no constraints on your very first credence distribution among axiological orderings. But there are always at least some constraints on your comparisons (e. g. Simplicity and Coherence). And the more evidence you gather, the more such constraints will apply to you (e. g. in light of Conservatism). So it's not the case that any such nonzero credence would allow you to make Nietzschean m-value judgments, let alone that those wouldn't even be judgments. Next, nothing about constructivism implies that there couldn't also be constraints your very first credence distribution among axiological orderings. Indeed, perhaps Simplicity is such a constraint: perhaps if you have no relevant evidence, it's simpler to have equal credences in both the pleasure- and the quasi-deontological theory. Or perhaps there are other, more specific such principles.[103] Now admittedly, such constraints may not *always* uniquely determine reasonable prior credences. So there might always be some discretion for subjectivity. But finally, that's true on every standard theory of rational degrees of belief. Even the most orthodox Objective Bayesians think that there aren't always uniquely determined rational prior probabilities.[104] So it's unclear why the degree of subjectivity that remains on constructivism should in any way be implausible.

Third, one might worry that our dependency on priors makes inter*personal* intertheoretic comparisons impossible. Suppose Albert thinks it would be m-better for us to sacrifice some equality to increase overall pleasure, while Lydia thinks it would be m-better not to. Intuitively, in some such cases, there's more at stake in terms of (m-)value for one person than for the other. And the truth of such interpersonal comparisons may be important in practice: we might need them, say, to make reasonable decisions from the point of view of society, aggregating individuals' m-value judgments. So there are analogous questions here as in the case of intrapersonal intertheoretic comparisons, about what these interpersonal comparisons of m-value mean, about which such comparisons hold, and what grounds them. Structural, metaphysical and absolutist accounts won't have any problems here. Their principles will apply across individuals just as for a single individual. But one might think the version of constructivism I've sketched faces problems due to the prior- and person-relativism it implies.

However, I don't think it does. The most natural approach for constructivism is to take the perspective of society, or perhaps a neutral decision-maker, and apply principles like Simplicity and Coherence again. Suppose Albert is certain of the pleasure-theory, while Lydia is certain of a pleasure/equality-theory on which both pleasure and equality are intrinsically good. From the point of view of society, the simplest assumption seems that they agree about the value of pleasure, but disagree about whether equality has value too. So this simplicity might ground the correct comparison between their judgments. Or suppose Albert believes in the pleasure-theory, while Lydia believes in the quasi-deontological theory on which there's an extra gravity to unjust or discriminatory harms. There might be some extra facts that help us make comparisons in light of Coherence. For in-

---

103 See footnote 100.
104 See Talbott (2016, sec. 4.2).

stance, perhaps both have plenty of experience of innocent pleasures, but only Lydia has first-hand experience of injustices. This might suggest that, conditional on Lydia being right, Albert simply underestimated the disvalue of injustices due to his lack of experience. And it might suggest that, conditional on Albert being right, Lydia overestimated the disvalue of such injustices precisely because of her personal involvement in them. In short, it might suggest that they agree about the value of pleasure, but disagree about the disvalue of these inequalities. The more general point is that there's no principled reason why our or similar principles couldn't ground interpersonal comparisons too.

4.4 Conclusion: constructivism and EVM

If all I've said is correct, we've answered the three sceptical worries. The prospect-explication explains what it is, or what it would be, for an intertheoretic comparison to hold. For a certain such comparison to hold would just be for certain m-value facts to be the case. This leaves open whether any such facts are the case, or which of them are, and what grounds them. The Minimal Argument suggests that some m-value facts must hold, and that there must be some further set of facts that grounds them. But it still doesn't tell us which m-value facts hold, or in what they ground. Constructivism is at least one plausible story to fill this gap for my overall argument. It suggests facts about m-value or intertheoretic comparisons are grounded constructively in epistemic norms. And so it's these norms, together perhaps with your priors, that determine which comparisons hold. In other words, we can answer radical scepticism. It's implausible that the m-value facts must be *radically* incomplete, or the idea of EVM fundamentally flawed in light of the problem of comparisons.

A follow-up question relevant for the framework of this book is whether given constructivism (and given our axiologies are vNM-conformable) it's plausible that the m-value facts satisfy Continuity and Completeness. Take Continuity first. As indicated in Section 3.2, m-value isn't continuous if some axiologies compare in a lexical way. So is it plausible, on constructivism, that some axiologies compare lexically? It doesn't seem so. Intuitively, credence distributions that don't feature lexical dominance seem simpler than credence distributions that do. And they'll cohere better with standard simple error theories. If you've so far believed in the pleasure-theory, but now have evidence for the value of beauty, it seems plausible that if beauty had value you'd simply have been insensitive to its worth. This explanation suggests there's nothing special about beauty or pleasure. Their being valuable are equal axiological possibilities. The idea that one of them is potentially infinitely more or less important than the other would lack any explanation, or not cohere well with this error theory. Constructivism suggest that m-value satisfies Continuity, or at least doesn't violate it due to lexical intertheoretic comparisons.

So consider Completeness. As indicated, m-value isn't complete if some axiologies aren't fully commensurable. So is it plausible, on constructivism, that some axiologies are to some extent incommensurable? It seems so. Perhaps for some axiologies and some belief-sets, it's plausible that the axiologies compare in a precise way. Perhaps it's plausible that if you have no relevant error theory, you should consider the value of pleasure to be precisely equally great on the pleasure- and the pleasure/beauty-theories. But it seems implausible that no matter what other beliefs you have, there's a precise specific number n of hangnails, such that you should consider the disvalue of breaking a particular promise, according to the quasi-deontological theory, as equally great as the disvalue of suffering n hangnails, according to the pleasure-theory. Among other things, any precise number n—or any precise comparison—would seem to some extent arbitrary or inexplicable, and thus less fully coherent with the rest of your beliefs. It can sometimes be most reasonable for you to assume that some axiologies compare only roughly. Sometimes, you should consider the disvalue of breaking a particular promise, according to the quasi-deontological theory, as being determinately greater than k and determinately smaller than m hangnails, according to the pleasure-theory, but not precisely equally as great as some number n between k and m. Or in other words, constructivism suggests the m-value facts aren't radically incomplete, but may not be fully complete either.

I suggested that one reason to explore axiomatisations of EVM without the Completeness condition is that many first-order axiologies aren't complete. But even if all axiologies under consideration are complete, at least under constructivism, there's another reason to do so. Under constructivism, plausibly, you may reasonably have credence in axiologies that aren't fully commensurable. And a representation theorem without the Completeness axiom would allow our argument to cover such axiologies. As indicated, we'll turn to that in Chapter 6.

5 The problem of probabilities

A second issue that the argument from the Basic Representation Theorem raised, besides the problem of intertheoretic comparisons, was the question of how to explicate probabilities. In the Basic Representation Theorem, the concept of a probability distribution over axiologies figured as a primitive. The prospects over which the m-value relation ranges were *defined* as leading to particular outcomes with particular probabilities, while different axiologies have particular probabilities of being true. So the concept of a probability distribution over axiologies appeared as a primitive in the very definition of these prospects. That was useful to focus on the other problems I've addressed. And it follows a trend in recent decision theory, where some authors have advocated taking credences as a primitive.[105] However, at least in the theory of axiological uncertainty, this primitivism seems ultimately unsatisfying. Suppose you say the human-welfare-theory has a probability of 0.05. Unless you give *some* account of what you mean by that, we arguably don't understand your assertion—or the difference between your statement and the claim that the probability is 0.1, or 0.01. That's particularly so because the notion of an axiological probability distribution is highly complex. It's triply quantitative: specifying quantitative probabilities attached to intratheoretically cardinal axiologies among which cardinally significant comparisons hold. The last point is especially important. It's not enough to know what it is for a particular axiological ordering to have considerable weight in your m-value facts, or even to be in some sense three times as weighty as another ordering. We also need to know what it is for such an axiology to have that weight in virtue of a high probability, but a relatively deflated value function, rather than in virtue of an inflated value function, but a relatively low probability. It's not plausible that our intuitive understanding of such a rich notion goes very far. So we need an explication of what we mean by axiological probabilities. That's the task of the present chapter.

The question of how to explicate probabilities is connected with a larger question about how to understand EVM and its normativity, which I've briefly indicated (on pages 23 and 60), but which requires further clarification. 'Axiological probabilities' could mean two different things. It could mean subjective probabilities—the actual credences you have in particular versions of axiological orderings. Or it could mean evidential probabilities—the credences your evidence warrants in particular versions of axiological orderings. Accordingly, the notion of 'm-value' and the core claim of EVM could be understood more, or less, subjectively. On a more subjective interpretation of m-value, a prospect is m-better than

---

105 See e. g. Eriksson and Hájek (2007).

another if it's better in light of *your* subjective credences in particular versions of axiological orderings—or in light of your credences in axiological orderings and the intertheoretic comparisons you make between them. (Again, we can interpret credences in axiological orderings plus specific comparisons between them simply as credences in specific versions of these orderings.) On this interpretation, EVM figures as a rational coherence constraint on your m-value judgments—your judgments about which prospects are m-better than which. It says that however precisely you're axiologically uncertain, you must assign certain probabilities to your axiologies, compare them in a certain way, and evaluate prospects in terms of their expectation relative to your credences and comparisons. If you do, your m-value judgments are (subjectively) correct. I'll call this *Subjectivist EVM*.

Let me clarify. I suggested in the last chapter (Section 4.1) that subjectivism can't be the whole story. Unless there's some norms about which credences and comparisons are more reasonable than which, as long as you satisfy our coherence constraints, we'll have no grounds at all to criticise your m-value judgments. This seems unduly permissive. Intuitively, m-value judgments on which it's always m-best for you to act as an Übermensch and do what you please seem in some sense worse than others (even if they satisfy our constraints). More fundamentally, unless there are such norms, we arguably can't speak of 'credences' in the first place. But constructivism provides a standard of reasonableness for credences and comparisons. In light of it, we can speak of credences, and criticise some of them as epistemically flawed. So given constructivism, a focus on subjective credences and comparisons seems viable. Subjectivist EVM doesn't deny that there are objective grounds for criticising your credences in particular versions of axiological orderings (even beyond coherence). Perhaps in light of Conservatism and Coherence, it's inappropriate for you to believe in such a massively inflated version of the Nietzschean axiology. Subjectivist EVM just isn't interested in whether your credences and comparisons are reasonable in this sense. Instead, it's interested in whether you evaluate your prospects in a subjectively reasonable manner, *given* your credences and comparisons. We might say it's analogous to a subjective version of decision theory. This theory doesn't deny that there are grounds for criticising your preferences and non-normative credences (even beyond coherence). It's not thoroughly Humean. Perhaps believing that the world will be destroyed in the coming ten years means a gross insensitivity to our evidence. Perhaps preferring the destruction of the world to the scratching of your finger means an overestimation of your itch. Subjective decision theory doesn't ask whether your beliefs and preferences are reasonable in this sense. It just asks which prospects you should, subjectively, prefer to which *given* your credences and preferences. What I'll call Subjectivist EVM does the same. It's interested in a thoroughly subjective 'ought', not denying there's a more objective one too. Thus it says that if you evaluate prospects in terms of their expectation relative to your credences and comparisons, your m-value judgments are (subjectively) correct. If we're interested in such Subjectivist EVM, we need to know what it is for you to have a certain subjective credence in a particular theory.

On a more objective interpretation of m-value, a prospect is m-better than another if it's better in light of the credences that your evidence *warrants*, and the intertheoretic comparisons that are *correct* (in a constructivist manner, in light of the relevant empistemic norms). On this interpretation, EVM figures as a more substantive theory of m-value. It says that axiologies have certain evidential probabilities and compare in a certain way, and that a prospect is m-better than another if and only if it has the greater expected moral value relative to *these* probabilities and comparisons. So even if you evaluate prospects in terms of their expectation relative to *your* credences and comparisons, your m-value judgments might be false. I'll call this *Objectivist EVM*. It's analogous to a thoroughly objective version of decision theory, which doesn't just ask which prospects you should prefer to which *given* your credences and concerns—but also which credences and concerns you should have in the first place. If we're interested in Objectivist EVM, we need to know what it is for your evidence to warrant a certain credence in a particular theory.

Both Subjectivist and Objectivist EVM are interesting. There are reasons to explore the objectivist theory. It's often more in line with our actual practice. Often when we reflect on what's (m-)best in the face of arguments for competing axiologies, we try to make judgments that are sensitive to our evidence and the correct comparisons. We don't try to make judgments that are sensitive to the credences and comparisons we happen to find ourselves with. Metaphorically speaking, our credences are *transparent* in our judgments: we don't look *at* them, but with them or through them in judging our options.[106] Moreover, Objectivist EVM is more thoroughly normative. If you satisfy Subjectivist EVM, but have wildly inappropriate axiological credences, your m-value judgments are still importantly suboptimal. But there are reasons to explore the subjectivist theory too. Subjectivist EVM doesn't seem alien to our practice. We can certainly try to make judgments that are sensitive to the credences and comparisons we happen to have, or that we settled upon after first reflecting on our evidence. It's not that we necessarily try to reach objectivist verdicts. More positively, there's a sense in which Subjectivist EVM focuses most clearly on the normativity of the theory of axiological uncertainty. Suppose you maximise expected value relative to your credences and comparisons, but have inappropriate credences. Then you aren't making a

106 I thank Felix Koch for pointing this out to me.

mistake about whether EVM, or My Favourite Theory, or some meta-deontological theory of axiological uncertainty is true, say. You're making an epistemic mistake. In this sense, as long as you're satisfying Subjectivist EVM, you're not making a mistake peculiar to the theory of axiological uncertainty. Finally, the notion of a subjective probability or credence is arguably conceptually more fundamental than that of an evidential probability or evidentially *warranted* credence. Only if we know what it is to have certain credences can we know what it is for certain credences to be warranted.

Fortunately, the two theories raise similar questions, and can be developed in similar fashions. So our focus doesn't matter very much. I'll generally start by elaborating on Subjectivist EVM, and then translate my arguments into Objectivist EVM. In line with my approach so far, I'll introduce an explication of axiological probabilities on the basis of a representation theorem (Section 5.1). I'll outline how we can apply a theory based on this explication in our practical decision-making (Section 5.2). And I'll then defend the explication against objections. I argue that representation theorems provide our best account of axiological probabilities, and outline the implications of this claim for the normativity of EVM (Section 5.3). Since all of this is controversial territory, I'll end the chapter by introducing Weighted Value Maximisation—a theory of axiological uncertainty that eschews the notion of credences altogether (Section 5.4).

5.1 The Representation Theorem for Probabilities

There are various possible answers to our question about what you mean by saying your credence in the human-welfare-theory is 0.05. But not all answers are equally good. Consider the

Simple Explication: That your credence in T_i is p_i means that when you consider the set of possible axiologies, consider how confident you feel about each axiology in light of the evidence for and against it, and try to associate a nonnegative number to each of them, such that the numbers add up to 1 and reflect your confidence, you associate with T_i the number p_i.

This might explain what you mean by saying your credence in the human-welfare-theory is 0.05. You might mean you distributed numbers to axiologies in accordance with your feelings of confidence and the human-welfare-theory ended up getting 0.05. However, this isn't a very good explication. For one thing, the Simple Explication doesn't seem to pick out something we'd intuitively identify as your degrees of belief. Suppose for some reason you associate the number zero to the human-welfare-theory on introspection. If in your actions and attitudes, and in your judgments about which prospects are m-best, you give considerable weight to that theory, then intuitively you *do* have credence in it. You simply misjudged your confidence. We need to pick out something closer to our intuitive concept of credences. For another thing, the Simple Explication doesn't seem to pick out something normatively very relevant. We can perform such an exercise of introspection. But assigning numbers to axiologies will soon seem a rather arbitrary stab in the dark. It would seem reckless to ground the most important decisions in our life solely on this intuitive list of numbers. We need to pick out something normatively more important.

A prominent candidate route is again via representation theorems. Let's start with some background. One of the first to explicate credences was Bruno de Finetti (1980, 62). He suggested that your credence in a proposition p is the rate x for which you'd be indifferent between receiving any sum of money S if p is true, and receiving xS with certainty. So for you to have a credence of 0.25 that it will rain today, say, is for you to be indifferent between receiving £1 if it rains and the certain gain of £0.25. The obvious problem with this is that it seems to misrepresent your beliefs if money has diminishing marginal value for you. If you prefer a sure gain of £1 million to the bet that gives you £2 millions if and only if some coin lands tails, you needn't think the coin isn't fair. You might simply care more about the first than the second million.[107] For this reason, the account given by Frank Ramsey (1990) was more promising. Ramsey provided a simple theorem showing that if your preferences satisfy certain conditions you can be represented as maximising expected utility with respect to relevantly unique probability and utility functions—which needn't conform linearly to any other independently specifiable quantity. According to Ramsey, this probability function can be interpreted as representing your credences. Ramsey's account was further refined by Leondard Savage (1954), who provided a conceptually more sophisticated theorem. The main tenet of all these explications is that to have a particular credence in a proposition is to give that proposition a particular weight in your preferences under uncertainty. Representation theorems show that if your preferences satisfy certain conditions, you maximise expected utility with respect to certain utility and probability functions. And according to the explications, we can then treat the probability function as specifying your actual credences.

I think this idea is promising. However, if we're to explain your *axiological* credences, we can't simply focus on your preferences. Perhaps you just don't care about moral value. Or perhaps you also care about many things besides it—your

---

107 See e. g. Eriksson and Hájek (2007) and Hájek (2019) for other famous objections against De Finetti's interpretation.

self-interest, the welfare of your family, deontological constraints, or whatever. So you may give little weight in your preferences to the human-welfare-theory, say, and still find it plausible *as* an axiology. We need to separate your axiological and non-axiological concerns. We can do so by focusing on which prospects you find m-better than which. In other words, instead of explicating credences in terms of preferences, we can do so in terms of *m-value judgments*. Your credence p_i in an axiology T_i is the weight you give that axiology in your m-value judgments. I'll refer to this as the *judgment-explication* of axiological credences. So what I'll look for is a set of conditions C such that, if your m-value judgments satisfy C, you maximise expected utility relative to a unique probability and a relevantly unique utility function. And I'll then assume that the probability function represents your axiological credences. Again, I treat this as an explication. The claim isn't that our theorem will identify the credences you *really* have. There's no such thing. Rather, the probabilities from this theorem pick out something close to our intuitive concept of credences, and something normatively important. That will be my claim in what follows.

Axiological Probabilities

So far, I've spoken rather impersonally about what '*our* axiologies' and '*the* m-value facts' are. But according to Subjectivist EVM, you should evaluate your prospects relative to *your* credences and values. So we now need to focus on the axiologies you consider, and the m-value facts relative to the credences you have in them. We need to reinterpret our formal framework slightly. To determine what your axiologies are, I'll assume you make (considered) judgments about prospects in $\mathcal{O}$, of the form 'according to axiology T_i, a is better than b'. I represent your judgments of this kind by 'your $\succeq_i$', to indicate that the set of these axiologies is the set you are considering. From these judgments, we can read off what axiological orderings you're considering. For instance, if you judge that according to T_1, a prospect is better than another if and only if it expectably leads to more human welfare, then, we'll assume, by T_1 you mean the human-welfare-theory.

However, we need to know not only what orderings, but also what *versions* of these orderings you're considering—or how you're comparing your orderings against each another. To that end, I'll assume you make (considered) m-value judgments about prospects in $\mathcal{Q}$. We might think of these as counterfactual judgments of the form 'if the probability distribution over axiologies was P, a would be m-better than b'. I represent these judgments by 'your $\succeq_m$', to indicate that these are what you take to be the counterfactual m-value facts. From these judgments, we can read off how you're comparing your axiologies against each other. Suppose you consider the human-welfare-theory T_1 and the non-human-animal-welfare-theory T_2. And you judge that if they had a probability of 1/3 and 2/3 respectively, it would be equally m-bad to inflict a given amount of pain on a human or on a non-human animal. Then, we'll assume, you think the value of a given amount of human welfare, according to T_1, is twice as great as that of the same amount of animal welfare, according to T_2.

However, we now also need to know what credence you have in these theories. To that end, we need a third set of prospects, beyond $\mathcal{O}$ and $\mathcal{Q}$. More specifically, we need a set $\mathcal{K}$ of probability distributions on X, in which the probability distribution over axiologies isn't specified. Intuitively, a prospect in $\mathcal{K}$ may be, say, that a person will suffer if and only if T_1 is true, or that a person will suffer if and only if T_1 is true and a non-human animal if and only if T_2 is true. I'll use cursive letters a, b, c... to refer to prospects in $\mathcal{K}$. Formally, these prospects can be represented as the set of theory-dependent probability distributions on X—i.e., $\mathcal{K} = \{a : I \times X \to \mathbb{R}_+ \mid \sum_{x \in X} a(i, x) = 1 \ \forall i \in I\}$. The second just-mentioned prospect, say—on which a person will suffer if and only if T_1 is true and a non-human animal if and only if T_2 is true—will thus be represented as the function a in $\mathcal{K}$ that assigns 1 to the pair of T_1 and the fact that the person suffers, 1 to the pair of T_2 and the fact that the non-human animal suffers, and 1 to the pairs of all other theories and the fact that nothing happens. Note that in a prospect in $\mathcal{K}$, the numbers assigned to outcomes sum to 1 *within* each axiology, not across axiologies. So a prospect in $\mathcal{K}$ doesn't specify an underlying probability distribution over axiologies. I'll assume you also make (considered) m-value judgments about prospects in $\mathcal{K}$. We might think of these as non-counterfactual judgments of the form 'a is m-better than b', relative to your credences. I represent these judgments by 'your $\tilde{\succsim}_m$,' (or 'your $\tilde{\succ}_m$' and 'your $\tilde{\approx}_m$'), to indicate that these are what you take to be the m-value facts relative to your credences. So I use a tilde to distinguish them from your judgments $\succsim_m$ on $\mathcal{Q}$.

If we know your judgments about $\mathcal{Q}$, then from your judgments about $\mathcal{K}$, we can read off what credences you have in your axiologies. By considering your counterfactual judgments ('If the probability distribution over theories was P, a would be m-better...'), we can detect your values. The function representing these judgments is a pure reflection of values, since the probabilities are already given in the prospects. And knowing your values, we can then detect your probability distribution by considering your ordinary judgments ('Actually, a is m-worse...'). Suppose, as we assumed above, that in your m-value judgments about $\mathcal{Q}$, you judge that *if* T_1 and T_2 had a probability of 1/3 and 2/3 respectively, it would be equally m-bad to inflict a given amount of pain on a human or on a non-human animal. So you think the value of a given amount of human welfare, according to T_1, is twice as great as that of the same amount of animal welfare, according to T_2.

And suppose that in your m-value judgments about $\mathcal{K}$, you judge that *actually* it's equally m-bad to inflict a given amount of pain on a human or *twice* that amount on a non-human animal. Then, if T_1 and T_2 are the only axiologies you consider, we'll assume you actually have a credence of 1/2 in both of them.

That's the rough idea. To sum up, we'll need three kinds of judgments from you in order to get a relevant expected utility representation: judgments about which prospects are better than which according to your axiologies (represented by your $\succeq_i$ on $\mathcal{O}$), judgments about which prospects *would* be m-better than which *given* that axiologies had certain probabilities (represented by your $\succeq_m$ on $\mathcal{Q}$) and judgments about which prospects *are* m-better than which relative to your credences (represented by your $\tilde{\succeq}_m$ on $\mathcal{K}$).

Three notes about this framework are in order. First, the set $\mathcal{Q}$ still presupposes that we understand what it means that a particular axiology has a particular probability. One may worry that we don't—indeed, that it's precisely because we don't understand this that we needed a new framework, and that this framework thus mustn't feature our set $\mathcal{Q}$. But I think we can answer this worry. What I'd doubt is a pretheoretic understanding of quantitative subjective or evidential probabilities. The relevant notion in $\mathcal{Q}$ can be understood differently. For example, we might imagine that God determined the true axiology on the basis of a device involving an unpredictable quantum mechanical phenomenon, and understand the prospects in $\mathcal{Q}$ in terms of objective propensities of that device. We can assume you satisfy Lewis' (1980) Principal Principle, as part of our understanding of subjective probabilities. And given this assumption, we can take your m-value judgments about $\mathcal{Q}$ to be a pure reflection of your values. Judgments like 'If the probability distribution over theories was P, ...' could be understood as meaning: 'Supposing God's device had propensities represented by P, ...'. This adds another complexity to my framework. But I think it's only that: an extra complexity. The presupposition of $\mathcal{Q}$ doesn't make our explications circular, incoherent, or overly primitivist.

Second, note that the sets $\mathcal{K}$ and $\mathcal{Q}$ both specify an underlying probability distribution over outcomes (relative to each axiology). In this sense, I'm still taking purely descriptive probabilities as given primitives. In principle, this is problematic, for similar reasons as it was problematic to take axiological credences as a primitive. However, my main concern is with axiological uncertainty. This problem is complicated enough. To keep it as simple as possible, I'll assume purely descriptive probabilities as primitives throughout.

Third, the set $\mathcal{K}$ includes *all* theory-dependent probability distributions over outcomes. In particular, and as illustrated by the above example, it includes prospects that lead to different (probability distributions over) outcomes, depending on which axiology is true. That is, for some a in $\mathcal{K}$, some x in X, and some

T_i and T_j, $a(i,x) \neq a(j,x)$. As with the analogous prospects in $\mathcal{Q}$, these prospects won't represent any natural, practical options. There's no natural act which leads to a non-human animal suffering if one theory is true, and a person suffering if another theory is true. But as with the prospects in $\mathcal{Q}$, such prospects seem conceptually possible (see page 23). So I think it isn't a problem for our framework that $\mathcal{K}$ includes them. On the contrary, it would be a drawback if it didn't. Apart from this somewhat non-practical aspect, judgments about $\mathcal{K}$ are fairly natural. Indeed, in some sense they're more straightforward than judgments about $\mathcal{Q}$. They don't require us to counterfactually imagine a specific probability distribution over axiologies. They just require us to judge how we'd evaluate prospects in light of our actual uncertainty or evidence. So I take it it's plausible to assume that we can make considered m-value judgments about $\mathcal{K}$ (as well as about $\mathcal{O}$ and $\mathcal{Q}$).

Given this framework, we can state our new theorem. It will again feature the three conditions of the Basic Representation Theorem: that all your $\succeq_i$ and your $\succeq_m$ are vNM-conformable, and that your $\succeq_m$ satisfies the Pareto Condition with respect to your $\succeq_i$. As we know from the Basic Representation Theorem, if your judgments satisfy these conditions, there's a function $u : I \times X \to \mathbb{R}$, unique up to positive affine transformation, such that for all $\boldsymbol{a}$ and $\boldsymbol{b}$ in $\mathcal{Q}$, all a and b in $\mathcal{O}$ and all i in I,

$$\boldsymbol{a} \succeq_m \boldsymbol{b} \quad \text{iff} \quad \sum_{i \in I, x \in X} \boldsymbol{a}(i,x)u(i,x) \geq \sum_{i \in I, x \in X} \boldsymbol{b}(i,x)u(i,x), \quad \text{and} \tag{5.1}$$

$$a \succeq_i b \quad \text{iff} \quad \sum_{x \in X} a(x)u(i,x) \geq \sum_{x \in X} b(x)u(i,x). \tag{5.2}$$

We now need to relate this to your judgments about $\mathcal{K}$. To that end, we need two new conditions. The first is that your $\succeq_m$ on $\mathcal{K}$ also satisfies the von Neumann-Morgenstern axioms. Define $pa + (1-p)b$ in $\mathcal{K}$ as the prospect that leads to a with probability p, and to b with probability $(1-p)$, hence $(pa+(1-p)b)(i,x) = pa(i,x) + (1-p)b(i,x)$ for all (i,x) in $I \times X$. For a reflexive binary relation $\succeq$ on $\mathcal{K}$, our axioms are

Transitivity$_\mathcal{K}$: for all a, b and c in $\mathcal{K}$, if $a \succeq b$ and $b \succeq c$, then $a \succeq c$;
Completeness$_\mathcal{K}$: for all a and b in $\mathcal{K}$, $a \succeq b$ or $b \succeq a$;
Independence$_\mathcal{K}$: for all a, b and c in $\mathcal{K}$ and $p \in]0,1[$, if $a \succ b$, then $pa + (1-p)c \succ pb + (1-p)c$; and
Continuity$_\mathcal{K}$: for all a, b and c in $\mathcal{K}$, if $a \succ b$ and $b \succ c$, then there exist $p, q \in]0,1[$, such that $pa + (1-p)c \succ b$ and $b \succ qa + (1-q)c$.

If a reflexive relation $\succeq$ on $\mathcal{K}$ satisfies these conditions, I'll again say it's 'vNM-conformable'. For two functions $u : I \times X \to \mathbb{R}$ and $v : I \times X \to \mathbb{R}$, say that v is a *positive unit-comparable transformation* of u if there are s and $t_i \in \mathbb{R}$, $s > 0$, such that $v(i, x) = su(i, x) + t_i$ for all i in I and x in X. It can be shown[108] that if $\tilde{\succeq}_m$ is vNM-conformable, there's a function $v : I \times X \to \mathbb{R}$, unique up to positive unit-comparable transformation, such that for all a and b in $\mathcal{K}$,

$$a \tilde{\succeq}_m b \quad \text{iff} \quad \sum_{i \in I, x \in X} a(i, x)v(i, x) \geq \sum_{i \in I, x \in X} b(i, x)v(i, x). \tag{5.3}$$

However, this isn't enough for our purposes. For all we know, v might be a random utility function without any relation to your axiologies or your m-value judgments about $\mathcal{Q}$. We need to ensure that the value functions v from (5.3) and u from (5.1) and (5.2) are related to each other—or more precisely, that the function v can be understood as a product of your values, as specified by u, and your credences, as specified by a probability function P on I.

So we need a further substantive condition. We need to assume that $\succeq_m$ and $\tilde{\succeq}_m$ are value-consistent—so that the differences between them can be fully explained by the underlying probabilities in $\mathcal{Q}$. To state this condition, let $\mathcal{Q}^+ \subset \mathcal{Q}$ be the set of prospects in $\mathcal{Q}$ on which all axiologies have a positive probability, i. e. $\mathcal{Q}^+ = \{a \in \mathcal{Q} \mid \sum_{x \in X} a(i, x) > 0 \ \forall i \in I\}$. Define a function $L : \mathcal{Q}^+ \to \mathcal{K}; a \mapsto L(a)$, such that for all i in I and x in X,

$$L(a)(i, x) = a(i, x)/ \sum_{y \in X} a(i, y). \tag{5.4}$$

Intuitively, L turns a prospect in $\mathcal{Q}^+$ into the corresponding prospect in $\mathcal{K}$ in which the underlying probabilities have been scraped out. For some i in I and a and b in $\mathcal{K}$, say that a and b *agree outside* i if for all j in I with $j \neq i$, and all x in X, $a(j, x) = b(j, x)$; and similarly for some a and b in $\mathcal{Q}$. For some i in I and binary relations $\succeq$ on $\mathcal{Q}$ and $\tilde{\succeq}$ on $\mathcal{K}$, say that i is *null* if (i) for all a and b in $\mathcal{K}$ that agree outside i, $a \approx b$, and (ii) there exist a and b in $\mathcal{Q}$ that agree outside i such that $a \succ b$. Say that i is *non-null* if there are a and b in $\mathcal{K}$ that agree outside i such that $a \tilde{\succ} b$. Now for binary relations $\succeq$ on $\mathcal{Q}$ and $\tilde{\succeq}$ on $\mathcal{K}$, define the

Consistency Axiom: For all i in I and all a and b in $\mathcal{Q}^+$, if a and b agree outside i and $L(a) \tilde{\succ} L(b)$, then $a \succ b$. Moreover, if i is non-null, then for all a and b in $\mathcal{Q}^+$ that agree outside i, if $a \succ b$, then $L(a) \tilde{\succ} L(b)$.

This condition ensures that your judgments about $\mathcal{K}$ and $\mathcal{Q}$, or the functions v from (5.3) and u from (5.1) and (5.2), are appropriately related. As a more technical assumption, we also need to assume that neither your axiologies nor your m-value judgments about $\mathcal{K}$ are uniform, or rank all prospects as equally (m-)good. So for

---

108 See Karni and Schmeidler (1980, 7).

some binary relations $\succeq_i$ on $\mathcal{O}$ and $\tilde{\succeq}$ on $\mathcal{K}$ say that $\succeq_i$ is *non-uniform* if there are a and b in $\mathcal{O}$ such that $a \succ_i b$, and that $\tilde{\succeq}$ is *non-uniform* if there are a and b in $\mathcal{K}$ such that $a \tilde{\succ} b$. We can now state the

Representation Theorem for Probabilities: *Suppose that all your $\succeq_i$ are vNM-conformable and non-uniform. If your $\succeq_m$ and your $\tilde{\succeq}_m$ are vNM-conformable and jointly satisfy the Consistency Axiom, if your $\succeq_m$ satisfies the Pareto Condition with respect to your $\succeq_i$, and your $\tilde{\succeq}_m$ is non-uniform, there's a unique probability distribution P on I and a function $u : I \times X \to \mathbb{R}$, unique up to positive affine transformation, such that for all a and b in $\mathcal{K}$, all $\mathbf{a}$ and $\mathbf{b}$ in $\mathcal{Q}$, all a and b in $\mathcal{O}$ and all i in I,*

$$a \tilde{\succeq}_m b \quad \text{iff} \quad \sum_{i \in I, x \in X} a(i,x)P(i)u(i,x) \geq \sum_{i \in I, x \in X} b(i,x)P(i)u(i,x), \tag{5.5}$$

$$\mathbf{a} \succeq_m \mathbf{b} \quad \text{iff} \quad \sum_{i \in I, x \in X} \mathbf{a}(i,x)u(i,x) \geq \sum_{i \in I, x \in X} \mathbf{b}(i,x)u(i,x), \quad \text{and} \tag{5.6}$$

$$a \succeq_i b \quad \text{iff} \quad \sum_{x \in X} a(x)u(i,x) \geq \sum_{x \in X} b(x)u(i,x), \tag{5.7}$$

and such that if i is null, $P(i) = 0$, and if i is non-null, $P(i) > 0$.[109]

This is a purely mathematical theorem. It says that if your $\succeq_i$, $\succeq_m$ and $\tilde{\succeq}_m$ satisfy these conditions, there are mathematical functions that represent these relations. To turn it into a philosophically significant result, we must again add the relevant conceptual assumptions. So let me express more formally the judgment-explication—or the idea that your credence in an axiology is the weight you give it in your m-value judgments. To restate the prospect-explication of intra-theoretic comparisons within the subjective framework we're now assuming, for your binary relation $\succeq_i$ on $\mathcal{O}$ and a function $u : X \to \mathbb{R}$, say that *u represents your $\succeq_i$ ordinally* if for all a and b in $\mathcal{O}$,

$$a \succeq_i b \quad \text{iff} \quad \sum_{x \in X} a(x)u(x) \geq \sum_{x \in X} b(x)u(x). \tag{5.8}$$

Furthermore, say that a function $u : X \to \mathbb{R}$ *represents your $\succeq_i$ cardinally* if for all x, y, z and t in X and $n \in \mathbb{R}$, the value-difference between outcomes x and y is n times as great as the value-difference between z and t, according to your T_i, if and only if $(u(x) - u(y))/(u(z) - u(t)) = n$. The *judgment-explication of intratheoretic comparisons* says that if there is a function $u : X \to \mathbb{R}$, unique up to positive affine transformation, which represents your $\succeq_i$ ordinally, then u represents your $\succeq_i$ cardinally. Now for binary relations $\succeq_m$ on $\mathcal{Q}$ and $\tilde{\succeq}_m$ on $\mathcal{K}$, a probability distribution

---

[109] See the appendix (Section A.2) for a proof.

P on I and a function $u : I \times X \rightarrow \mathbb{R}$, say that (P, u) *represents your* $\succeq_m$ *and* $\tilde{\succeq}_m$ *ordinally* if for all $\boldsymbol{a}$ and $\boldsymbol{b}$ in $\mathcal{Q}$ and all a and 6 in $\mathcal{K}$,

$$\boldsymbol{a} \succeq_m \boldsymbol{b} \quad \text{iff} \quad \sum_{i \in I, x \in X} \boldsymbol{a}(i, x) u(i, x) \geq \sum_{i \in I, x \in X} \boldsymbol{b}(i, x) u(i, x), \quad \text{and} \tag{5.9}$$

$$a \tilde{\succeq}_m 6 \quad \text{iff} \quad \sum_{i \in I, x \in X} a(i, x) P(i) u(i, x) \geq \sum_{i \in I, x \in X} 6(i, x) P(i) u(i, x). \tag{5.10}$$

Furthermore, suppose that for some probability distribution P on I and some function $u : I \times X \rightarrow \mathbb{R}$, the crosscutting cardinal intertheoretic comparisons between all outcomes and all theories are the same as the ratios among the utility differences between these outcomes according to u, and that your credences in any axiology T_i is $P(i)$—that is, for all x, y, z, t in X, all i, j, h, k in I and $n \in \mathbb{R}$, the difference between the value of x, according to your T_i, and the value of y, according to your T_j, is n times as great as the difference between the value of z, according to your T_h, and the value of t, according to your T_k, if and only if $(u(i, x) - u(j, y))/(u(h, z) - u(k, t)) = n$, with $p_i = P(i)$, $p_j = P(j)$, $p_h = P(h)$ and $p_k = P(k)$. I'll then say that (P, u) *represents your intertheoretic comparisons cardinally and your axiological probabilities quantitatively.* The *judgment-explication of your intertheoretic comparisons and axiological probabilities* says that if there is such a pair (P, u), with P being unique and u unique up to positive affine transformation, which represents your $\succeq_m$ and $\tilde{\succeq}_m$ ordinally, and if for all i in I, $u(i, \cdot)$ represents your $\succeq_i$ cardinally, then (P, u) represents your intertheoretic comparisons cardinally and your axiological probabilities quantitatively. So we can interpret all utility functions $u(i, \cdot)$ jointly as value functions G_i, and the probabilities $P(i)$ as your credences p_i.

Given this explication, the following theorem holds:

Expected Value Theorem for Probabilities: *Suppose that all your* $\succeq_i$ *are vNM-conformable and non-uniform. If your* $\succeq_m$ *and your* $\tilde{\succeq}_m$ *are vNM-conformable and jointly satisfy the Consistency Axiom, if your* $\succeq_m$ *satisfies the Pareto Condition with respect to your* $\succeq_i$ *and your* $\tilde{\succeq}_m$ *is non-uniform, then for all a and 6 in* $\mathcal{K}$,

$$a \tilde{\succeq}_m 6 \quad \text{iff} \quad \sum_{i \in I, x \in X} a(i, x) p_i G_i(x) \geq \sum_{i \in I, x \in X} 6(i, x) p_i G_i(x).^{[110]} \tag{5.11}$$

This is a non-mathematical result. But it's still only a conditional. It says that if your m-value judgments satisfy the relevant conditions, you're as a matter of fact

---

[110] See the appendix (Section A.2) for the derivation of this theorem from the Representation Theorem for Probabilities and the judgment-explications.

following (5.11)—and that is, EVM. Clearly, the converse is also true: if there exist a probability distribution P, and functions G_i that represent your axiologies cardinally, and your judgments satisfy (5.11) (and its equivalent regarding Q) with respect to them, then your judgments will satisfy the relevant conditions. So if we're interested in Subjectivist EVM, we can now turn this into an argument for the normative truth of (5.11). Denote the conditions in the antecedent of this theorem ('If your $\succeq_m$ and your $\tilde{\succeq}_m$...') by 'C'. And say that you satisfy C, or that your judgments are 'C-conformable', if your judgments satisfy these conditions. If all your axiologies are vNM-conformable and non-uniform, we can then argue:

(R) your m-value judgments are (subjectively) correct if and only if you satisfy C;
(S) as a matter of logical equivalence, you satisfy C if and only if you follow Subjectivist EVM; therefore
(T) your m-value judgments are (subjectively) correct if and only if you follow Subjectivist EVM; Subjectivist EVM is true.

This is the main argument for a form of Subjectivist EVM.[111]

As mentioned, the Representation Theorem for Probabilities can be used to ground Objectivist EVM too. To that end, we can interpret the relations $\succeq_i$ as denoting which prospects are better than which according to our axiologies—or as inducing the axiological orderings under consideration. We can interpret the relation $\succeq_m$ as denoting which prospects *would* be m-better than which for you, if axiological orderings had certain antecedently specified probabilities—or as inducing the intertheoretic comparisons that are *reasonable* for you to make between these orderings. And we can interpret the relation $\tilde{\succeq}_m$ as denoting which prospects are m-better than which, given your evidence—or as inducing the credences that your evidence *warrants* in the respective versions of our axiologies. The resulting argument would be similar to the argument outlined in Chapter 2: the m-value facts satisfy C; if they satisfy C, Objectivist EVM is true; therefore Objectivist EVM is true. For simplicity, I'll continue to focus on the subjectivist version of the theorem, the argument and EVM. But much of what I say applies *mutatis mutandis* to the objectivist version as well.

A brief note about the plausibility of the meta-axiological assumptions. Most of the conditions of the Representation Theorem for Probabilities are familiar from

---

111 Note that this argument is only sound if you make *subjective* judgments, about which prospects are m-better than which relative to your credences and the comparisons you make. If you make objectivist judgments, about which prospects are m-better than which relative to the credences your evidence warrants and the comparisons that are (constructively) correct, your judgments may satisfy C and still be false—by embodying unwarranted credences or mistaken comparisons.

the Basic Representation Theorem. So my discussion of these conditions in Chapter 3 (and Chapter 6) clarifies how plausible they are as normative constraints on your (m-)value judgments. The problem of incommensurabilities carries over to the present context. Your $\succeq_i$ needn't satisfy Completeness, because according to some of your axiologies, some prospects might not be fully commensurable. And in addition, your $\succeq_m$ and $\tilde{\succeq}_m$ needn't satisfy Completeness, because some of your axiologies may be less than fully commensurable to each other. However, in the context of your $\tilde{\succeq}_m$ on $\mathcal{K}$, there might be an additional reason for why your judgments needn't be complete. To assume that your $\tilde{\succeq}_m$ should satisfy Completeness is to assume that your credences ought to be sharp, or representable by single real numbers. If your credences can justifiably be 'fuzzy'—or less than fully sharp—your $\tilde{\succeq}_m$ needn't be complete. And this is so even if all your axiologies are complete and fully commensurable. There are strong arguments to the effect that your non-normative credences needn't be precise, and these plausibly carry over to axiological credences.[112] But since the problem of fuzzy credences is not specific to axiological uncertainty, I'll rule out fuzzy credences throughout this book. So this is another important restriction of our arguments. It's plausible that your axiological credences can justifiably be fuzzy, but I'll ignore this.

5.2 Applying Subjectivist EVM in practice

I'll presently discuss objections to the argument just outlined. But first, it might help to spell out how the theory of axiological uncertainty based on the Expected Value Theorem for Probabilities and the judgment-explication of credences can be applied in real-life cases. In principle, the theory is silent on this. EVM is a criterion of m-betterness, not a procedure for how to arrive at m-value judgments in practice. So in principle we might satisfy EVM by just following the advice of a fortuneteller. But that seems unlikely. And taking our criterion of m-betterness as a decision procedure often seems a good way of arriving at m-value judgments. So let's see how this could be done. As an example, suppose you consider becoming a vegan. You believe that doing so would increase animal welfare by some amount, but reduce human welfare by 60 % of that amount (since it would require resources you're currently using to your and other people's benefit). You're certain that welfare and only welfare has value, but uncertain about whether animal welfare is equally as valuable as human welfare. And you want to know whether it's m-better for you to become a vegan. How do you answer this question?

---

112 See e. g. Joyce (2005; 2010); see e. g. Elga (2010) and White (2010) for arguments that subjective probabilities should be sharp.

First, you need to determine what axiological orderings you're uncertain about. You need to determine your orderings $\succeq_i$. To that end, you can consider simple examples like the following:

Tab. 5.1: Example to illustrate axiological orderings.

a	b_q	
$p = 1$	$p = q$	$p = (1 - q)$
Bruin killed	Maria killed	status quo

If you choose prospect a, bear Bruin will be killed with certainty. If you choose prospect b_q, human Maria will be killed with probability q, and nothing will happen otherwise. Let's assume that their death would be equally bad for Bruin and Maria. Now if according to some axiology, $a \sim_i b_1$, the value of animal welfare is equally as great as the value of human welfare according to this axiology. If according to an axiology, $a \sim_j b_{0.5}$, the value of animal welfare is half as great as the value of human welfare according to it. Suppose you think that these two and only these two axiologies are plausible. Let's call them welfare-theory (T_W), and species-weighted-welfare-theory (T_{SWW}) respectively.

Next, you need to determine how your theories compare intertheoretically, or in what relative versions of these orderings you have credence. To that end, you have to consider your m-value judgments about $\mathcal{Q}$. This will be easiest with unnatural toy examples, like the following:

Tab. 5.2: Example to illustrate intertheoretic comparisons.

a_x		b_x	
T_W	T_{SWW}	T_W	T_{SWW}
$p_W = x$	$p_{SWW} = (1 - x)$	$p_W = x$	$p_{SWW} = (1 - x)$
Maria killed	status quo	status quo	Maria killed

If you choose a_x, Maria will be killed if T_W is true, and nothing will happen if T_{SWW} is true. If you choose b_x, Maria will be killed if T_{SWW} is true, and nothing will happen if T_W is true. And these prospects are such that the probability of T_W and T_{SWW} are x and $(1 - x)$ respectively. So in judging that $a_{2/3} \sim_m b_{2/3}$, say, you'd judge that killing Maria was twice as bad on T_{SWW} as on T_W. But suppose you actually judge that $a_{1/2} \sim_m b_{1/2}$. This means you think a_x and b_x are equally m-good if T_W and T_{SWW} are equiprobable, or that the value of human welfare is the same on both theories. You might think this, say, because you think this is the simplest assumption, or the least radical way of reforming your credence in light of the evidence you've just found for T_W.

Finally, you need to determine what credence you have in these theories. To that end, you have to consider your m-value judgments about $\mathcal{K}$. This will again be easiest with unnatural toy examples, like the following:

Tab. 5.3: Example to illustrate axiological credences.

a_n		b_m	
T_W	T_{SWW}	T_W	T_{SWW}
n people killed	status quo	status quo	m people killed

If you choose a_n then n people will be killed if T_W is true, and nothing will happen if T_{SWW} is true. If you choose b_m then m people will be killed if T_{SWW} is true, and nothing will happen if T_W is true. Their death would be equally bad for all of these people. So in judging that $a_1 \sim_m b_1$, say, you'd judge it equally m-good to risk the death of a person conditional on T_W as conditional on T_{SWW}. And since we already know you find these deaths equally *bad* on either theory, this means you'd assign both T_W and T_{SWW} the same probability. But suppose you actually judge that $a_2 \sim_m b_1$. This means you think it's equally m-good to risk the death two people conditional on T_W as the death of one person conditional on T_{SWW}. It means that the credence you have in T_W is half of that you have in T_{SWW}.

So your judgments about these toy examples imply what axiological orderings you have credence in, how they compare, and how much credence you have in them. You can now use these probabilities and values to determine whether it's m-better for you to turn vegan. We were assuming that according to your non-normative beliefs, your becoming a vegan increases animal welfare (a-welfare) by some amount w, but reduces human welfare (h-welfare) by 60 % of that amount:

Tab. 5.4: Example to illustrate Subjectivist EVM.

Becoming a vegan		Not becoming a vegan	
T_W	T_{SWW}	T_W	T_{SWW}
a-welfare $+w$, h-welfare $-0.6w$	a-welfare $+w$, h-welfare $-0.6w$	status quo	status quo

We can assume (without loss of generality) that the value of the status quo is 0 on both theories, and that the disvalue of decreasing human welfare by w is -1. Note that according to the theory you find more plausible (T_{SWW}), it's better not to become a vegan. The value of becoming a vegan, according to T_{SWW} is

$$\frac{1}{2} - \frac{6}{10} = -\frac{1}{10} < 0. \tag{5.12}$$

Nonetheless, it's m-better for you to become a vegan. The expected value of becoming a vegan is

$$\frac{1}{3}\left(1 - \frac{6}{10}\right) + \frac{2}{3}\left(\frac{1}{2} - \frac{6}{10}\right) = \frac{1}{15} > 0. \tag{5.13}$$

So relative to your credences, it's m-better for you to become a vegan, even though you think it's more likely worse.

This is at least the beginning of the full story of how our theory can—in Savage's terms—help you to 'police [your] own decisions for consistency and, when possible, to make complicated decisions depend on simpler ones' (1954, 20). Of course, in practice, you might also have credence in other versions of these theories which compare differently; or you might have credence in other species-weighted-welfare-theories, which imply a different ordering; or you might have still other views that affect this decision. Then the above calculations are only a first approximation of whether it's m-better for you to become a vegan. Your calculation will be more accurate the more of these alternatives you take into account. Moreover, you might also have an intuition concerning the m-value of becoming a vegan. If you intuitively judge it *m-worse* to turn vegan, your m-value judgments can't all be correct. So you need to revise some of these judgments, until you attain a reflective equilibrium in which they satisfy all of our constraints. As an aside, note that the ability to construct unnatural prospects like a_x, b_x, a_n and b_m is helpful in thinking about these questions. In this respect, as indicated on page 24, the unnatural aspects of our framework are actually an advantage.

5.3 Objections and implications

The argument in Section 5.1 again suggested that representation theorems can serve the two foundational purposes indicated in Section 1.2: clarify what EVM means, and corroborate that it is true. But especially with respect to the notion of credences, many philosophers are sceptical of the significance of representation theorems for these purposes. Christopher Meacham and Jonathan Weisberg, for instance, claim that 'representation theorems cannot serve either of these foundational purposes', and that, 'we should [...] lay the foundations of decision theory on firmer ground' than that provided by such theorems (2011, 641). So it's time to address some objections. Most of these objections have been levelled against preference-based representation theorems in decision theory. But they apply *mutatis mutandis* to Subjectivist EVM in the context of axiological uncertainty. And I'll only be concerned with that. I'll argue that the judgment-explication is the best explication of axiological credences. But I won't claim that preference-based theorems can serve these purposes in decision theory or epistemology more generally. That's another question.[113]

Relationship to the ordinary concept

A technical concept may diverge from the ordinary language notion in some respects. It may be more precise, and may perhaps also shift the original meaning slightly. However, if it's to be an *explication* of that notion—rather than a stipulative definition of a completely new term—it shouldn't deviate too much from the explicandum. Preference-based definitions of credences have been criticised in this respect, and some worries carry over to our context. Here's a first worry. Intuitively, most of us have varying credences in axiologies: we find some axiologies quite plausible, others somewhat less, and still others highly unlikely. Yet we generally don't satisfy C. So we can rarely be ascribed credences as defined by our explication. Thus our technical notion diverges from its explicandum. Among others, Meacham and Weisberg (2011) raised this objection against preference-based definitions in decision theory.[114] Referring to the technical notions of utilities and degrees of belief as 'utilities*' and 'degrees of belief*', they say:

> To make degrees of belief* and utilities* relevant to epistemology and normative decision theory, these states must be linked to the states that are the topic of our normative theorizing in these domains. And since agents like us generally don't have degrees of belief* and utilities*, it's hard to see how they're relevant. (2011, 655)

The same worry applies *mutatis mutandis* in our context.

---

113 In particular, I'll ignore the debate about probabilism—the view that your credences should satisfy the axioms of probability theory. According to the judgment-explication and my main argument, probabilism is true. But I don't understand it as an *argument* for probabilism. I understand it as an argument for how your credences and values should interact to determine your m-value judgments.

114 Eriksson and Hájek (2007, 200 f.; 203 f.) and Zynda (2000, 62) make the same point.

There are three replies to this objection. First, we must keep the purpose of our explication in mind. Since you'll rarely satisfy C, the specific explication I've given may be relatively useless in descriptive or predictive accounts of your mental states or behaviour. But Subjectivist EVM isn't a descriptive or predictive account. It's a normative account of what your m-value judgments should be, or of when they're correct. It says your m-value judgments are (subjectively) correct if and only if you satisfy C in one way or another; and that if you do, you satisfy EVM with respect to your credences. The fact that we can't assign credences to you on the basis of our explication if you fail to satisfy C is irrelevant for whether *this* claim is convincing, or close enough to our ordinary concept of credences. All that's relevant is that our explication resembles our intuitive concept when you satisfy C. And Meacham and Weisberg's argument does nothing to challenge that. Against the specific *normative* interpretation of EVM I've adopted, their argument is simply a red herring.

Second, we need to distinguish between the specific explication I've given and the general idea behind it. The general idea of the judgment-explication is simply that your credence in an axiology is the weight you give it in your m-value judgments. And this idea isn't limited to the ideal cases where you satisfy C, or to the narrowly normative interpretation of EVM I've invoked. The Representation Theorem for Probabilities shows that if you satisfy C, there's a unique weight you give all your axiologies. But even when you don't satisfy these conditions, there might be facts about the weights you give your axiologies in your m-value judgments. And through slightly broader interpretations of our general explicative idea, and perhaps slightly more complex theorems, these facts might still allow credence-interpretations of you. For instance, suppose you don't satisfy Completeness. Intuitively, this might mean you don't assign unique probabilities to your axiologies in the manner my explication presupposes, but have fuzzy credences in them. And our general explicative idea could capture this. There are representation theorems without the Completeness axiom, which in such cases can represent you as assigning a range of weights to your axiologies. Thus we could interpret you as assigning probability-ranges to them. Alternatively, suppose you don't satisfy C for the full range of axiologies $\mathcal{T}$ (and the corresponding sets $\mathcal{K}$ and $\mathcal{Q}$). You satisfy C only for the set $\mathcal{T} \setminus T_i$ (and the corresponding prospects). Intuitively, this might mean you've decided how likely all other axiologies are, relative to each other. But you haven't yet made up your mind about what credence you assign to T_i. Again, our general idea could capture this. We could use the Representation Theorem for Probabilities, and my judgment-explication, as applied to the set $\mathcal{T} \setminus T_i$—and add the caveat that you haven't yet fully made up your mind regarding T_i. Or again, suppose you don't satisfy C for the full set of outcomes X (and the corresponding sets $\mathcal{K}$ and $\mathcal{Q}$). You satisfy C only for the set $X \setminus x$ (and the corresponding prospects). Intuitively, this might mean you've basically decided how likely your axiologies are. But for some reason, you just get confused when considering the outcome x. Again, our general idea could capture this. We could use the Representation Theorem for Probabilities, and my judgment-explication, as applied to the set $X \setminus x$—and add the caveat that x seems to confuse you. Or perhaps all these qualifications apply: you satisfy only Transitivity, Independence and Continuity, with respect to a restricted set of axiologies, and a restricted set of outcomes. Even then, there might be certain facts about the weights you give your axiologies, which would allow certain claims about your credences in light of our explication.

Third, we must not be too lenient in assigning credences to people. The cases I've just described are still to some extent ideal: they presuppose that you satisfy Transitivity, Independence and Continuity with respect to some theories and outcomes. Perhaps when people don't even show any such traces of satisfying C, there's no way for our explication to assign credences to them. But this seems intuitively plausible too. Intuitively, some people simply don't allow any meaningful assignments of degrees of belief. They're just too incoherent. So arguably, these remaining limitations even speak in favour of our explication. The core idea of the judgment-explication can explain when credence-assignments intuitively become impossible.

A more promising strategy might be to attack the core idea of the judgment-explication directly, and question whether the explication is adequate *when* you satisfy C. And this may be questioned. One pertinent worry is that our ordinary notion of credences is much *richer* than the concept I've introduced. Among others, David Christensen (2001) stressed this point in decision theory—suggesting that 'the preference-based definition leaves out important parts of our pretheoretic notion' (2001, 361).[115] For one thing, 'a person's beliefs [...] affect the way she behaves in countless ways that have nothing directly to do with the decision theorist's paradigm of cost-benefit calculation' (2001, 361). For another thing, degrees of belief not only help to explain behaviour, but also 'other psychological states and processes' (2001, 361). Your self-deprecating beliefs may explain why you're performing poorly in a competition, or why you're being sad or afraid, or why you release stress hormones or are physically unhealthy. Beliefs are involved in a plethora of explanatory connections, even when our preferences satisfy the

---

115 The same point is endorsed by Eriksson and Hájek (2007, 208). Meacham and Weisberg (2011, 646) also highlight the rich explanatory connections of beliefs (though not as an objection against what they call the 'Explicative View', and what is basically the view I suggested); see also Hájek (2008, 803 ff.).

axioms. This being so, Christensen claimed, 'the move of settling on just one of these connections—even an important one—as definitional comes to look highly suspicious' (2001, 362). And this worry carries over to our context. Your axiological beliefs arguably play a much richer role than just determining your m-value judgments: they may explain your behaviour, your immediate reactions, attitudes and emotions and so on, even when you satisfy C.

This is a more pertinent worry. But again it can be answered. Christensen focused on Patrick Maher's (1993) understanding of probabilities and utilities, according to which 'an attribution of probabilities and utilities is correct just in case it's part of an overall interpretation of the person's preferences that makes sufficiently good sense of them and better sense than any competing interpretation does' (1993, 9). Christensen objected:

> a given interpretation of an agent's degrees of belief might maximize expected-utility fit with the agent's preferences while a different interpretation might fit much better with other psychological-explanatory principles. In such cases of conflict [...] there's no guarantee that the best interpretation will be the one on which the agent's preferences accord perfectly with maximizing [expected utility]. (2001, 362)

But my understanding of the explication differs from Maher's. I don't offer it as the best overall interpretation of an agent. On the contrary, at least if 'best' means 'descriptively best' as opposed to 'best for our purposes', I'd doubt there generally *is* a uniquely best interpretation. Suppose in my m-value judgments I give much more weight to the welfare- than the human-welfare-theory. But in my emotional reactions, implicit attitudes, hormone levels and in my actual behaviour, I give somewhat more weight to the human-welfare- than to the welfare-theory. In which theory do I then have a higher degree of belief? Do my reactions and behaviour show that I don't really have a higher credence in the welfare-theory? Or do I act and react against my true credences, due to akrasia or biases or whatever? Very plausibly, our intuitive concept of credence isn't sharp enough to imply anything definitive in all such cases. There is often no uniquely 'best interpretation'. There are several viable interpretations that don't seem outright misleading, and that might all pick out a theoretically useful phenomenon.[116] All I claim is that the judgment-explication is one of them. If you satisfy C, and thus give each axiology a constant weight in your m-value judgments under uncertainty, it's not

---

116 There's a literature on whether, if you profess to believe that p but act contrary to that professed belief, you truly believe that p (see e. g. Schwitzgebel 2010 for an overview, and a position similar to the one expressed above). I'm not aware of a discussion of such cases with regards to a *graded* notion of belief.

determinately wrong or completely misleading to call the relevant weights your 'credences'. And it picks out something that's useful for our purposes.

Let me elaborate on the latter point. Why focus on your m-value judgments, of all possible connections, to explicate credences? There are at least two reasons. First, we want to say you should satisfy EVM with respect to your 'credences'. So we need to pick out 'credences' that should be relevant in your decision-making. But many aspects Christensen emphasises arguably shouldn't be. Many of us won't have the moral emotions we judge to be fitting.[117] Our implicit attitudes often contradict what we explicitly claim to believe and take to reflect our evidence—and often in a sexist or racist manner.[118] And presumably, many of us fail to act in accordance with what we judge to be good.[119] And this isn't surprising. Among other things, our judgments can adapt to new evidence very quickly. Our behaviour, emotions and implicit attitudes are much more resistant to such changes. But plausibly, when there's a conflict between your considered judgments and other aspects of your psychology, you shouldn't satisfy EVM with respect to the latter. You should satisfy EVM with respect to the 'credences' induced by your judgments. Our explication picks out something relevant to what you ought to do.

Second, our explication is very simple. In response to Christensen's conflict cases, we could provide an explication involving other aspects of our psychology. For example, we could introduce conditions on attitudes, of the sort: 'if you have a favouring attitude for a over b, then for any c in $\mathcal{K}$ and any $p \in]0,1[$, you have a favouring attitude for $pa+(1-p)c$ over $pb+(1-p)c$'. These conditions may imply an attitude-relative 'credence'-function. Perhaps we could do the same for your behaviour, your hormone level, and so on. And we could then take a weighted average of these relativized 'credence'-functions to get your overall credence-function. Or we could assume bridging principles of the form 'if you judge that a is m-better than b, you have a favouring attitude for a over b', guaranteeing that all these credence functions are the same. No one has done this, and it would involve serious difficulties.[120] But even if it were possible, the complexity of such an account of

---

117 See e. g. Greene et al. (2001, 2107) on people judging 'in spite of their emotions'.

118 See e. g. Greenwald and Banaji (1995), Gaertner and McLaughlin (1983) or Dovidio and Gaertner (2000) for relatively early works; Strohminger et al. (2014) for a recent methodological survey about implicit *moral* attitudes.

119 See e. g. the findings of Schwitzgebel and Rust (2014) or Schwitzgebel (2014), suggesting that more stringent moral views don't imply more stringent moral behaviour.

120 For instance, different people seem to react differently to the belief that one prospect is m-better than another; no such reaction might be a necessary condition for that belief, and the choice of any one might be somewhat arbitrary.

credences would be a major drawback. Our explication is much simpler. So the judgment-explication may not provide the uniquely overall best interpretation of you. There often won't be any such interpretation. But our explication picks out a feature of 'beliefs' that's descriptively very salient, normatively relevant, and still comparatively straightforward.

Here's a third, related worry. One might worry, not that there are *additional* connections between our credences and our psychology, but that sometimes the presumed connection with our m-value judgments doesn't exist. Lina Eriksson and Alan Hájek (2007) have claimed this with respect to standard preference-explications in decision theory:

> Credences and preferences are certainly separable in thought, and sometimes in practice. Imagine a Zen Buddhist monk who has credences but no preferences [i. e., 'is indifferent among all things']. [...] If the monk is conceptually possible, then any account that concep-tually ties credences to preferences is refuted. [...] Or consider a chronic apathetic who has lost all his desires, but who has kept all his credences. To be sure, these characters are not recognizably like us, although some of us may approximate them over certain domains, and to the extent that we do, bets and preferences more generally ill-reflect our true credences. (2007, 194)

Others have provided similar arguments.[121] And a similar point seems to apply in our context. Axiological credences and m-value judgments are 'separable in thought', it seems, since we can imagine someone who has axiological beliefs but doesn't make any m-value judgments.

But what precisely is the argument here? On the face of it, first, mere 'ap-proximation' of monk-like apathy doesn't distort preference-based explications at all. It will simply result in an attenuated utility function, and this seems precisely appropriate. Second, the perfectly indifferent monk is such that our theorem just doesn't apply to them. The Expected Value Theorem for Probabilities presupposes that you make (non-uniform) m-value judgments. Thus monk-cases can't show that the explication is flawed *when* it applies.[122]

But perhaps Eriksson and Hájek raise a deeper worry. As applied to our con-text, their argument seems to be that the mere possibility of axiological credences

---

121 See Christensen (2001, 363).

122 True, there's arguably a difference between the monk and someone with, say, intransitive preferences: the latter is (presumably) making some sort of mistake, whereas the monk perhaps needn't make any mistake. So the monk shows that the Representation Theorem for Probabilities can't ground a fully general normative theory. But I've already admitted that many constraints in that theorem are too strong as normative constraints, and are only plausible given certain restric-tions or simplifications (e. g., the assumption that all axiologies are non-uniform).

and m-value judgments coming apart shows that any *definition* of the former in terms of the latter must be flawed. If they can come apart, the thought seems to go, any connection between them must be contingent and can't be conceptual. But that's simply a *non-sequitur*. A condition may be sufficient but not necessary for a concept to apply, and this may be a conceptual truth. It seems to be a conceptual matter, say, that if you have the ability repeatedly to play the first prelude from the *Well-Tempered Clavier*, then you know how to play it. And yet, you can also know how to play it without having that ability, as when your arms are broken or all pianos have been destroyed. Our explication only says that *if* you satisfy C, then as a matter of explication, you have the credences that make you satisfy EVM. And this may be correct, or a legitimate explication, even if intuitively you may have credences even if you don't make m-value judgments.

Perhaps Eriksson and Hájek have in mind yet another argument: that we anyway need an explication of the perfect monk's credences; that *that* explication can't be preference-based; that it will apply to any other agent as well; and that therefore the preference-explication is redundant. However, for reasons I've indicated, it's unclear whether we *can* give an adequate explication of someone's quantitative credences if they don't make any m-value judgments. So unless Eriksson and Hájek present a better or more general explication (which they don't) this argument doesn't get off the ground. And more generally, perfectly indifferent monks are very rare, or indeed presumably inexistent. And so are people who don't make any m-value judgments. If we have an otherwise useful explication, that's silent on these highly exceptional cases, that seems like a limitation we can live with.[123]

Normative relevance

Let's turn to a different set of worries about the judgment-explication. These worries concern the *normative relevance* of the resulting theory. They challenge

---

123 There are other objections against preference-based explications in decision theory; Eriksson and Hájek (2007) offer an overview. Another worry that carries over to our context is that explicating credences in terms of preferences gets the order of explanation wrong (see Eriksson and Hájek 2007, 207 f.). I've replied to the equivalent objection concerning value in Section 3.3. A similar reply could be given concerning credences. As far as I see, the remaining objections don't apply to my explication of axiological credences. In particular, a prominent objection against explicating degrees of belief in terms of preferences is that this explication is overly 'pragmatic', reducing a doxastic attitude (credence) to a conative one (preferences) (see Joyce 1999, 89 ff. or Eriksson and Hájek 2007, 194). However, my explication explains a doxastic attitude (axiological credences) in terms of another doxastic attitude (m-value judgments). So this objection doesn't apply.

that Subjectivist EVM as understood by the judgment-explication can play the normative role we want a theory of axiological uncertainty to play. A first such worry is that Subjectivist EVM is normatively *trivial*. A theory of axiological uncertainty should constrain your judgments about what's m-best. But Subjectivist EVM seems to take your m-value judgments as *given* to define your credences and values. So it may seem that it will just guarantee that your m-value judgments are correct, and thus can't constrain or guide you at all.[124]

That's a misunderstanding. Subjectivist EVM does put constraints on you. These constraints are simply the axioms. In the version I've outlined, your m-value judgments can't be correct if you violate C. So you may use these conditions to guide your evaluation of prospects, or make more complex evaluations depend on simpler ones. What's true is that—as far as the correctness of your m-value judgments *as* subjective m-value judgments is concerned—these conditions are all that Subjectivist EVM implies. And these conditions only rule out certain *sets* of m-value judgments, but no individual judgment in itself: they're mere coherence constraints (as I've put it), rather than unconditional local constraints on individual judgments themselves. Thus Subjectivist EVM reduces to a set of coherence constraints. This doesn't mean that any C-conformable set of judgments is as good as any other *in all respects*. Some such judgments will reflect inadequate credences, and thus be epistemically problematic, say. But on Subjectivist EVM, your m-value judgments are correct *as* subjective m-value judgments relative to your credences if and only if they're C-conformable.

Here's a second, related worry. Even if that's not outright trivial, one might still find it disappointing. Meacham and Weisberg do. They argue that the view that you ought to maximise the expectation of utility* relative to your credences* (in the technical senses of these terms) is 'prescriptively useless' (2011, 656) or 'uninteresting' (2011, 642; 645; 655; 661): 'Normative decision theory applies only to agents who have degrees of belief and utilities. But agents who have degrees of belief* and utilities* are automatically [...] expected utility maximizers with respect to them.' So, they suggested, 'it will be true by definition that all agents subject to the norms of decision theory satisfy them'. (2011, 653) The worry is that the norm to maximise expected utility only applies to you if you have credences and utilities; but that once you have credences* and utilities* you automatically maximise

---

124 Sepielli (2010, 169) raised this objection against preference-based explications in decision theory: 'The standard way of assigning credences and utilities in decision theory assigns them in such a way that the agent's preferences will necessarily come out as maximizing expected utility. Since the going assumption in decision theory is that maximizing expected utility is necessarily rational, this means that agents will necessarily have fully rational preferences.' This is 'highly counterintuitive' (2010, 168), he says.

expected utility with respect to them. But that's again just false. The coherence conditions C of Subjectivist EVM don't just apply to you once you have axiological credences. They apply to you whenever. They say you always ought to make m-value judgments that satisfy Completeness, Transitivity, Independence, and so on. We might say Subjectivist EVM requires you, among else, to *have* axiological credences.

Meacham and Weisberg consider this reply in a footnote. But all they say in response is that

> this proposal represents a substantive shift in the content of normative decision theory. We're no longer dealing with the same norms, and these replacements can't do the same work as the originals. For example, normative decision theory is supposed to say which of an agent's options she ought to take. But the injunction to have degrees of belief and utilities will be silent on this, since every option will maximize expected utility relative to some pair of probability and utility functions. (2011, 648, n.15)

This is merely to say that if we thought EVM could imply local constraints, Subjectivist EVM constitutes a shift in our understanding. But it doesn't show why that should make it uninteresting, or why we thus have to 'lay the foundations of decision theory on firmer ground' than that provided by representation theorems (2011, 641).

In fact, the shift from an understanding of EVM on which it implies local to one on which it implies coherence constraints is much less dramatic than it may seem. On the one hand, at least on a reflective-equilibrium-type view in (meta-)axiological epistemology, there's anyway ultimately just coherence constraints. Suppose we can take axiological credences as primitives, and have some intuitive, introspective sense of what our credences are. If the numbers you gathered through introspection imply m-value judgments you find highly implausible (giving far too much weight to the average-welfare-theory, say) you shouldn't stick slavishly to these judgments. You should adjust your 'credences' until they cohere with a set of m-value judgments you find plausible. Thus ultimately, our norms concerning m-value judgments anyway reduce to coherence constraints. In Subjectivist EVM this reduction is internal to the theory. But it's not clear why that should be problematic.[125] On the other hand, nothing in the judgment-explication implies that you may not *also*, say, consult your feelings of confidence when determining a set of m-value judgments. If you start with an intuitive list of numbers, and these

---

125 In fact, at least in the present case, I think it's preferable to have the coherence constraints built into the theory. Note that according to EVM as understood in terms of the Simple Explication, your first (extremely implausible seeming) m-value judgments were *true* as subjective m-value judgments. That seems to show that, in itself, this theory is of little normative significance.

numbers lead you to a set of m-value judgments that satisfy our conditions and that you find plausible, there's nothing wrong with that. The reduction to coherence constraints doesn't prohibit the use of introspection or local constraints in practice.

Here's a third worry Subjectivist EVM invites. If it normatively boils down to C, why should it even matter whether we interpret your m-value judgments this way or another once you satisfy C? It now seems all the work is done by the axioms, and that the *formula* (5.11) for EVM has become entirely redundant. So why should we even care about the EVM-representation? Why should we care about the relevant theorem and the bulk of my argument in this chapter?

The reason is that we may ultimately not just be interested in the truth of your m-value judgments *as* subjective m-value judgments. As far as that is concerned, the formula for EVM indeed doesn't add an additional norm. But we may also be interested in whether your m-value judgments reflect reasonable credences. And the EVM-representation helps express the connection between the theory of axiological uncertainty on the one hand, and axiological epistemology on the other. Judging that it's m-better to benefit people significantly more than non-human animals, say, seems epistemically unreasonable. But it's not perspicuous from the axioms alone how we can capture this in a unified way. Representation theorems show that if your judgments satisfy C, you attach a constant weight to each axiology. So they allow us to say, not just that this or that m-value judgment is unreasonable, but that you're giving too much *weight* to speciesism. And if we can interpret these weights as credences, that's a congenial way to link the norms of the theory of axiological uncertainty to epistemology. It does justice to the intuitive idea that some axiologies are more plausible or likely true than others, and that these likelihoods are relevant in determining m-value. And it allows us to say that the normative relationship between our evidence and these weights is one between evidence and a doxastic state, which may provide more unity to our overall picture of what an epistemic norm is, or what norms there exist.[126]

There's a fourth, more specific worry about employing coherence constraints on your m-value judgments. We all have some pretheoretic *preferences*, and can thus use coherence constraints to determine what further preferences we ought to have in cases where we haven't yet formed any. So coherence constraints might be good and well in standard decision theory. But one might worry that we can't make *any* m-value judgments without prior theoretic guidance. Indeed this, one

---

126 Representation theorems can also serve a practical purpose. Instead of working with the axioms alone, it's often easier to derive your probabilities and values from simple cases, and then apply the formula for EVM for more complex ones. That's what I did in Section 5.2.

might say, is why we need a theory of axiological uncertainty in the first place. Hence such a theory must be able to constrain us without assuming that we make prior m-value judgments, on pain of presupposing that we know already what it was supposed to tell us. This was argued by Brian Hedden, who reports to have 'few if any brute intuitions' (2016, 114) concerning which prospects are m-better than which, and suspects that this is true for most people.[127]

This is a more pertinent worry. But I'm much less pessimistic than Hedden about our ability to make m-value judgments. Axiological uncertainty raises difficult philosophical questions and presents intricate formal problems. But in an important sense, it's also a fairly straightforward phenomenon. It can be explained to non-specialists in a couple of sentences. And it doesn't seem to engender anything like intellectual paralysis as far as m-value judgments go. I suspect most people would say they aren't entirely certain about the value of equality or deserved punishment or the creation of an extra person. But I also suspect that, when pressed to judge *in light* of this uncertainty, most people would consider it m-better to bring about an equal distribution of some amount of welfare rather than a grossly unequal distribution of a marginally greater amount of it; or m-better to punish the guilty rather than an innocent person for some moral wrong, even if this involves somewhat greater costs for society; but perhaps m-worse to create a person and thereby greatly harm an existing one rather than to leave the population as it is. Or perhaps they'd judge differently. But I'd be surprised if people were entirely clueless about which of such prospects are m-better. If anything, a sense of cluelessness seems to be *post*-theoretic, issuing perhaps from one's view about the problem of intertheoretic comparisons or one's metaethical assumptions.

Now of course, there will be many cases where we lack a firm intuition. We won't have a firm intuition about precisely which increase in overall welfare makes an unfair distribution equally as m-good as a fair one. But this needn't indicate a defect. Recall what I said in the last chapter. Plausibly, your m-value judgments needn't satisfy Completeness: there often *aren't* any positive facts about which

---

127 This worry is analogous to one about Harsanyi's theorem. Standardly, the theory of 'social preferences' is supposed to take individual preferences as inputs and tell you which of your prospects is socially best. But Harsanyi's theorem *starts* with social and individual preferences, and then tells you that if they satisfy certain axioms, you can pick utility functions that represent them and relate in a certain way. Again, Harsanyi's axioms might well help you derive some social preferences if you know some such preferences to start from. But you might worry that you don't have brute intuitions about what's socially best and thus can't know any such preferences—in particular, not unless you're *antecedently* told how to make interpersonal comparisons of welfare (see Hedden 2016, 114).

prospects are m-better than which, since our axiologies aren't fully commensurable. And if this is so, our lack of firm intuitions needn't indicate that there are facts we're not grasping, and that our intuitions are poor. It may indicate that there aren't any facts, and that our intuitions *are* a good guide to *that*. The absence of a firm intuition might be the intuition of the absence of a fact.

Even if this is granted, and the practical usefulness of our theory accepted, there might be a fifth and final worry. One might object that a reduction to coherence constraints just makes EVM too permissive—that it's simply *wrong* that any judgments satisfying C are correct.

But there's an answer to this too, and it's perhaps a general answer to all remaining worries concerning the normativity of Subjectivist EVM. Recall that according to Subjectivist EVM, such judgments are only correct *as* subjective m-value judgments. They might of course still reflect unreasonable credence distributions over axiological orderings, or implicate credences in versions of these orderings, or intertheoretic comparisons, that violate our prior constructivist norms. In other words, your judgments might still be false by the lights of Objectivist EVM. Subjectivist EVM only says they're correct by subjectivist standards. And any theory of subjective m-value is necessarily rather permissive. On any such theory, your m-best prospect depends on your credences. Hence no such theory will imply a local m-value judgment unless something about your credences is known. And it will render correct whatever judgments are implied by your credences. The difference is merely that on Subjectivist EVM, your credences are determined by your m-value judgments, rather than your brute introspection, say. But as I've argued, that doesn't seem problematic.

I've granted that there are reasons for thinking objective m-value is ultimately more important normatively speaking, or more more naturally the object of our judgments. But that doesn't threaten Subjectivist EVM as a theory about subjective m-value. And more importantly, it doesn't threaten the general approach of this book or this chapter. If you think objective m-value is more important, you can understand the Expected Value Theorem for Probabilities, and the argument it grounds, in objectivist terms—as indicated on page 94. It's not true that any judgments about objective m-value satisfying C will be correct. You might make C-conformable judgments that imply unwarranted credences. So Objectivist EVM doesn't boil down to coherence constraints. And any remaining worries one might have about such constraints might be answerable by focusing on it, rather than its subjectivist cousin.

5.4 Conclusion: Weighted Value Maximisation

Let me conclude. In this chapter, I've examined the question of how to understand axiological credences. I argued that we shouldn't take such credences as primitives, and introduced the judgment-explication to explain them. According to this explication, your credence in an axiology is the weight you give this axiology in your m-value judgments. After providing the formal background for this explication, I argued that it's adequately related to our intuitive concept and picks out something normatively relevant—or doesn't trivialise EVM, make it uninteresting or redundant. This suggests an explication of credences in terms of representation theorems on your m-value judgments is the best explication we can get.

More fundamentally, I've argued that it's preferable to interpret the weights that axiological orderings have in determining m-value as being composed of their value function on the one hand, and their probability on the other. If we can make this distinction, we can capture the idea that some axiologies are more likely than others, and that these likelihoods are relevant in determining m-value. And we can thus express the intuitive connection between the theory of axiological uncertainty and axiological epistemology. However, I've admitted that in light of the import of the axioms, the distinction might be somewhat less relevant than it first appeared. So it might be worth indicating how the alternative view, which eschews the distinction between probabilities and values altogether, can be axiomatised in our framework. We can do that with a simple analogue of the Expected Value Theorem, concerning $\mathcal{K}$ instead of $\mathcal{Q}$. Define for each i in I a function $K_i : \mathcal{K} \to \mathcal{O}$; $a \mapsto K_i(a)$, such that for all x in X,

$$K_i(a)(x) = a(i, x). \tag{5.14}$$

The mapping K_i thus formally turns a prospect a in $\mathcal{K}$ into the prospect that a represents, given T_i. Now for a set of binary relations $\{\succeq_i \mid i \in I\}$ on $\mathcal{O}$ and a binary relation $\tilde{\succeq}$ on $\mathcal{K}$, define the

Pareto Condition for K: If for some a and b in $\mathcal{K}$, $K_i(a) \sim_i K_i(b)$ for all i in I, then $a \tilde{\approx} b$; and if $K_i(a) \succeq_i K_i(b)$ for all i in I, and $K_j(a) \succ_j K_j(b)$ for some j in I, then $a \tilde{\succ} b$.

That your $\tilde{\succeq}_m$ should satisfy this condition is only plausible if you don't rule out the truth of any axiology under consideration completely. If there's some T_j, which you believe with certainty is false, the second clause of the condition is implausible with regards to that theory. So to ground an argument on this condition, we need to restrict the set of theories under consideration to those you don't rule out completely. The simplest way to do so is to restrict the theories to those for which your $\tilde{\succeq}_m$ does, as a matter of fact, satisfy the Pareto Condition for $\mathcal{K}$. In any case, the following theorem holds:

Weighted Value Theorem: *Suppose that all your $\succeq_i$ are vNM-conformable, and that your $\tilde{\succeq}_m$ satisfies the Pareto Condition for $\mathcal{K}$ with respect to them. If your $\tilde{\succeq}_m$ is vNM-conformable, there's a function $u : I \times X \rightarrow \mathbb{R}$, unique up to positive unit-comparable transformation, that represents each axiology cardinally, and is such that for all a and b in $\mathcal{K}$,*

$$a \tilde{\succeq}_m b \quad iff \quad \sum_{i \in I, x \in X} a(i, x)u(i, x) \geq \sum_{i \in I, x \in X} b(i, x)u(i, x).^{[128]} \qquad (5.15)$$

In other words, if your m-value judgments satisfy the von Neumann-Morgenstern axioms and the Pareto Condition for $\mathcal{K}$, then to each axiology you're attaching a constant weight in the form of a utility function. This doesn't establish that we can treat such a function $u(i, \cdot)$ as a product $p_i G_i$ of your credence in, and the value function of, theory T_i. So (5.15) expresses *Weighted Value Maximisation*, rather than EVM. This is a genuine theory of axiological uncertainty. To my knowledge, no one has defended that theory so far. If we can establish EVM, EVM is preferable to Weighted Value Maximisation. But Weighted Value Maximisation is a relevant alternative.

---

128 See the appendix (Section A.2) for a proof.

6 The problem of incommensurabilities

The third issue that the argument from the Basic Representation Theorem raised, besides the problem of intertheoretic comparisons and that of probabilities, was the problem of incommensurabilities. By assuming Completeness, the arguments so far rule out any incommensurabilities, and thus suffer from two major restrictions. As indicated in Chapter 3, many plausible axiologies allow for incommensurabilities at the level of first-order value, and are thus themselves incomplete. And as substantiated in Chapter 4, even if there's no fundamental problem with intertheoretic comparisons or the idea of EVM, plausibly, some axiologies aren't fully commensurable with each other, and thus induce an incomplete m-value relation. A theorem presupposing Completeness can't allow for such incommensurabilities. So it's time to introduce a representation theorem that doesn't presuppose this axiom. I'll do that in the present chapter (Section 6.1). The emerging theorem will be the most encompassing result of this book.

Having dropped Completeness, we'll be in a better position to assess whether representation theorems can ground EVM as a general theory of *moral*—rather than just axiological—uncertainty. So to round off my exploration of the axiomatic approach, I'll identify the most promising strategies to extend my arguments beyond axiology, and the most serious difficulties these strategies face (Section 6.2). I'll end the chapter with a conclusion, summarising the main positive and negative upshots of the book, and indicating possible directions for further research (Section 6.3).

6.1 Axiomatising incomplete m-value relations

To explicate and defend a form of EVM covering incommensurabilities, I'll again first state a relevant theorem in terms of mathematical functions, and then interpret it in a philosophically significant manner. And I'll again start with a theorem that assumes probabilities as given, before extending it to allow for an explication of them.

The Expected Value Theorem for Incompleteness

Consider the relation $\succeq_m$ on $\mathcal{Q}$. To allow for incompleteness, we'll need a slightly different set of axioms. Let $\boldsymbol{a}_{(i,x)}$ be the prospect that certainly leads to (i, x): $\boldsymbol{a}_{(i,x)}(i, x) = 1$. For a reflexive binary relation $\succeq$ on $\mathcal{Q}$, define

Transitivity$_\varrho$: for all a, b and c in ϱ, if $a \succeq b$ and $b \succeq c$, then $a \succeq c$;

Mixture-Independence$_\varrho$: for all a and b in ϱ, $a \succeq b$ if and only if $pa + (1-p)c \succeq pb + (1-p)c$ for all $p \in]0,1[$ and all c in ϱ;

Sequence-Continuity$_\varrho$: if $\{a_n\}$ and $\{b_n\}$ are convergent sequences such that $a_n \succeq b_n$ for all n, then $\lim(a_n) \succeq \lim(b_n)$;

Existence of Best and Worst$_\varrho$: there are $(\bar{i}, \bar{x})$ and $(\underline{i}, \underline{x})$ in $(I \times X)$ such that for all (i,x) in $(I \times X)$, $a_{(\bar{i},\bar{x})} \succeq a_{(i,x)}$, and $a_{(i,x)} \succeq a_{(\underline{i},\underline{x})}$; and

Non-Triviality$_\varrho$: $a_{(\bar{i},\bar{x})} \succ a_{(\underline{i},\underline{x})}$ (i.e., not $a_{(\underline{i},\underline{x})} \succeq a_{(\bar{i},\bar{x})}$).

If a reflexive relation $\succeq$ on ϱ satisfies these axioms, I'll say it is '*N-conformable*' (since my results are based on Nau 2006). Note that Existence of Best and Worst implies that $\succeq$ can't be *totally* incomplete. But apart from this, these conditions don't assume that $\succeq$ is complete. Now instead of defining a uniqueness criterion for our utility functions—which is somewhat more complicated if we're dealing with incomplete relations[129]—we'll simply introduce a *normalisation* for these functions, and then focus on normalised functions only. So define a normalised set of utility functions

$$U^\star = \{u : I \times X \to \mathbb{R} \mid u(\underline{i},\underline{x}) = 0; \ 0 \le u(i,x) \le 1 \ \forall (i,x) \in (I,X);$$
$$u(\bar{i},\bar{x}) = 1\}. \tag{6.1}$$

Call a collection of preferences $\{a_n \succeq b_n\}$ a *basis* for $\succeq$ under an axiom system if every preference $a \succeq b$ can be deduced from $\{a_n \succeq b_n\}$ by application of these axioms. Finally, for simplicity, for some function $u : I \times X \to \mathbb{R}$, define

$$\mathbf{U}_u(a) = \sum_{i \in I, x \in X} a(i,x)u(i,x). \tag{6.2}$$

It can be shown[130] that if $\succeq_m$ is N-conformable, there exists a nonempty closed convex set $U \subset U^\star$ of functions, such that for all a and b in ϱ,

$$a \succeq_m b \quad \text{iff} \quad \sum_{i \in I, x \in X} a(i,x)u(i,x) \ge \sum_{i \in I, x \in X} b(i,x)u(i,x) \quad \forall u \in U. \tag{6.3}$$

In particular, if $\{a_n \succeq_m b_n\}$ is a basis for $\succeq_m$ under these axioms, then U is the set of u in $U^\star$ satisfying $\{\mathbf{U}_u(a_n) \ge \mathbf{U}_u(b_n)\}$. (6.3) is a representation in terms of a *set* of utility functions. This straightforwardly allows for incompleteness in $\succeq_m$: neither

---

129 See Nau (2006) for a fully spelt out uniqueness criterion.

130 See the appendix (Section A.3; 'The Representation Theorem for Incompleteness') for a proof.

$a \succeq_m b$ nor $b \succeq_m a$ are true if there are u and v in W with $\mathbf{U}_u(a) > \mathbf{U}_u(b)$ and $\mathbf{U}_v(b) > \mathbf{U}_v(a)$.

We again need to ensure that the relevant utility functions u in U^* are appropriately related to our axiologies, by assuming that our axiologies satisfy certain conditions, and that $\succeq_m$ is related to them via a Pareto condition. For a reflexive binary relation $\succeq$ on $\mathcal{O}$, define

Transitivity$_\mathcal{O}$: for all a, b and c in $\mathcal{O}$, if $a \succeq b$ and $b \succeq c$, then $a \succeq c$;

Mixture-Independence$_\mathcal{O}$: for all a and b in $\mathcal{O}$, $a \succeq b$ if and only if $pa + (1-p)c \succeq pb + (1-p)c$ for all $p \in]0,1[$ and all c in $\mathcal{O}$; and

Sequence-Continuity$_\mathcal{O}$: if $\{a_n\}$ and $\{b_n\}$ are convergent sequences such that $a_n \succeq b_n$ for all n, then $\lim(a_n) \succeq \lim(b_n)$.

If a reflexive relation $\succeq$ on $\mathcal{O}$ satisfies these conditions, I'll say it's *N*-conformable*. For a set of binary relations $\{\succeq_i \mid i \in I\}$ on $\mathcal{O}$ and a binary relation $\succeq$ on $\mathcal{Q}$, define the

Strong Pareto Condition: For any probability distribution P on I, and for all a and b in $\mathcal{Q}^P$, if $H_i(a) \sim_i H_i(b)$ for all i in I with $P(i) > 0$, then $a \sim b$; if $H_i(a) \succeq_i H_i(b)$ for all i in I with $P(i) > 0$ and $H_j(a) \succ_j H_j(b)$ for some j in I with $P(j) > 0$, then $a \succ b$; and if for some j in I with $P(j) > 0$, $H_i(a) \sim_i H_i(b)$ for all i in I with $i \neq j$ and $P(i) > 0$, then $a \succeq b$ only if $H_j(a) \succeq_j H_j(b)$.

The third clause of this condition guarantees that the value functions in our representation will not represent *sharpenings* of our axiologies.

Now the following theorem holds:

Representation Theorem for Incompleteness: *Suppose that all our $\succeq_i$ are N*-conformable. If $\succeq_m$ is N-conformable and satisfies the Strong Pareto Condition with respect to our $\succeq_i$, there's a nonempty closed convex set $U \subset U^*$ of functions, such that for all $\mathbf{a}$ and $\mathbf{b}$ in $\mathcal{Q}$, all a and b in $\mathcal{O}$ and all i in I,*

$$a \succeq_m b \quad \text{iff} \quad \sum_{i \in I, x \in X} a(i,x)u(i,x) \geq \sum_{i \in I, x \in X} b(i,x)u(i,x) \quad \forall u \in U, \quad \text{and} \quad (6.4)$$

$$a \succeq_i b \quad \text{iff} \quad \sum_{x \in X} a(x)u(i,x) \geq \sum_{x \in X} b(x)u(i,x) \quad \forall u \in U. \quad (6.5)$$

In particular, if $\{a_n \succeq_m b_n\}$ is a basis for $\succeq_m$ under these axioms, then U is the set of u in U^* satisfying $\{\mathbf{U}_u(a_n) \geq \mathbf{U}_u(b_n)\}$.[131]

---

131 See the appendix (Section A.3) for a proof.

To turn this into a non-mathematical theorem, we again need prospect-explications of intra- and intertheoretic comparisons. These will have to be slightly different from the ones we've got so far. If we want to represent an axiology on which outcomes are less than fully commensurable, we can't interpret it as implying determinate value-difference ratios of the form 'the value-difference between x and y is n times as great as the value-difference between z and t'. Similarly, if we want to represent two axiologies that aren't fully commensurable, we can't interpret them as implying determinate intertheoretic value-difference ratios of the form 'the value-difference between x and y, according to T_i, is n times as great as the value-difference between z and t, according to T_j'. Instead, as far as intratheoretic comparisons are concerned we're interested in *rough cardinal intratheoretic value comparisons*, or facts of the form

(U) according to T_i, the value-difference between x and y is at least (or at most) n times as great as the value-difference between z and t.

As far as intertheoretic comparisons are concerned, we're interested in *rough cardinal intertheoretic value comparisons*, or facts of the form

(V) the value-difference between x and y, according to T_i, is at least (or at most) n times as great as the value-difference between z and t, according to T_j.

Again, our theorem guarantees that we can explicate level-comparisons too. That is, we can actually explicate *rough crosscutting cardinal intertheoretic value comparisons*, or facts of the form

(W) the difference between the value of x, according to T_i, and the value of y, according to T_j, is at least (or at most) n times as great as the difference between the value of z, according to T_h, and the value of t, according to T_k.

To state our explications, let U be a nonempty closed convex set of utility functions $u : I \times X \to \mathbb{R}$. Suppose that for some axiology T_i, and for all a and b in $\mathcal{O}$,

$$a \succeq_i b \quad \text{iff} \quad \sum_{x \in X} a(x)u(i,x) \geq \sum_{x \in X} b(x)u(i,x) \quad \forall u \in U. \tag{6.6}$$

I'll then say that U *represents T_i ordinally*. And I'll use equivalent, self-explanatory definitions for the claims that some nonempty closed convex set U of utility functions represents the m-value relation $\succeq_m$ ordinally, or (below) that some pair (U, P) represents your $\succeq_m$ and $\tilde{\succeq}_m$ ordinally. Now suppose that for some nonempty closed convex set U of real-valued functions on $I \times X$, and some axiology T_i, the rough cardinal intratheoretic comparisons between outcomes, according to T_i, are true if and only if they are true for all functions $u(i, \cdot)$ with u in U—that is, for all x, y, z, t in X (with $a_x \succeq_i a_y$ and $a_z \succeq_i a_t$), and $n \in \mathbb{R}$, the value-difference between x and y is at least n times as great as the value-difference between z and t, according to T_i, if and only if $(u(i, x) - u(i, y))/(u(i, z) - u(i, t)) \geq n$ for all u in U. I'll then say that U *represents* T_i *cardinally*. The *prospect-explication of rough intratheoretic comparisons* says that if there's a nonempty closed convex set $U \subset U^*$ of utility functions, which represents an axiology ordinally, then it also represents it cardinally. Similarly, suppose that for some nonempty closed convex set U of real-valued functions on $I \times X$, the rough crosscutting cardinal intertheoretic comparisons are true, according to our theories, if and only if they are true for all functions u in U—that is, for all x, y, z, t in X, all i, j, h, k in I (with $a_{(i,x)} \succeq_m a_{(j,y)}$ and $a_{(h,z)} \succeq_m a_{(k,t)}$) and $n \in \mathbb{R}$, the difference between the value of x, according to T_i, and the value of y, according to T_j, is at least n times as great as the difference between the value of z, according to T_h, and the value of t, according to T_k, if and only if $(u(i, x) - u(j, y))/(u(h, z) - u(k, t)) \geq n$ for all u in U. I'll then say that U *jointly represents all axiologies cardinally*. The *prospect-explication of rough intertheoretic comparisons* says that if there's a nonempty closed convex set $U \subset U^*$ of theory-dependent utility functions, which represents the m-value relation ordinally, and represents each axiology cardinally, then it jointly represents all axiologies cardinally. If that's so, we can assume, say, that our theories are represented by the set of value functions $\mathcal{G} = \{G : I \times X \rightarrow \mathbb{R} \mid G = u, u \in U\}$, and accordingly, that each theory T_i is represented by the set of value functions $\mathcal{G}_i = \{G_i : X \rightarrow \mathbb{R} \mid G_i = G(i, \cdot), G \in \mathcal{G}\}$.

Given these explications, the following theorem holds:

Expected Value Theorem for Incompleteness: *Suppose that all our $\succeq_i$ are N^*-conformable. If $\succeq_m$ is N-conformable and satisfies the Strong Pareto Condition with respect to our $\succeq_i$, then for all a and b in $\mathcal{Q}$,*

$$a \succeq_m b \quad \text{iff} \quad \sum_{i \in I, x \in X} a(i, x) G_i(x) \geq \sum_{i \in I, x \in X} b(i, x) G_i(x) \quad \forall G \in \mathcal{G}.^{132} \qquad (6.7)$$

Existence of Best and Worst implies that our axiologies can't be fully incomparable. Sequence-Continuity implies they can't compare in a lexical way. But I take it that such theories are extreme and comparatively very implausible. So this is a much less severe restriction than that imposed by Completeness. What's important is that (6.7) allows for both (non-radical) intra- and intertheoretic incomparability. If a theory T_i features some intratheoretic incomparability, then some two functions in $\mathcal{G}_i$ aren't positive affine transformations of each other. If no axiology

---

132 See the appendix (Section A.3) for the derivation of this theorem from the Representation Theorem for Incompleteness and the prospect-explications.

under consideration features intratheoretic incomparability, then for all i in I, all functions in $\mathcal{G}_i$ are positive affine transformations of each other. There may then still be *inter*theoretic incomparability. In that case, for at least some theory T_i, not all functions in $\mathcal{G}_i$ are the same. Some of them are *nontrivial* positive affine transformations of each other.

The Expected Value Theorem for Incompleteness and Probabilities

Let's now make first steps towards axiomatising incomplete m-value relations without given probabilities. To that end, we'll have to consider the relation $\succsim_m$ on $\mathcal{K}$ again. And we must define our new axioms for this relation. Let a_x be the prospect that for all i in I certainly leads to x: $a_x(i, x) = 1$ for all i. For a reflexive binary relation $\succsim$ on $\mathcal{K}$, define

Transitivity$_\mathcal{K}$: for all a, b and c in $\mathcal{K}$, if $a \succsim b$ and $b \succsim c$, then $a \succsim c$;

Mixture-Independence$_\mathcal{K}$: for all a and b in $\mathcal{K}$, $a \succsim b$ if and only if $pa + (1 - p)c \succsim pb + (1 - p)c$ for all $p \in]0, 1[$ and all c in $\mathcal{K}$;

Sequence-Continuity$_\mathcal{K}$: if $\{a_n\}$ and $\{b_n\}$ are convergent sequences such that $a_n \succsim b_n$ for all n, then $\lim(a_n) \succsim \lim(b_n)$;

Existence of Best and Worst$_\mathcal{K}$: there are $\bar{x}$ and $\underline{x}$ in X such that for all x in X, $a_{\bar{x}} \succsim a_x$, and $a_x \succsim a_{\underline{x}}$; and

Non-Triviality$_\mathcal{K}$: $a_{\bar{x}} \succ a_{\underline{x}}$ (i.e., not $a_{\underline{x}} \succsim a_{\bar{x}}$).

If a reflexive relation $\succsim$ on $\mathcal{K}$ satisfies these axioms, I'll again say it's *N-conformable*. The incompleteness of $\succsim_m$ on $\mathcal{K}$ raises a further complexity, noted on page 95. There are two reasons for why the m-value relation relative to your credences may be incomplete. You may have credence in theories that give rise to incommensurability; or you may have fuzzy credences. As mentioned, for simplicity I'll ignore the latter case, and assume that the incompleteness of your m-value judgments is entirely due to incommensurability in your values.

To model this, say that a probability distribution P on I is *positive* if $P(i) > 0$ for all i in I. For binary relations $\succeq$ on $\mathcal{Q}$ and $\succsim$ on $\mathcal{K}$, define the

Reduction Axiom: There's a positive probability distribution P on I such that for all a and b in $\mathcal{Q}^P$, $a \succeq b$ if and only if $L(a) \succsim L(b)$.

If your preferences on $\mathcal{K}$ satisfy the Reduction Axiom, they're exactly equal to your preferences on prospects conditional on the probability distribution P. I'm not aware that this axiom has been used in the literature for reducing incompleteness in preferences to incompleteness in values. Similar axioms have been used, but the ones I know of all depend on the assumption of state-*independent* preferences.[133] It's undoubtedly very strong. It not only rules out fuzzy credences, but also basically gives us the required probabilities. But at least as a first step towards bringing together axiomatisations without Completeness and axiomatisations for state-dependent utilities, it's interesting to see what this axiom implies.

Say that $\succeq_i$ is *strictly non-uniform* if there are $\bar{x}_i, \tilde{x}_i, x_i$ and $\underline{x}_i$ in X such that $a_{\bar{x}} \succ_i a_{\tilde{x}}, a_{\tilde{x}} \succ_i a_x$ and $a_x \succ_i a_{\underline{x}}$. Given this definition, we can state the

Representation Theorem for Incompleteness and Probabilities: *Suppose that all your $\succeq_i$ are N^*-conformable and strictly non-uniform. If your $\succeq_m$ and your $\tilde{\succeq}_m$ are N-conformable and jointly satisfy the Reduction Axiom for some positive probability distribution P on I, and if your $\succeq_m$ satisfies the Strong Pareto Condition with respect to your $\succeq_i$, there's a nonempty closed convex set $U \subset U^*$ of functions such that for all a and b in $\mathcal{K}$, all **a** and **b** in $\mathcal{Q}$, all a and b in $\mathcal{O}$ and all i in I,*

$$a \tilde{\succeq}_m b \quad \text{iff} \quad \sum_{i \in I, x \in X} a(i,x)P(i)u(i,x) \geq \sum_{i \in I, x \in X} b(i,x)P(i)u(i,x) \quad \forall u \in U, \qquad (6.8)$$

$$\boldsymbol{a} \succeq_m \boldsymbol{b} \quad \text{iff} \quad \sum_{i \in I, x \in X} \boldsymbol{a}(i,x)u(i,x) \geq \sum_{i \in I, x \in X} \boldsymbol{b}(i,x)u(i,x) \quad \forall u \in U, \quad and \qquad (6.9)$$

$$a \succeq_i b \quad \text{iff} \quad \sum_{x \in X} a(x)u(i,x) \geq \sum_{x \in X} b(x)u(i,x) \quad \forall u \in U. \qquad (6.10)$$

In particular, if $\{\boldsymbol{a}_n \succeq_m \boldsymbol{b}_n\}$ is a basis for $\succeq_m$ under these axioms, then U is the set of $u \in U^*$ satisfying $\{U_u(\boldsymbol{a}_n) \geq U_u(\boldsymbol{b}_n)\}$. And there's no other probability distribution $Q \neq P$ for which this is true.[134]

To turn this into a philosophically significant result, we can expand the judgment-explication from Chapter 5. Suppose that for some probability distribution P on I and some nonempty closed convex set U of real-valued functions on $I \times X$, the rough crosscutting cardinal intertheoretic comparisons are true, according to your theories, if and only if they are true for all functions u in U, and that your credence in any axiology T_i is $P(i)$—that is, for all x, y, z, t in X, all i, j, h, k in I (with $\boldsymbol{a}_{(i,x)} \succeq_m \boldsymbol{a}_{(j,y)}$ and $\boldsymbol{a}_{(h,z)} \succeq_m \boldsymbol{a}_{(k,t)}$) and $n \in \mathbb{R}$, the difference between the value of x, according to T_i, and the value of y, according to T_j, is at least n times as great as the difference between the value of z, according to T_h, and the value of t, according to T_k, if and only if $(u(i,x) - u(j,y))/(u(h,z) - u(k,t)) \geq n$ for all u in U, with $p_i = P(i)$, $p_j = P(j)$, $p_h = P(h)$ and $p_k = P(k)$. I'll then say that (U, P) *represents your intertheoretic comparisons cardinally and your axiological probabilities*

---

133 See e. g. the 'Reduction Axiom' in Ok et al. (2012).
134 See the appendix (Section A.3) for a proof.

quantitatively. The *judgment-explication of your rough intertheoretic comparisons and axiological probabilities* says that if there's a unique pair $(U \subset U^\star, P)$, which represents your $\succeq_m$ and $\tilde{\succeq}_m$ ordinally, and if U represents each of your axiologies cardinally, then (U, P) represents your intertheoretic comparisons cardinally and your axiological probabilities quantitatively. Hence if that's so, we can assume that $P(i)$ represents your credence p_i in the theory represented by the functions $\mathcal{G}_i = \{G_i : X \to \mathbb{R} \mid G_i = G(i, \cdot), G \in \mathcal{G}\}$.

Given this explication, the following theorem holds:

Expected Value Theorem for Incompleteness and Probabilities: *Suppose that all your $\succeq_i$ are N*-conformable and strictly non-uniform. If your $\succeq_m$ and your $\tilde{\succeq}_m$ are N-conformable and jointly satisfy the Reduction Axiom for some positive probability distribution P on I, and if your $\succeq_m$ satisfies the Strong Pareto Condition with respect to your $\succeq_i$, then for all a and b in $\mathcal{K}$,*

$$a \tilde{\succeq}_m b \quad iff \quad \sum_{i \in I, x \in X} a(i, x) p_i G_i(x) \geq \sum_{i \in I, x \in X} b(i, x) p_i G_i(x) \quad \forall G \in \mathcal{G}.^{135} \tag{6.11}$$

This is the most encompassing theorem of this book. Again, it doesn't allow us to represent fully incomparable theories, or theories that compare in a lexical way. And it doesn't allow for fuzzy credences. Moreover, that your $\succeq_m$ and $\tilde{\succeq}_m$ should satisfy the Reduction Axiom is only plausible if you assign nonzero credence to all axiologies under consideration. So to ground a normative argument on this theorem, we'd have to restrict the set of axiologies under consideration accordingly. But these seem relatively minor restrictions. Given these restrictions, and in light of our account of intertheoretic comparisons, the remaining axioms seem plausible. So we've now overcome all the major problems that affected the argument from the Basic Representation Theorem. We have an axiomatic foundation for EVM that doesn't suffer from any fundamental problem of intertheoretic comparisons, doesn't take axiological probabilities as primitives, and doesn't rule out either intra- or intertheoretic incommensurabilities.

6.2 General moral uncertainty

We're now in a position to explore a final question the axiomatic approach raises. Can the argument I've given ground a general theory of *normative* rather than

---

135 See the appendix (Section A.3) for the derivation of this theorem from the Representation Theorem for Incompleteness and Probabilities and the judgment-explications.

merely axiological uncertainty? That's the question of this section. Or more precisely, for simplicity, I'll ask whether our argument can ground a general theory of *moral* uncertainty. I'll set aside other forms of normative uncertainty such as uncertainty about prudence or rationality. I won't introduce new labels. So in this section, when I speak of 'EVM', I don't mean the theory of axiological uncertainty I've so far discussed. I mean the more general idea that under moral uncertainty, you ought to maximise the expectation of a quantity that represents the moral worth, or choiceworthiness, or the amount of moral reasons, assigned to options by moral theories. For this idea to make sense, EVM mustn't range over *betterness*-relations only. There must be a more general relation between options that all moral theories induce. I'll take 'moral preferability' to be such a relation. So in this section, by 'T_1', 'T_2', 'T_3', ... I'll mean theories about moral preferability. And by '$a \succeq_i b$', '$a \succ_i b$' and '$a \sim_i b$' I'll mean, respectively, that a is morally weakly preferable to, or strictly preferable to, or equally as preferable as b, according to T_i.[136]

The application of EVM to moral theories raises various questions.[137] In what follows, I'll focus on one issue only: on whether moral theories generally satisfy the axioms of decision theory. If they don't, this raises our two familiar problems for EVM. First, it's unclear how to explicate cardinal intra- and intertheoretic comparisons for such theories—or how to even understand EVM. Second, it's implausible that the m-value facts satisfy these axioms if they range over such theories—or that EVM is true. These problems (or at least the first one) are sometimes acknowledged. But my sense is that their urgency is underestimated. In response to the question of how to represent moral theories by value functions, Jacob Ross says:

> [F]or any theory that tells us what to do in [...] cases of uncertainty and that satisfies certain minimal coherence conditions, we can construct a value function that indicates not just the ordinal values of one's options, but also ratios among the value intervals between them. (2006a, 25; see 2006b, 754 f.)

---

136 In applying EVM to moral uncertainty, some authors have taken moral theories to imply 'moral choice-worthiness' relations (see MacAskill 2014), or moral 'value' relations (where that is somehow understood more broadly than axiological value; see Sepielli 2010 or Ross 2006b). However, both 'more choice-worthy than' and 'more valuable than' are, as a matter of meaning, transitive. So these interpretations threaten to rule out intransitive theories from the outset.

137 One important problem is supererogation, for which most standard deontological theories allow. According to these theories, there are options a and b such that a is morally preferable to b, but it's not the case that you *ought* to choose a. This raises the problem of how moral preferability and the moral 'ought' are weighed under uncertainty. See e. g. Sepielli (2010, ch. 6) or Tarsney (2019b) for a discussion.

This suggests that any 'minimally coherent' theory will be representable by a value function.[138] But that's anything but clear. To begin with, a theory can only be represented by '*a*' (single) value function if it satisfies Completeness. But incompleteness abounds among deontological theories, just as among axiologies. There are many plausible pluralist views, say, on which what's morally preferable depends on a range of factors—special obligations, rights, impersonal goodness, and so on. On many such views, there aren't determinate facts about how these considerations weigh against each other in cases of conflict.[139] These theories are incomplete. Now as the theorems from the last section show, EVM doesn't presuppose Completeness, or representability by a single value function. That's one reason why these theorems were crucial to even begin examining how far EVM can cover moral uncertainty. But similar problems arise for Transitivity, Continuity and Independence.

Transitivity

Start with Transitivity. There are many moral theories that *prima facie* violate this axiom. Consider a person-affecting view of population ethics according to which, if you have a choice between bringing about two worlds, it's preferable to bring about the world in which the total wellbeing of all the people existing in both worlds is greater, and if this total wellbeing is equal in both worlds, the worlds are equally preferable.[140] Suppose we have some cardinal concept of wellbeing, and consider the following five worlds—where the first number refers to Therese's and the second number to Philine's level of wellbeing, and 'Ω' indicates that the person doesn't exist in that world:

$$a: (2, \Omega), \quad b: (1, 3), \quad c: (\Omega, 2), \quad d: (3, 1), \quad \text{and} \quad e: (2, \Omega).$$

According to the person-affecting view, $a \succ b$, $b \succ c$, $c \succ d$ and $d \succ e$. Since a and e seem to be the same options, our view is *prima facie* intransitive.[141]

---

138 Sepielli (2010, ch. 5) also suggests the same method for cardinalisation. However, he doesn't even mention that a theory has to satisfy certain conditions for this method to be applicable. MacAskill (2014) also suggests the same method, and does mention that moral theories have to satisfy certain axioms for that method to work, but doesn't discuss whether they generally do.
139 Such a pluralist theory, explicitly implying incompleteness, is defended in Nagel (1979). Views that allow for moral dilemmas are also plausibly construed as incomplete. See e.g. Richardson (1994, 115 ff.).
140 For a defence of such a view, see e.g. Roberts (2003).
141 I thank John Broome for this example. Note that for simplicity, in this section, I'll consider a transitivity-condition on the non-reflexive relation $\succ$ rather than the reflexive relation $\succeq$. As is

The intransitivity arises because according to our view, whether the wellbeing of a person in a world matters depends on whether she exists in the world we *compare* it with. More generally, the view features 'alternative-dependency': it says that the moral worth of an option depends on its alternative. This easily leads to such intransitivities. And unfortunately, as Tim Willenken (2012) has shown, common sense morality is full of alternative-dependency. Consider, for example, the following common sense principles:

Numbers: If faced with a pairwise choice between saving a lesser number of people from some harm and a greater number of people from that same harm, it's morally preferable to save the greater number.

Dominance: If faced with a pairwise choice between two options a and b, where each individual is at least as well off and someone is much better off if you choose a rather than b, it's morally preferable to choose a.

No Pushing: If faced with a pairwise choice between pushing one person off a bridge to his death in order to block a trolley and letting several other people get killed by that trolley, it's morally preferable to let the greater number get killed.

As Willenken has shown, these three principles generate a *prima facie* deontic cycle.[142] And such examples could be multiplied with ease. Common sense morality is full of alternative-dependency, and thus full of *prima facie* intransitivities.

However, the case isn't as simple. These examples raise the question of how options, or outcomes, should be individuated. Suppose a theory implies that $a \succ b$, $b \succ c$, and $c \succ a$, on grounds of alternative-dependency. One might say it treats a-when-b-was-the-alternative (a_b) as different from a-when-c-was-the-alternative (a_c). After all, it takes the relevant alternatives to matter. For instance, one might say that our person-affecting theory treats $(2, \Omega)_{(3,1)}$ as distinct from $(2, \Omega)_{(1,3)}$. If we bring about $(2, \Omega)$ by rejecting $(3, 1)$, we've made Therese worse off than she could have been. But there's no one for whom that's true if we bring about $(2, \Omega)$ by rejecting $(1, 3)$. And since our theory is particularly concerned with such harms, this more fine-grained description is a better specification of (what matters in) an outcome for our theory. In individuating outcomes coarsely, we ignore features of the world that according to our view matter morally. Now if we do individuate outcomes according to their alternatives, alternative-dependency no longer grounds

---

easily verified, the condition on $\succeq$ implies that on $\succ$. Suppose $a \succ b$ and $b \succ c$. Then by the transitivity of $\succeq$, $a \succeq c$. Moreover, if $c \succeq a$ were to hold, by the transitivity of $\succeq$, $c \succeq b$ would hold—which contradicts $b \succ c$. So $c \succeq a$ cannot hold, and we have $a \succ c$.

142 See Willenken (2012, 546) for an example.

intransitivity. The claims $a_b \succ b_a$, $b_c \succ c_b$, and $c_a \succ a_c$ are perfectly consistent with Transitivity. So there's a general strategy by which we can render theories that seem to violate this axiom consistent with it.

There's a downside to this strategy. Many theories that are complete under a coarse-grained individuation of outcomes will become very incomplete under such a fine-grained one. Take the person-affecting view again. If we individuate outcomes only by the people who exist in them and their level of wellbeing, the theory tells us for any two outcomes which of them is preferable. That isn't so if we individuate outcomes more finely. The theory doesn't imply any ordering of the worlds $(2, \Omega)_{(3,1)}$ and $(1, 3)_{(2,\Omega)}$. Therese could have been better off in both $(2, \Omega)_{(3,1)}$ and $(1, 3)_{(2,\Omega)}$. But are these worlds equally preferable because the harm is the same (1 unit of wellbeing); or is $(2, \Omega)_{(3,1)}$ preferable because in this world Therese is better off than in $(1, 3)_{(2,\Omega)}$? The theory is silent on this. It's not defined to order these two outcomes. And there's no reason why it should be. It's logically impossible for you to face a choice between $(2, \Omega)_{(3,1)}$ and $(1, 3)_{(2,\Omega)}$. In such a choice, you could either choose $(1, 3)$ by rejecting world $(2, \Omega)$, or choose $(2, \Omega)$ by rejecting the altogether different world $(3, 1)$. But you can't possibly have these two options. It's an *impractical comparison*. Individuation of outcomes in terms of their alternatives always leads to impractical comparisons. But deontic moral theories are designed to guide your decision-making. And they can do this perfectly well while being silent on impractical comparisons. So as they stand, they generally won't give advice about such comparisons.

There's an important structural difference here between axiologies and deontic moral theories. An axiology is a claim about which worlds are better than which, or about which properties contribute to the value of worlds. But actual worlds are infinitely fine-grained, or characterised by an infinite number of properties. And for each of these properties, an axiology should say whether it contributes to value or not. An axiology is fragmentary, not fully specified or well-defined, if it's silent on how fine-grained outcomes or prospects are ordered. This isn't to say that an axiology must be 'complete' in my technical sense—that it must imply that any two options are *comparable*. But it must imply for any two outcomes or prospects that they're equally good, or that one is better, *or* that they're incomparable. If it's simply *silent* on the comparison, then to at least one of them it hasn't assigned any (precise or rough) value, which by its nature it should. A fully specified axiology may feature the verdict of an absence (of precise value-comparisons); but it can't feature the absence of any verdict.

So axiologies must imply a verdict on impractical comparisons. Modal properties, such as what could have been the case instead of a world, are properties of worlds just like the number of people or the amount of welfare they contain. So an axiology is fragmentary if it doesn't specify whether such modal properties contribute to value or not. Whether we can face a *choice* between two worlds is irrelevant from an axiological point of view. Indeed, our framework featured other impractical comparisons, like comparisons between prospects with different underlying probability distributions over axiologies. This wasn't a principled problem. In contrast, deontic moral theories (especially deontological ones[143]) aren't in the business of saying which properties contribute to value. They're designed to guide your decision-making. So by their standard, whether we can face a choice between two worlds is pivotal. There's nothing fragmentary or underspecified if a deontic moral theory is silent on impractical comparisons.

What does that mean for present purposes? Fortunately, from the point of view of Completeness and Transitivity, I think this difference doesn't matter much. There are representation theorems that allow for incompleteness, and *if* the other conditions of these theorems could be satisfied even under a fine-grained individuation of outcomes, these theorems would serve their purpose. If for some two options a and b, a deontic theory neither implies that $a \succeq b$ nor that $b \succeq a$, nothing in the theorems requires that this must be because of an explicit verdict of incomparability. So for the purposes of representation, we could treat the absence of a verdict like the verdict of an absence. We'd blur this distinction on a formal level. But we could bear it in mind, and no great harm would be done. So given that we have theorems allowing for incompleteness, the incompleteness emerging from reindividuation wouldn't *in itself* present a problem. Let's thus turn to Continuity and Independence.

Continuity

Questions of continuity are less often discussed in deontological ethics. But as with Transitivity, many standard deontological theories *prima facie* violate this axiom. That's because, *prima facie*, many deontological constraints are best captured by probability-thresholds. Consider the violation of rights. According to common sense deontology, you can respect a person's rights even if you take *some*

---

143 There's a question about whether deontic consequentialist theories imply verdicts concerning impractical comparisons. One might say they're also just designed to guide your decision-making, and since you can't face impractical comparisons, they won't imply any verdict about them either. However, there's a straightforward sense in which a deontic consequentialist theory can be extended or interpreted to imply such verdicts: we can interpret it as saying an option is 'weakly morally preferable' to another if and only if the prospect it represents is at least as good. Interpreted thus, it will inherit all the richness of its underlying axiology. So when I speak of the problems of deontic moral theories, I generally have in mind deontological theories especially.

risk of killing her for the sake of a minor pleasure—driving past her at sufficient distance on your way to a restaurant, say. But you violate her rights if you take a *considerable* risk of killing her for that pleasure. Yet whether you violate her rights isn't a matter of degree: you either violate them or you don't. So when does the constraint that you ought to respect people's rights apply? It seems congenial to deontology to accept a probability threshold.[144] But such thresholds lead to incontinuity. Suppose you violate someone's rights if you take more than a 1% risk of killing her for the sake of a minor pleasure. Suppose there's thus a constraint against taking such a risk, but not against taking a risk of 1% or less. And suppose not violating anyone's rights is always preferable to violating someone's, and that if you don't violate anyone's rights, risking fewer deaths is preferable to risking more. Now consider

f   killing Juliette with 100 % probability;
g   killing Lenardo and Valerine with 1 % probability; and
h   killing Juliette with 1 % probability.

Our view implies that $h > g$ and $g > f$. But there's no probability $p \in]0, 1[$ such that $pf + (1 - p)h > g$. For any $p > 0$, $pf + (1 - p)h$ involves a risk of more than 1 % of killing Juliette, and thus violates her rights. So g will be preferable to it.

Again, it's easy to find other examples where such thresholds seem congenial to deontology. Consider whether it's permissible to kill one person to save ten others. On common sense deontology, this depends on whether that person forfeited her right not to be killed—by intending to kill the ten, say. Yet you don't need *absolute* certainty that she forfeited her right, or else the permission would be irrelevant in practice. You only need it to be clear 'beyond reasonable doubt'. What does that mean? A natural interpretation is again that there's a threshold, such that you can permissibly kill someone for the sake of saving ten others if and only if the probability of her innocence isn't more than this threshold. Suppose this threshold is 3 %. And suppose not killing anyone impermissibly is always preferable to killing someone impermissibly, and that permissibly killing fewer people is preferable to permissibly killing more. Consider

i   killing William, where William has a 10 % probability of being innocent;
j   killing Margaret and Clara, where Margaret and Clara both have a 3 % probability of being innocent; and
k   killing William, where William has a 3 % probability of being innocent.

---

144 For further reflections on deontological approaches to uncertainty, see e. g. Jackson and Smith (2006), Tenenbaum (2017), Lazar (2018) or Tarsney (2018b).

Our view says that $k > j$ and $j > i$. But there's no probability $p \in]0, 1[$ such that $pi + (1 - p)k > j$. For any $p > 0$, $pi + (1 - p)k$ involves killing someone who has a probability of more than 3% of being innocent, and is thus impermissible. So j will be preferable to it.[145]

More examples could easily be given—concerning cases where it's unclear whether you have a promissory obligation to someone, are using them as a mere means, are violating their autonomy, and so on. *Prima facie*, many standard deontological theories violate Continuity. Is there a strategy to resist this? Reindividuating outcomes might again be natural. Consider our first example. Option f was to kill Juliette with certainty, option h to kill her with a 1% chance. Suppose you chose h, and it resulted in Juliette's death. For our theory there will have been a categorical difference between your action and the action of choosing f and Juliette's certain demise. You didn't violate her rights. So we might say our theory treats the resulting deaths as distinct—implying that Juliette is suffering mere injury as an outcome of h, but injury and insult (i. e. rights-violation) after f. More generally, probability threshold-views seem to posit a categorical difference between an outcome that had more and one that had less than this probability of coming about, however similar they otherwise are.

Yet, natural as such a reindividuation may be, it doesn't help make our deontic theories continuous. Once we've distinguished the outcome 'Juliette is dead, and suffered the insult of a rights-violation' (of f) from 'Juliette is dead, but suffered no insult' (of h), we'll again face impracticalities. Consider the option '$pf + (1 - p)h$', with $p \in]0, 1[$. One possible outcome of this option is that Juliette suffered an insult, and another is that she suffered none. But on common sense views of rights, rights violations are determined *ex ante*, rather than *ex post* through brute moral luck. So you can't face such a prospect in practice. Whatever you do, you'll either violate her rights or you won't, for all possible outcomes of your choice. So you can't face a prospect like '$pf + (1 - p)h$'. This option not only contributes to impractical comparisons with others, as in the cases we've encountered above. It's an *impractical option*, all in itself. Deontic theories (especially deontological ones) generally won't imply verdicts concerning such options. There's no reason why they should. So they generally won't imply any verdicts of the form '$pf + (1-p)h > g$', or '$g > pf + (1 - p)h$'. But such verdicts are precisely what Continuity would require. So reindividuating outcomes won't help with this axiom.

The difference between Continuity and Transitivity is this. In either case, the pertinent reindividuation will lead to impracticalities, and thus to widespread

---

145 This example is taken from Jackson and Smith (2006); the threshold view is accepted by Aboodi et al. (2008).

incompleteness. This is a problem with Continuity. Continuity features what we might call a 'conditional minimal completeness constraint'. It requires that, if a theory implies that $a \succ b$ and $b \succ c$, it must also make some third judgment involving $pa + (1-p)c$ (viz., that $pa + (1-p)c \succ b$ for some $p \in]0, 1[$)—or can't be *fully* incomplete with respect to this latter option. Now even under a fine-grained individuation of outcomes via their probabilities, there'll be many (standard, practical) options for which deontic moral theories imply the first two judgments, and thus satisfy the antecedent of the conditional completeness constraint. So then Continuity will require at least minimal completeness with respect to $pa + (1-p)c$, which the theories will fail to deliver. Transitivity also features a conditional minimal completeness constraint. It requires that if a theory implies that $a \succ b$ and $b \succ c$, it must also make some third judgment involving a and c (viz., that $a \succ c$). However, under a fine-grained individuation of outcomes via their alternatives, there won't be any options for which our theories imply the first two judgments, and thus satisfy the antecedent of the conditional constraint. They might imply that $a_b \succ b_a$ and $b_c \succ c_b$. But this doesn't force them to any third judgment. They would be so forced if they implied that $a_b \succ b_a$ and $b_a \succ c_b$. But this they won't imply. So even if theories fail to deliver judgments like $a_b \succ c_b$, that's no problem, since Transitivity won't require them to.

Again, I take it, there's an important difference here between axiologies and deontic moral theories. Axiologies aren't designed to guide your decision-making. So there doesn't seem to be a principled reason why they shouldn't imply verdicts concerning impractical options, or deliver the minimal completeness that Continuity requires. Our framework featured other impractical options, like prospects in which it depends on the correct axiology whether you'll kill a non-human animal. So as indicated in Section 3.2, I take it the strategy of reindividuating outcomes can more successfully be applied in the case of axiologies—e. g., axiologies that treat rights infringements as a bad thing. It can help us render axiologies that *prima facie* violate Continuity consistent with it. It just cannot help with deontic views.

Is there another strategy to resist *prima facie* violations of Continuity? One might think there is. Intuitively, discontinuities arise through thresholds, or sudden leaps in the graph that designates our options' worth. So perhaps we could assume that the relevant deontological worth-functions have continuous drops instead of discontinuous leaps. Rather than saying that a risk of 1 % marks a cut-off point for the violation of rights, say, we could say it marks a point where our options' worth decreases drastically but continuously—as in the following illustration:

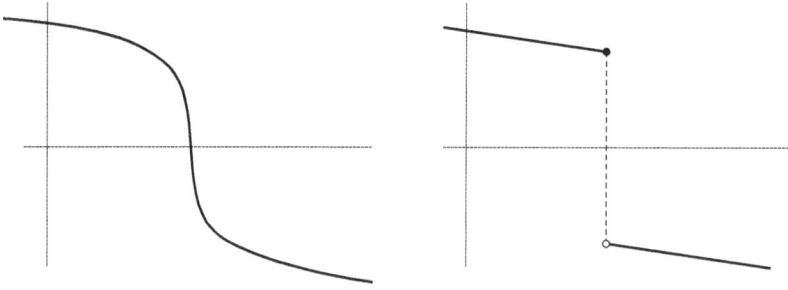

Fig. 6.1: Graphs to illustrate continuous drop (left) versus discontinuous leap (right).

Indeed, one might think that's a more charitable interpretation of deontological views, as thresholds seem mysterious or arbitrary.

But this strategy isn't fully satisfying either, at least with standard deontological theories like the ones we've been considering. Such views operate with all-or-nothing concepts. There's an important qualitative difference in whether or not you violate rights, say. Your actions are generally permissible as long as you don't, and impermissible as soon as you do. And you can't violate rights *a little bit*. Of course, not all rights violations are equally grievous, as there are more and less weighty rights. But even the less important rights will either be violated or not, and that will be a qualitative difference. All-or-nothing concepts are at the heart of deontology, and in the face of uncertainty, it seems they'll have to be captured by thresholds. If we reinterpret such views as continuous, we may produce extensionally similar analogues of them. And working with these analogues may be the best we can do. But it doesn't present a fully satisfying theoretical solution to the problem of discontinuous theories. Moreover, as we'll presently see, even if we render our views continuous, this won't help make them satisfy Independence. So even if we accept this strategy in the face of Continuity, it won't solve the general problem we're concerned with.

There's a final strategy one could propose. It's also a possible strategy concerning Independence. So let me discuss it in that context, and turn to this final axiom now.

Independence

If what I've said is correct, the case of Independence is even more problematic. As with the other axioms, many standard moral theories *prima facie* violate it. Consider fairness. According to a common sense idea, a distribution of a good is fair if and only if people's claims to this good are satisfied in proportion to their strength. If a good can't be divided, it's fairest to put on a lottery, in which people's chances of receiving this good are proportional to the strength of their claims.[146] And a distribution or lottery is less fair the further away it is from (expected) proportionate satisfaction of claims. Now suppose Care and Helen both have a claim to some indivisible good G, but Care's is twice as strong as Helen's. Consider the options

l Care gets G; and
m Helen gets G.

On the present theory, $l > m$, since l comes closer to a distribution in which their claims are satisfied in proportion to their strength. However, suppose you have a biased coin that lands tails 2/3 of the time, and you can choose among the lotteries

n Care gets G no matter how the coin lands; and
o Helen gets G if the coin lands heads, and Care if it lands tails.

Given that G is indivisible, o is the fairest option available. So we have $o > n$. However, since n seems equivalent to $1/3l + 2/3l$, and o equivalent to $1/3m + 2/3l$, this theory seems to violate Independence.[147]

Again, it's clear why it does. According to this theory, what matters about an outcome is not only what actually happens in it, but also what *could* have happened, and with what probability, instead of it. So we can't evaluate the outcomes of our actions independently of one another. For the same reason, the above view of rights will also violate Independence. On this view, again, you violate someone's rights if you take a risk of more than 1 % of killing her for the sake of a minor pleasure, but not if the risk is 1 % or less. Consider our options

f killing Juliette with 100 % probability;
g killing Lenardo and Valerine with 1 % probability; and
h killing Juliette with 1 % probability.

The theory implies that $h > g$. But for $p = 0.99$, it implies that $pg + (1 - p)f > ph + (1 - p)f$—since the latter but not the former option violates someone's rights. And something similar will hold for many related views. *Prima facie*, violations of Independence are again very common in standard deontology.

Unfortunately, however, neither of the two strategies we encountered with Transitivity and Continuity works with Independence. First, the problem with reindividuating outcomes via the probability with which they came about is

---

146 For a defence of such a view, see e. g. Broome (1990).
147 See Diamond (1967) for a similar example.

exactly the same as with Continuity. Independence also features a conditional minimal completeness constraint. It requires that, if a theory implies that $a > b$, it must also make verdicts involving some compound option $pa + (1 - p)c$ (viz., that $pa + (1 - p)c > pb + (1 - p)c$ for all c). And even under a fine-grained individuation of outcomes via their probabilities, there'll be many standard, practical options for which deontic moral theories imply the first judgment, and thus satisfy the antecedent of the conditional completeness constraint. So then Independence will require minimal completeness with respect to $pa + (1 - p)c$. But this will be an impractical option. This won't be a problem for axiologies. So as indicated in Section 3.2, I take it the strategy of reindividuating outcomes can help us render axiologies that *prima facie* violate Independence consistent with it. But theories designed to guide action will remain silent on such impractical options, and won't deliver the relevant minimal completeness.

Second, violations of Independence don't depend on probability-thresholds. Even if we interpret our theories in terms of continuous drops rather than discontinuous leaps, it remains true that what matters according to them is not only what actually happened, but also what could have happened instead. This very general fact causes violations of Independence, and we don't avoid it by making our theories continuous. Consider our view of rights-violations again. Suppose the moral worth of options decreases drastically but continuously when we take a risk of more than 1 % of killing someone. Then adding an additional risk of killing Juliette will decrease the worth of 'killing Lenardo and Valerine with 1 % probability' less than it will decrease the worth of 'killing Juliette with 1 % probability'. And this will lead to violations of Independence. So even if we grant that this strategy allows us to satisfy Continuity, it doesn't help with Independence. Whatever we think about interpreting deontological views as continuous, doing so doesn't help with the general problem we're concerned with.

As indicated, there's a final move in response to violations of Independence, which could also be made with respect to Continuity. It builds on reindividuating outcomes. I've shown that reindividuating outcomes will render our theories too incomplete even to satisfy the axioms of Continuity and Independence. This is because reindividuating outcomes will produce impractical options, and our theories aren't designed to order such options. So what we could do is this. We could *extend* our theories and *make* them imply verdicts on impractical options; and we could do that in ways that accord with the relevant Continuity and Independence constraints. As far as I see, that would be possible. And as first-order judgments of moral preferability go, it wouldn't alter these views in any practically relevant manner. We'd keep all their verdicts on practically possible options and comparisons, and only extend them with respect to options and comparisons you can't face in practice. So one might argue that such extensions would be innocuous, and not distort our views in any problematic respect.

However, there are problems with this move too. For one thing, by so extending our views, we'd turn them into different theories—indeed, theories of a different kind. Again, deontic moral theories have a specific nature, and that's fundamentally different from that of axiologies. From an axiological point of view, it's irrelevant whether options can figure in practical choice. So there's something fragmentary about an axiology that implies no verdict on impractical options. But deontic moral theories are just designed to guide choice. By a deontic standard, there's nothing fragmentary about silence on impracticalities. In fact, at least with the deontological theories we've been considering, there will often be no basis *within* these views on which they could imply verdicts on impractical comparisons or options. Hence by making our moral theories order impractical options, we wouldn't somehow finish them, complement them where otherwise they'd be fragmentary. We'd change their very nature. We'd basically turn them into axiologies, without any basis for doing so implied by the theories themselves.

Moreover, even though our extensions would have no practical implications as far as first-order judgments of moral preferability are concerned, they *would* have practical implications under uncertainty. Consider again the options of killing Juliette with 100 % probability (f), killing Lenardo and Valerine with 1 % probability (g), and killing Juliette with 1 % probability (h). And suppose we reindividuate outcomes and supplement our theories with verdicts such that, for some p and $q \in]0, 1[$, $pf + (1-p)h > g$ and $g > qf + (1-q)h$. The precise verdicts will determine where on the value scale between f and h the value of g lies. And that in turn will determine how important it is to choose g rather than f, according to our theory. And while this may be irrelevant if we're certain of this theory and face a choice between f and g, it's not irrelevant if we have to weigh it against a theory according to which f is morally preferable to g. So there'd be no basis within the deontological views to make these extensions, and yet they'd have significant implications under uncertainty. Thus even if these extensions are the best we can work with in practice, they don't present a fully convincing theoretical solution to our problem. In providing a theory of uncertainty about these extended cousins of our deontological views, we're not giving a theory of uncertainty about *these* deontological views.

Conclusion

In conclusion, a great number of standard deontic views don't satisfy our axioms, and there's no altogether convincing way in which we can interpret them as doing so. This casts doubt on whether the argument I've been developing can readily ground a general theory of moral uncertainty. *A fortiori*, it casts doubt on whether our argument can readily ground an even more general theory of normative uncertainty. Also, I've now addressed only one problem with understanding EVM as a general theory of moral or normative uncertainty. There remain other problems—for instance, the question of how to accommodate supererogation.[148] Even disregarding the question I've discussed, these other problems would still need to be solved.

Let me turn back to axiologies again. I've considered whether the strategy of reindividuating outcomes can render theories that *prima facie* violate Continuity and Independence consistent with these axioms. I've pointed out a problem with this strategy when applied to deontic views: once we individuate outcomes finely, many standard deontic theories will be too incomplete to satisfy Continuity and Independence, since they're designed to guide your decision-making. But I've suggested this isn't a problem when we apply the strategy to axiologies: axiologies aren't designed to guide your decision-making. Does this mean we can *always* apply this strategy to axiologies? In other words, does it mean we can see *all* possible axiologies as satisfying Independence and Continuity, provided we individuate outcomes properly?

It doesn't. Importantly, the strategy only works for axiologies on which the relevant fine-grained features of outcomes—such as facts about what could have happened, or about the probability with which something happened—*are* indeed good- or bad-making features of outcomes.[149] I take it that on the most natural axiological versions of the deontic views we've considered, this is the case. For instance, I take it the most natural rights- or fairness-sensitive axiologies say that the fact that someone's rights have been violated (e. g., that Juliette had more than a 1 % chance of being killed) or that some state of affairs came about unfairly (e. g., that Helen had a disproportionately low chance of getting some good) *are* bad-making features of outcomes. They say that how good some state of affairs is depends among else on its modal properties. So they say the relevant fine-grained features of outcomes do indeed matter axiologically.

In principle, however, this needn't be. There are axiologies that violate Continuity and Independence, but not because they consider such features as good- or bad-making properties of outcomes. Consider Continuity. Take an axiology on which the value of wellbeing lexically dominates that of beauty—in that a prospect is better than another whenever it expectably leads to more wellbeing, but *ceteris*

---

148 See footnote 137.
149 For similar considerations, see e. g. Broome (1991, 103 f.).

paribus better if it expectably leads to more beauty. This welfare/beauty-theory doesn't satisfy Continuity. But the reason for this isn't that on this axiology, some extra modal feature of an outcome makes an axiological difference. The theory doesn't, for example, treat an instance of beauty as more or less valuable depending on whether some wellbeing could have materialised instead of it. It just treats wellbeing as lexically better. Or at least, that's the most natural version or interpretation of this view. So as far as I see, the strategy of reindividuating outcomes couldn't successfully be applied to it. Or consider Independence. Take an axiology on which fairness is purely a consideration at the level of prospects. On this axiology, *ceteris paribus*, one prospect is better than another if on that prospect people's chances of receiving some good are proportional to the strength of their claims. But an unfair causal history isn't a bad-making feature of an *outcome*. So on this axiology, *ex ante* it's best to give people fair chances. But *ex post* the chances that people have had are irrelevant, and it's only the actual distribution of goods that matters. This too is a possible theory. And as far as I see, the strategy of reindividuating outcomes couldn't successfully be applied to it. So I think we can't understand all possible axiologies as satisfying Continuity and Independence. Or again, our argument cannot ground a fully general theory of axiological uncertainty. It can only ground a theory of uncertainty about those axiologies that are, or can successfully be seen as being, N*-conformable.

However, in contrast to the case of deontic view, my sense is that most standard *axiologies* satisfy our conditions, and that the axiologies we ultimately strictly exclude are comparatively rare and implausible. Take the two axiologies I've just mentioned. Presumably, we should have *some* nonzero credence in them. But they certainly don't seem very plausible. On the contrary, the extreme kind of lexical priority contended by the former, and the distinction between *ex ante* and *ex post* considerations assumed by the latter, make them rather dubious. More generally, at the level of axiologies, Continuity and Independence do seem to express compelling thoughts. Thus while its restrictions are non-trivial, I think our theory is still an interestingly general theory of axiological uncertainty. That's part of why, in this book, I've focused on the narrower problem of axiological, rather than the general problem of moral or normative uncertainty.

6.3 Conclusion

In this book, I've explored an axiomatic approach to the problem of axiological uncertainty, and to the idea of Expected Value Maximisation in particular. I first introduced a basic representation theorem (Chapter 2), and argued that—*modulo* the fundamental metaphysical problem of intertheoretic comparisons, the pre-supposition of axiological probabilities as primitives, and the existence of intra- and intertheoretic incommensurabilities—this theorem can help answer the question of meaning and the question of truth about EVM (Chapter 3). I then addressed these restrictions one by one. I argued that epistemic norms can provide a constructivist ground for intertheoretic comparisons (Chapter 4). I furnished the overall theory with an account of axiological credences, and thus paved the way for applying it in real life (Chapter 5). And I extended the theorem to cover axiologies that involve intra- or give rise to intertheoretic incommensurabilities (Chapter 6).

Naturally, there remain many problems for further research. On the one hand, there are further philosophical questions. For instance, in discussing the axioms, I've often restricted myself to comparing their plausibility in our context with their status in other contexts. To make a more complete case for EVM, it would be necessary to say more in their defence. Similarly, it would be interesting to explore constructivism about intertheoretic comparisons in more depth, and spell out some plausible actual implications of it. And most urgently perhaps, this last chapter raised problems for the theory of *moral* uncertainty, and it would be important to make progress on these. On the other hand, there remain many open technical problems. It may be worthwhile to seek theorems for incomplete orderings that yield unique separations of subjective probabilities and state-dependent utilities and don't rely on the strong Reduction Axiom. It ultimately seems important to explore results for state-dependent utilities that allow for incomparability in values as well as fuzzy credences. And since there are infinitely many axiologies, it would certainly be desirable to extend the results of this book to a framework that allows for an infinite state-space.

As usual in moral philosophy, I can't be certain that my arguments are sound. But I hope this book has at least shed a new light on some difficulties in the theory of normative or evaluative uncertainty and on a possible path to a solution. In particular, I hope I've shown that Expected Value Maximisation is neither self-explanatorily clear nor trivially true, but that the axiomatic approach provides a promising strategy to explicate and ground it. And I hope this has some value.

A Appendix

In this appendix, I'll provide the proofs of the theorems in the foregoing chapters.

A.1 Proofs for Chapter 2

The Basic Representation Theorem

As indicated in footnotes 38 and 40, Karni and Schmeidler (1980, 8) and Karni (1985, 14) prove that if your $\succeq_m$ and all your $\succeq_i$ are vNM-conformable, there's a function $u : I \times X \rightarrow \mathbb{R}$, unique up to positive affine transformation, such that for all a and b in $\mathcal{Q}$,

$$a \succeq_m b \quad \text{iff} \quad \sum_{i \in I, x \in X} a(i, x) u(i, x) \geq \sum_{i \in I, x \in X} b(i, x) u(i, x), \tag{A.1}$$

and for each i in I, there's a function u_i, unique up to positive affine transformation, such that for all a and b in $\mathcal{O}$,

$$a \succeq_i b \quad \text{iff} \quad \sum_{x \in X} a(x) u_i(x) \geq \sum_{x \in X} b(x) u_i(x). \tag{A.2}$$

It remains to show that if your $\succeq_m$ satisfies the Pareto Condition with respect to your $\succeq_i$, then for each i in I, $u(i, \cdot)$ is a positive affine transformation of u_i, or also represents the relation $\succeq_i$ in the sense of (A.2). So for some theory T_i, consider the set of prospects in $\mathcal{Q}$ in which the probability of T_i is 1, $\mathcal{Q}^i_{p=1} = \{a \in \mathcal{Q} \mid \sum_{x \in X} a(i, x) = 1\}$. This set is isomorphic to $\mathcal{O}$. So for any a in $\mathcal{O}$, we have a prospect $H_i^{-1}(a)$ in $\mathcal{Q}^i_{p=1}$, with $H_i^{-1}(a)(i, x) = a(x)$ for all x. The Pareto Condition implies that for all a and b in $\mathcal{O}$,

$$a \succeq_i b \quad \text{iff} \quad H_i^{-1}(a) \succeq_m H_i^{-1}(b). \tag{A.3}$$

From (A.1), we know that for all such $H_i^{-1}(a)$ and $H_i^{-1}(b)$ in $\mathcal{Q}^i_{p=1}$,

$$H_i^{-1}(a) \succeq_m H_i^{-1}(b) \quad \text{iff} \quad \sum_{x \in X} a(x) u(i, x) \geq \sum_{x \in X} b(x) u(i, x). \tag{A.4}$$

So $u(i, \cdot)$ constitutes a utility function on X that represents T_i in the sense of (A.2).

$\square$

The Expected Value Theorem

The derivation of the Expected Value Theorem from the Basic Representation Theorem and the prospect-explications is straightforward. The Basic Representation Theorem implies that if your $\succsim_m$ and all your $\succsim_i$ are vNM-conformable, and your $\succsim_m$ satisfies the Pareto Condition with respect to your $\succsim_i$, there's a function $u : I \times X \to \mathbb{R}$, unique up to positive affine transformation, that represents your $\succsim_m$ ordinally, and is such that for each i, $u(i, \cdot)$ represents $\succsim_i$ ordinally. Since any other function that represents $\succsim_i$ ordinally must be a positive affine transformation of $u(i, \cdot)$ (see footnote 40), by the prospect-explication of intratheoretic comparisons, each $u(i, \cdot)$ thus represents $\succsim_i$ cardinally. So u represents each axiology cardinally. By the prospect-explication of intertheoretic comparisons, it thus jointly represents all axiologies cardinally.

A.2 Proofs for Chapter 5

The Representation Theorem for Probabilities

Karni and Schmeidler (1980, 9; also 2016) prove that if your $\succsim_m$ and your $\tilde{\succsim}_m$ are vNM-conformable and jointly satisfy the Consistency Axiom, and if your $\tilde{\succsim}_m$ is non-uniform, there's a function $u : I \times X \to \mathbb{R}$ and a probability distribution P on I such that for all a and b in $\mathcal{K}$ and all $\boldsymbol{a}$ and $\boldsymbol{b}$ in $\mathcal{Q}$,

$$a \tilde{\succsim}_m b \quad \text{iff} \quad \sum_{i \in I, x \in X} a(i,x)P(i)u(i,x) \geq \sum_{i \in I, x \in X} b(i,x)P(i)u(i,x), \quad \text{and} \quad (\text{A.5})$$

$$\boldsymbol{a} \succsim_m \boldsymbol{b} \quad \text{iff} \quad \sum_{i \in I, x \in X} \boldsymbol{a}(i,x)u(i,x) \geq \sum_{i \in I, x \in X} \boldsymbol{b}(i,x)u(i,x). \quad (\text{A.6})$$

Moreover, u is unique up to positive affine transformation; if i is null, $P(i) = 0$, and if i is non-null, $P(i) > 0$; and if for all i in I there are $\boldsymbol{a}$ and $\boldsymbol{b}$ in $\mathcal{Q}$ that agree outside i such that $\boldsymbol{a} \succ_m \boldsymbol{b}$, then P is unique. By the same reasoning as in the proof of the Basic Representation Theorem, if your $\succsim_i$ are vNM-conformable and your $\succsim_m$ satisfies the Pareto Condition with respect to your $\succsim_i$, then for each i in I, $u(i, \cdot)$ also represents the relation $\succsim_i$ in the sense of (A.2). It remains to show that the uniqueness condition of P is satisfied. We've assumed that all your $\succsim_i$ are non-uniform, or that for each i in I there are $\bar{a}_i$ and $\underline{b}_i$ in $\mathcal{O}$ such that $\bar{a}_i \succ_i \underline{b}_i$. So consider $\bar{a}_i$ and $\underline{b}_i$ in the set $\mathcal{Q}^i_{p=1}$ (from the proof of the Basic Representation Theorem), with $\bar{\boldsymbol{a}}_i(i,x) = \bar{a}_i(x)$ and $\underline{\boldsymbol{b}}_i(i,x) = \underline{b}_i(x)$ for all x in X. $\bar{\boldsymbol{a}}_i$ and $\underline{\boldsymbol{b}}_i$ agree outside i, and by the Pareto Condition, we have $\bar{\boldsymbol{a}}_i \succ_m \underline{\boldsymbol{b}}_i$. So P is unique. $\qquad\square$

The Expected Value Theorem for Probabilities

The derivation of the Expected Value Theorem for Probabilities from the Representation Theorem for Probabilities and the judgment-explications is parallel to that of the Expected Value Theorem from the Basic Representation Theorem.

The Weighted Value Theorem

Karni and Schmeidler (1980, 7) prove that if your $\tilde{\succeq}_m$ is vNM-conformable, there's a function $u : I \times X \rightarrow \mathbb{R}$, unique up to positive unit-comparable transformation, such that for all a and b in $\mathcal{K}$,

$$a \; \tilde{\succeq}_m \; b \quad \text{iff} \quad \sum_{i \in I, x \in X} a(i,x)u(i,x) \geq \sum_{i \in I, x \in X} b(i,x)u(i,x). \tag{A.7}$$

We also know (see footnote 40) that if all your $\succeq_i$ are vNM-conformable, then for each i in I, there's a function u_i, unique up to positive affine transformation, such that for all a and b in $\mathcal{O}$,

$$a \succeq_i b \quad \text{iff} \quad \sum_{x \in X} a(x)u_i(x) \geq \sum_{x \in X} b(x)u_i(x). \tag{A.8}$$

It remains to show that if your $\tilde{\succeq}_m$ satisfies the Pareto Condition for $\mathcal{K}$ with respect to your $\succeq_i$, then for each i in I, $u(i, \cdot)$ represents $\succeq_i$ cardinally. So for some theory T_i and some outcome y, consider the set of prospects in $\mathcal{K}$ that if T_i is false lead to y with probability 1, $\mathcal{K}_y^i = \{a \in \mathcal{K} \mid a(j,y) = 1 \; \forall j \neq i\}$. This set is isomorphic to $\mathcal{O}$. So for any a in $\mathcal{O}$, we have a prospect $K_i^{-1}(a)$ in $\mathcal{K}_y^i$, with $K_i^{-1}(a)(i,x) = a(x)$ for all x. Since all $\succeq_i$ are reflexive and complete, the Pareto Condition for $\mathcal{K}$ implies that for all a and b in $\mathcal{O}$,

$$a \succeq_i b \quad \text{iff} \quad K_i^{-1}(a) \; \tilde{\succeq}_m \; K_i^{-1}(b). \tag{A.9}$$

From (A.7), we know that for all such $K_i^{-1}(a)$ and $K_i^{-1}(b)$ in $\mathcal{K}_y^i$,

$$K_i^{-1}(a) \; \tilde{\succeq}_m \; K_i^{-1}(b) \quad \text{iff} \quad \sum_{x \in X} a(x)u(i,x) \geq \sum_{x \in X} b(x)u(i,x). \tag{A.10}$$

So $u(i, \cdot)$ constitutes a utility function on X that represents T_i in the sense of (A.2). By the prospect-explication of intratheoretic comparisons, it thus represents $\succeq_i$ cardinally. $\qquad\square$

A.3 Proofs for Chapter 6

The Representation Theorem for Incompleteness

As a first lemma, we prove that if $\succeq_m$ is N-conformable, there exists a nonempty closed convex set $U \subset U^*$ of functions, such that for all $\boldsymbol{a}$ and $\boldsymbol{b}$ in $\mathcal{Q}$,

$$\boldsymbol{a} \succeq_m \boldsymbol{b} \quad \text{iff} \quad \sum_{i \in I, x \in X} a(i,x)u(i,x) \geq \sum_{i \in I, x \in X} b(i,x)u(i,x) \quad \forall u \in U, \tag{A.11}$$

where if $\{\boldsymbol{a}_n \succeq_m \boldsymbol{b}_n\}$ is a basis for $\succeq_m$ under these axioms, U is the set of u in U^* satisfying $\{\mathbf{U}_u(\boldsymbol{a}_n) \geq \mathbf{U}_u(\boldsymbol{b}_n)\}$. Suppose that a reflexive binary relation $\tilde{\succeq}$ on $\mathcal{K}$ is N-conformable for some $\bar{x}$ and $\underline{x}$. We can then define a normalised set of functions

$$W^* = \left\{ w : I \times X \to \mathbb{R} \mid w(i,\underline{x}) = 0 \;\; \forall i \in I; \;\; 0 \leq \sum_{i \in I} w(i,x) \leq 1 \right.$$

$$\left. \forall x \in X; \sum_{i \in I} w(i,\bar{x}) = 1 \right\}. \tag{A.12}$$

Nau (2006, Theorem 2) proves that if a reflexive binary relation $\tilde{\succeq}$ on $\mathcal{K}$ is N-conformable, there's a nonempty closed convex set $W \subset W^*$ of functions, such that for all a and b in $\mathcal{K}$,

$$a \tilde{\succeq} b \quad \text{iff} \quad \sum_{i \in I, x \in X} a(i,x)w(i,x) \geq \sum_{i \in I, x \in X} b(i,x)w(i,x) \quad \forall w \in W. \tag{A.13}$$

And in particular, if $\{a_n \tilde{\succeq} b_n\}$ is a basis for $\tilde{\succeq}$ under these axioms, then W is the set of $w \in W^*$ satisfying $\{\mathbf{U}_w(a_n) \geq \mathbf{U}_w(b_n)\}$. Note that this holds for any finite sets of states and outcomes. So let I' be the singleton $\{k\}$, let X' be a set of $|X| \cdot |I|$ outcomes, and define $\mathcal{K}' = \{a : I' \times X' \to \mathbb{R}_+ \mid \sum_{x \in X'} a(k,x) = 1\}$. According to Nau's result, if a reflexive relation $\tilde{\succeq}$ on $\mathcal{K}'$ is N-conformable, there's a nonempty closed convex set $W \subset W^*$ of functions representing it in the sense of (A.13). Since $\mathcal{K}'$ is isomorphic to $\mathcal{Q}$ (and to each $\boldsymbol{a}_{(i,x)}$ in $\mathcal{Q}$ there corresponds an a_x in $\mathcal{K}'$), this implies our representation of $\succeq_m$.

Let's spell this out in detail. To see the bijection between $\mathcal{Q}$ and $\mathcal{K}'$, label the outcomes in X by $X = \{x_1, x_2, \ldots, x_k\}$, and the outcomes in X' by:

$$X' = \{x_{11}, x_{12}, \ldots, x_{1k},$$

$$x_{21}, x_{22}, \ldots, x_{2k},$$

$$\ldots,$$

$$x_{n1}, x_{n2}, \ldots, x_{nk}\}$$

For all $\boldsymbol{a}$ in $\mathcal{Q}$ and a in $\mathcal{K}'$, we have

$$\sum_{i\in I, x\in X} \boldsymbol{a}(i,x) = \sum_{i\in I', x\in X'} a(i,x) = \sum_{x\in X'} a(k,x) = 1. \tag{A.14}$$

So with each $\boldsymbol{a}$ in $\mathcal{Q}$ we can associate an a in $\mathcal{K}'$ such that $a(k, x_{ij}) = \boldsymbol{a}(i, x_j)$, and vice versa. That is, there's a bijection $M : \mathcal{K}' \to \mathcal{Q}$,

$$M : a \mapsto M(a), \ M(a)(i, x_j) = a(k, x_{ij}), \quad \text{with}$$
$$M^{-1} : \boldsymbol{a} \mapsto M^{-1}(\boldsymbol{a}), \ M^{-1}(\boldsymbol{a})(k, x_{ij}) = \boldsymbol{a}(i, x_j). \tag{A.15}$$

For some best and worst outcomes $\bar{x}$ and $\underline{x}$ in X', we can define

$$W'^\star = \{w : I' \times X' \to \mathbb{R} \mid w(k, \underline{x}) = 0; \ 0 \le w(k, x) \le 1 \ \forall x \in X;$$
$$w(k, \bar{x}) = 1\}. \tag{A.16}$$

Now define a binary relation $\gtrsim$ on $\mathcal{K}'$ such that $a \gtrsim b$ if and only if $M(a) \succsim_m M(b)$. Then if $\succsim_m$ is N-conformable (for $(\overline{i, x}) = (m, x_n)$ and $(\underline{i, x}) = (p, x_q)$), $\gtrsim$ is N-conformable (for $\bar{x} = x_{mn}$ and $\underline{x} = x_{pq}$). By Nau's result, there's thus a nonempty closed convex set $W \subset W'^\star$ of functions, such that for all a and b in $\mathcal{K}'$,

$$a \gtrsim b \quad \text{iff} \quad \sum_{x\in X'} a(k, x)w(k, x) \ge \sum_{x\in X'} b(k, x)w(k, x) \quad \forall w \in W. \tag{A.17}$$

For any $w \in W$, define a corresponding function $u : I \times X \to \mathbb{R}$, such that $u(i, x_j) = w(k, x_{ij})$, and let U be the set of all such u. Since W is nonempty, closed and convex, and $W \subset W'^\star$, U is nonempty, closed and convex, and $U \subset U^\star$. Also, for any $\boldsymbol{a}$ and $\boldsymbol{b}$ in $\mathcal{Q}$, we have

$$\boldsymbol{a} \succsim_m \boldsymbol{b} \quad \text{iff} \quad M^{-1}(\boldsymbol{a}) \gtrsim M^{-1}(\boldsymbol{b})$$
$$\text{iff} \quad \sum_{x\in X'} M^{-1}(\boldsymbol{a})(k, x)w(k, x)$$
$$\ge \sum_{x\in X'} M^{-1}(\boldsymbol{b})(k, x)w(k, x) \quad \forall w \in W$$
$$\text{iff} \quad \sum_{i\in I, x\in X} \boldsymbol{a}(i, x)u(i, x) \ge \sum_{i\in I, x\in X} \boldsymbol{b}(i, x)u(i, x) \quad \forall u \in U. \tag{A.18}$$

And if $\{\boldsymbol{a}_n \succsim_m \boldsymbol{b}_n\}$ is a basis for $\succsim_m$ under our axioms, then $\{M^{-1}(\boldsymbol{a}_n) \gtrsim M^{-1}(\boldsymbol{b}_n)\}$ is a basis for $\gtrsim$. So by Nau's result, W is the set of w in $W^\star$ satisfying $\{U_w(M^{-1}(\boldsymbol{a}_n)) \ge U_w(M^{-1}(\boldsymbol{b}_n))\}$. So U is the set of u in $U^\star$ satisfying $\{U_u(\boldsymbol{a}_n) \ge U_u(\boldsymbol{b}_n)\}$. This proves our lemma.

It remains to show that if all our $\succsim_i$ are N*-conformable, and if $\succsim_m$ satisfies the Strong Pareto Condition with respect to our $\succsim_i$, then for each i in I, the set

$U_i = \{u(i, \cdot) \mid u \in U\}$ represents $\succeq_i$ in the sense of (6.5). This follows by a reasoning parallel to that in the proof of the Basic Representation Theorem, in light of the bijection H between $\mathcal{O}$ and $\mathcal{Q}^i_{p=1} = \{a \in \mathcal{Q} \mid \sum_{x \in X} a(i, x) = 1\}$. □

The Expected Value Theorem for Incompleteness

The derivation of the Expected Value Theorem for Incompleteness from the Representation Theorem for Incompleteness and the prospect-explications is parallel to that of the Expected Value Theorem from the Basic Representation Theorem.

The Representation Theorem for Incompleteness and Probabilities

From the Representation Theorem for Incompleteness we know that if all your $\succeq_i$ are N*-conformable and strictly non-uniform, and if your $\succeq_m$ is N-conformable and satisfies the Strong Pareto Condition with respect to your $\succeq_i$, there's a non-empty closed convex set $U \subset U^*$ of functions, such that for all a and b in $\mathcal{Q}$, all a and b in $\mathcal{O}$ and all i in I,

$$a \succeq_m b \quad \text{iff} \quad \sum_{i \in I, x \in X} a(i, x) u(i, x) \geq \sum_{i \in I, x \in X} b(i, x) u(i, x) \quad \forall u \in U, \quad \text{and} \quad \text{(A.19)}$$

$$a \succeq_i b \quad \text{iff} \quad \sum_{x \in X} a(x) u(i, x) \geq \sum_{x \in X} b(x) u(i, x) \quad \forall u \in U, \quad \text{(A.20)}$$

where if $\{a_n \succeq_m b_n\}$ is a basis for $\succeq_m$ under these axioms, then U is the set of u in U^* satisfying $\{U_u(a_n) \geq U_u(b_n)\}$. We first prove that if your $\tilde{\succeq}_m$ is N-conformable and satisfies the Reduction Axiom for some positive probability distribution P on I together with your $\succeq_m$, P and U represent your $\tilde{\succeq}_m$ in the sense of (6.8). To see this, define a function $N_P : \mathcal{K} \to \mathcal{Q}^P$; $a \mapsto N_P(a)$, such that for all i in I and x in X,

$$N_P(a)(i, x) = P(i) a(i, x). \quad \text{(A.21)}$$

Since $a = L(N_P(a))$, (A.19) and the Reduction Axiom imply that for all a and b in $\mathcal{K}$,

$$a \tilde{\succeq}_m b \quad \text{iff} \quad N_P(a) \succeq_m N_P(b)$$

$$\text{iff} \quad \sum_{i \in I, x \in X} N_P(a)(i, x) u(i, x)$$

$$\geq \sum_{i \in I, x \in X} N_P(b)(i, x) u(i, x) \quad \forall u \in U$$

$$\text{iff} \quad \sum_{i \in I, x \in X} a(i,x)P(i)u(i,x)$$

$$\geq \sum_{i \in I, x \in X} b(i,x)P(i)u(i,x) \quad \forall u \in U. \tag{A.22}$$

It remains to show that there's no other probability distribution $Q \neq P$ that represents your $\succsim_m$ in the sense of (6.8). By way of negation, suppose there is such a probability distribution Q. We define lotteries in $\mathcal{Q}^P$ and $\mathcal{K}$ that lead to contradiction. Since $Q \neq P$, there must be h and k in I with $P(h) > Q(h)$ and $P(k) < Q(k)$. Since each i is strictly non-uniform, for each i, there are $\bar{x}_i, \tilde{x}_i, x_i, \underline{x}_i$ in X such that $a_{(i,\bar{x}_i)} \succ_m a_{(i,\tilde{x}_i)} \succ_m a_{(i,x_i)} \succ_m a_{(i,\underline{x}_i)}$. Now for any $r \in [0,1]$, define a_r and b_r in $\mathcal{Q}^P$ by

$$\begin{aligned}
a_r(h, \bar{x}_h) &= r \cdot P(h), & b_r(k, \underline{x}_k) &= r \cdot P(k), \\
a_r(h, \underline{x}_h) &= (1-r) \cdot P(h), & b_r(k, \bar{x}_k) &= (1-r) \cdot P(k), \\
a_r(k, \underline{x}_k) &= P(k), & b_r(h, \underline{x}_h) &= P(h),
\end{aligned}$$

and assume that a_r and b_r agree outside h and k (i.e. that $a_r(i,x) = b_r(i,x)$ for all x in X and i in $I \smallsetminus \{h,k\}$). Similarly, define a_r and b_r in $\mathcal{K}$ by

$$\begin{aligned}
a_r(h, \bar{x}_h) &= r, & b_r(k, \underline{x}_k) &= r, \\
a_r(h, \underline{x}_h) &= (1-r), & b_r(k, \bar{x}_k) &= (1-r), \\
a_r(k, \underline{x}_k) &= 1, & b_r(h, \underline{x}_h) &= 1,
\end{aligned}$$

and assume that a_r and b_r agree outside h and k. Since $a_r = L(a_r)$, and $b_r = L(b_r)$, the Reduction Axiom implies that $a_r \succsim_m b_r$ if and only if $a_r \succsim_m b_r$ for any $r \in [0,1]$. So if Q represents your $\succsim_m$, then for any $r \in [0,1]$,

$$\sum_{i \in I, x \in X} a_r(i,x)u(i,x) \geq \sum_{i \in I, x \in X} b_r(i,x)u(i,x) \quad \forall u \in U \quad \text{iff}$$

$$\sum_{i \in I, x \in X} a_r(i,x)Q(i)u(i,x) \geq \sum_{i \in I, x \in X} b_r(i,x)Q(i)u(i,x) \quad \forall u \in U. \tag{A.23}$$

The left-hand side of the biconditional (A.23) is equivalent to

$$rP(h)u(h, \bar{x}_h) + (1-r)P(h)u(h, \underline{x}_h) + P(k)u(k, \underline{x}_k)$$
$$\geq rP(k)u(k, \underline{x}_k) + (1-r)P(k)u(k, \bar{x}_k) + P(h)u(h, \underline{x}_h) \quad \forall u \in U, \tag{A.24}$$

or

$$rP(h)\big(u(h, \bar{x}_h) - u(h, \underline{x}_h)\big)$$
$$\geq (1-r)P(k)\big(u(k, \bar{x}_k) - u(k, \underline{x}_k)\big) \quad \forall u \in U. \tag{A.25}$$

Similarly, the right-hand side of (A.23) is equivalent to

$$rQ(h)\big(u(h,\bar{x}_h) - u(h,\underline{x}_h)\big)$$
$$\geq (1-r)Q(k)\big(u(k,\bar{x}_k) - u(k,\underline{x}_k)\big) \quad \forall u \in U. \tag{A.26}$$

Now, define $\tilde{r} = \inf\{r \in [0,1] \mid$ (A.25) holds$\}$. Such an infimum must exist, since the set $\{r \in [0,1] \mid$ (A.25) holds$\}$ is nonempty and bounded. Suppose $\tilde{r} = 0$. Then $\{\boldsymbol{a}_{1/n}\}$ and $\{\boldsymbol{b}_{1/n}\}$ would be two sequences with $\boldsymbol{a}_{1/n} \succeq \boldsymbol{b}_{1/n}$ for all $n \in \mathbb{N}$; hence Sequence-Continuity would imply that $\boldsymbol{a}_0 \succeq \boldsymbol{b}_0$, which (given that P is positive) contradicts our assumptions about $\bar{x}_k$ and $\underline{x}_k$. So $\tilde{r} > 0$. Similarly, suppose $\tilde{r} = 1$. Then

$$\sup\left\{\frac{u(k,\bar{x}_k) - u(k,\underline{x}_k)}{u(h,\bar{x}_h) - u(h,\underline{x}_h)} \;\middle|\; u \in U\right\} = \infty. \tag{A.27}$$

Since $U \in U^\star$, $1 \geq u(k,\bar{x}_k) - u(k,\underline{x}_k)$ for all u in U. Hence

$$\inf\{u(h,\bar{x}_h) - u(h,\underline{x}_h) \mid u \in U\} = 0, \tag{A.28}$$

which contradicts our assumptions about $\bar{x}_h$ and $\underline{x}_h$. So $1 > \tilde{r}$. Moreover, given Sequence-Continuity, we have $\boldsymbol{a}_{\tilde{r}} \succeq_m \boldsymbol{b}_{\tilde{r}}$. However, since $P(h) > Q(h)$ and $P(k) < Q(k)$, (A.26) can't hold for $r = \tilde{r}$. So Q can't represent your $\tilde{\succeq}_m$.[150] $\qquad \square$

The Expected Value Theorem for Incompleteness and Probabilities

The derivation of the Expected Value Theorem for Incompleteness and Probabilities from the Representation Theorem for Incompleteness and Probabilities and the judgment-explications is parallel to that of the Expected Value Theorem from the Basic Representation Theorem.

---

[150] A similar proof is given by Karni and Schmeidler (1980, 12 f.) for the uniqueness of a probability distribution in a theorem featuring simple utility functions rather than sets.

Bibliography

Aboodi, R. (2017). One thought too few: Where de dicto moral motivation is necessary. Ethical Theory and Moral Practice, 20(2), 223–237.

Aboodi, R., Borer, A. and Enoch, D. (2008). Deontology, individualism, and uncertainty: A reply to Jackson and Smith. Journal of Philosophy, 105(5), 259–272.

Allais, M. (1953). Le comportement de l'homme rationnel devant le risque: Critique des postulats et axiomes de l'école américaine. Econometrica, 21(4), 503–546.

Arrhenius, G. (forthcoming). Population Ethics: The Challenge of Future Generations. Oxford: Oxford University Press.

Bader, R. (forthcoming). Person-affecting utilitarianism. In G. Arrhenius, K. Bykvist, T. Campbell and E. Finneron-Burns (Eds.), Oxford Handbook of Population Ethics, Oxford: Oxford University Press.

Bales, R. E. (1971). Act-utilitarianism: Account of right-making characteristics or decision-making procedure? American Philosophical Quarterly, 8(3), 257–265.

Barnett, Z. (forthcoming). Rational moral ignorance. Philosophy and Phenomenological Research.

Barry, C. and Tomlin, P. (2016). Moral uncertainty and permissibility: Evaluating option sets. Canadian Journal of Philosophy, 46(6), 1–26.

Barry, C. and Tomlin, P. (2019). Moral uncertainty and the criminal law. In L. Alexander and K. K. Ferzan (Eds.), The Palgrave Handbook of Applied Ethics and the Criminal Law, London: Palgrave Macmillan.

Basu, K. (1983). Cardinal utility, utilitarianism, and a class of invariance axioms in welfare analysis. Journal of Mathematical Economies, 12(3), 193–206.

Beckstead, N. (2013). On the Overwhelming Importance of Shaping the Far Future. PhD thesis, Rutgers University.

Beddor, B. (2020). Fallibility for expressivists. Australasian Journal of Philosophy, 98(4), 763–777.

Bernoulli, D. (1954). Exposition of a new theory on the measurement of risk. Econometrica, 22(1), 23–36.

Binmore, K. and Voorhoeve, A. (2003). Defending transitivity against Zeno's paradox. Philosophy and Public Affairs, 31(3), 272–279.

Björkholm, S., Bykvist, K. and Olson, J. (forthcoming). Quasi-realism and normative certitude. Synthese.

Bossert, W. (1991). On intra- and interpersonal utility comparisons. Social Choice and Welfare, 8(3), 207–219.

Bossert, W., Blackorby, C. and Donaldson, D. (2005). Population Issues in Social Choice Theory, Welfare Economics, and Ethics. Cambridge: Cambridge University Press.

Bossert, W. and Stehling, F. (1994). On the uniqueness of cardinally interpreted utility functions. In W. Eichhorn (Ed.), Models and Measurement of Welfare and Inequality, Berlin: Springer.

Bossert, W. and Weymark, J. A. (2004). Utility in social choice. In S. Barbera, P. Hammond and C. Seidl (Eds.), Handbook of Utility Theory, Volume 2: Extensions, Dordrecht: Kluwer.

Bostrom, N. (2003). Astronomical waste: The opportunity cost of delayed technological development. Utilitas, 15(3), 308–314.

Briggs, R. A. (2019). Normative theories of rational choice: Expected utility. In E. N. Zalta (Ed.), The Stanford Encyclopedia of Philosophy, Metaphysics Research Lab, Stanford University, Fall 2019 Edition.

Broome, J. (1990). Fairness. Proceedings of the Aristotelian Society, 91(1), 87–102.

Broome, J. (1991). Weighing Goods. Oxford: Blackwell.

Broome, J. (1997). Is incommensurability vagueness? In R. Chang (Ed.), Incommensurability, Incomparability and Practical Reason, Cambridge, MA: Harvard University Press.

Broome, J. (2004). Weighing Lives. Oxford: Oxford University Press.

Broome, J. (2012). Climate Matters: Ethics in a Warming World. New York: W.W. Norton and Company.

Broome, J. (2013). Rationality Through Reasoning. Oxford: Oxford University Press.

Buchak, L. (2013). Risk and Rationality. Oxford: Oxford University Press.

Bykvist, K. (2009a). No good fit: Why the fitting attitude analysis of value fails. Mind, 118(469), 1–30.

Bykvist, K. (2009b). Objective versus subjective moral oughts. Uppsala Philosophical Studies, 57, 39–65.

Bykvist, K. (2013). Evaluative uncertainty and consequentialist environmental ethics. In L. Kahn and A. Hiller (Eds.), Environmental Ethics and Consequentialism, London: Routledge.

Bykvist, K. (2017). Moral uncertainty. Philosophy Compass, 12(3), 1–8.

Bykvist, K. and Olson, J. (2009). Expressivism and moral certitude. Philosophical Quarterly, 59(235), 202–215.

Bykvist, K. and Olson, J. (2012). Against the being for account of normative certitude. Journal of Ethics and Social Philosophy, 6(2), 1–8.

Bykvist, K. and Olson, J. (2017). Non-cognitivism and fundamental moral certitude: Reply to Eriksson and Francén Olinder. Australasian Journal of Philosophy, 95(4), 794–799.

Callicott, J. B. (1989). In Defense of the Land Ethic: Essays in Environmental Philosophy. New York: State University of New York Press.

Carr, J. R. (forthcoming). Normative uncertainty without theories. Australasian Journal of Philosophy.

Chisholm, R. (1980). A version of foundationalism. Midwest Studies in Philosophy, 5(1), 543–564.

Christensen, D. (1994). Conservatism in epistemology. Noûs, 28(1), 69–89.

Christensen, D. (2001). Preference-based arguments for probabilism. Philosophy of Science, 68(3), 356–376.

Cohen, G. A. (1989). On the currency of egalitarian justice. Ethics, 99(4), 906–944.

Crisp, R. (2000). Review of 'Value . . . and What Follows', by Joel Kupperman. Philosophy, 75(3), 458–462.

Crisp, R. (2006). Hedonism reconsidered. Philosophy and Phenomenological Research, 73(3), 619–645.

D'Arms, J. and Jacobson, D. (2000). The moralistic fallacy: On the 'appropriateness' of emotions. Philosophy and Phenomenological Research, 61(1), 65–90.

de Finetti, B. (1980). Foresight: Its logical laws, its subjective sources. In H. E. Kyburg and H. E. Smokler (Eds.), Studies in Subjective Probability, Malabar: Robert E. Krieger Publishing Company.

Diamond, P. (1967). Cardinal welfare, individualistic ethics, and interpersonal comparison of utility: A comment. Journal of Political Economy, 75(5), 765–766.

Dietrich, F. and Jabarian, B. (2018). Decision under normative uncertainty. Documents de travail du Centre d'Economie de la Sorbonne, Université Panthéon-Sorbonne, Centre d'Economie de la Sorbonne.

Dietrich, F. and Jabarian, B. (2021). Expected value under normative uncertainty. Documents de travail du Centre d'Economie de la Sorbonne, Université Panthéon-Sorbonne, Centre d'Economie de la Sorbonne.

Doob, J. L. (1971). What is a martingale? The American Mathematical Monthly, 78(5), 451–463.

Dovidio, J. F. and Gaertner, S. L. (2000). Aversive racism and selection decisions: 1989 and 1999. Psychological Science, 11(4), 315–319.

Drèze, J. (1987). Decision theory with moral hazard and state-dependent preferences. In Essays on Economic Decisions under Uncertainty, Cambridge: Cambridge University Press.

Elga, A. (2010). Subjective probabilities should be sharp. Philosophers' Imprint, 10(5), 1–11.

Elgin, C. (1996). Considered Judgment. Princeton: Princeton University Press.

Ellsberg, D. (1961). Risk, ambiguity, and the Savage axioms. The Quarterly Journal of Economics, 75(4), 643–669.

Eriksson, J. and Francén Olinder, R. (2016). Non-cognitivism and the classification account of moral uncertainty. Australasian Journal of Philosophy, 94(4), 719–735.

Eriksson, L. and Hájek, A. (2007). What are degrees of belief? Studia Logica, 86(2), 183–213.

Feldman, F. (2006). Actual utility, the objection from impracticality, and the move to expected utility. Philosophical Studies, 129(1), 49–79.

FitzPatrick, W. J. (2017). Unwitting wrongdoing, reasonable expectations, and blameworthiness. In P. Robichaud and J. W. Wieland (Eds.), Responsibility: The Epistemic Condition, Oxford: Oxford University Press.

Fleurbaey, M. and Voorhoeve, A. (2013). Decide as you would with full information! An argument against ex ante Pareto. In N. Eyal, S. Hurst, O. Norheim and D. Wikler (Eds.), Inequalities in Health: Concepts, Measures, and Ethics, Oxford: Oxford University Press.

Foley, R. (1983). Epistemic conservatism. Philosophical Studies, 43(2), 165–182.

Fox, P. (2019). Revisiting the argument from action guidance. Journal of Ethics and Social Philosophy, 15(3), 222–254.

Gaertner, S. L. and McLaughlin, J. P. (1983). Racial stereotypes: Associations and ascriptions of positive and negative characteristics. Social Psychology Quarterly, 46(1), 23–30.

Geyer, J. (2018). Moral uncertainty and moral culpability. Utilitas, 30(4), 399–416.

Gilboa, I., Samuelson, L. and Schmeidler, D. (2014). No-betting Pareto dominance. Econometrica, 82(4), 1405–1442.

Good, I. (1967). On the principle of total evidence. British Journal for the Philosophy of Science, 17(4), 319–321.

Gracely, E. (1996). On the noncomparability of judgments made by different ethical theories. Metaphilosophy, 27(3), 327–332.

Greaves, H. (2015). Antiprioritarianism. Utilitas, 1(27), 1–42.

Greaves, H. (2017). A reconsideration of the Harsanyi-Sen-Weymark debate on utilitarianism. Utilitas, 29(2), 175–213.

Greaves, H. and Ord, T. (2017). Moral uncertainty about population axiology. Journal of Ethics and Social Philosophy, 12(2), 135–167.

Greene, J. D., Sommerville, R. B., Nystrom, L. E., Darley, J. M. and Cohen, J. D. (2001). An fMRI investigation of emotional engagement in moral judgment. Science, 293(5537), 2105–2108.

Greenwald, A. G. and Banaji, M. R. (1995). Implicit social cognition: Attitudes, self-esteem, and stereotypes. Psychological Review, 102(1), 4–27.

Guerrero, A. A. (2007). Don't know, don't kill: Moral ignorance, culpability, and caution. Philosophical Studies, 136(1), 59–97.

Gustafsson, J. E. and Torpman, T. O. (2014). In defence of My Favourite Theory. Pacific Philosophical Quarterly, 95(2), 159–174.

Hájek, A. (2008). Arguments for – or against – probabilism? British Journal for the Philosophy of Science, 59(4), 793–819.

Hájek, A. (2019). Interpretations of probability. In E. N. Zalta (Ed.), The Stanford Encyclopedia of Philosophy, Metaphysics Research Lab, Stanford University, Fall 2019 Edition.

Harman, E. (2015). The irrelevance of moral uncertainty. In R. Shafer-Landau (Ed.), Oxford Studies in Metaethics, Vol. 10, Oxford: Oxford University Press.

Harsanyi, J. (1955). Cardinal welfare, individualistic ethics and interpersonal comparisons of utility. Journal of Political Economy, 63(4), 309–321.

Hedden, B. (2016). Does MITE make right? On decision-making under normative uncertainty. In R. Shafer-Landau (Ed.), Oxford Studies in Metaethics, Vol. 11, Oxford: Oxford University Press.

Hicks, A. (2018). Moral uncertainty and value comparison. In R. Shafer-Landau (Ed.), Oxford Studies in Metaethics, Vol. 13, Oxford: Oxford University Press.

Hicks, A. (2019). Moral hedging and responding to reasons. Pacific Philosophical Quarterly, 100(3), 765–789.

Howard-Synder, F. (1997). The rejection of objective consequentialism. Utilitas, 9(2), 241–248.

Hudson, J. (1989). Subjectivization in ethics. American Philosophical Quarterly, 26(3), 221–229.

Huemer, M. (2008). In defence of repugnance. Mind, 117(468), 899–933.

Jackson, F. (1991). Decision-theoretic consequentialism and the nearest and dearest objection. Ethics, 101(3), 461–482.

Jackson, F. and Smith, M. (2006). Absolutist moral theories and uncertainty. Journal of Philosophy, 103(6), 267–283.

Jaynes, E. T. (1957a). Information theory and statistical mechanics. Physical Review, 106(4), 620–630.

Jaynes, E. T. (1957b). Information theory and statistical mechanics ii. Physical Review, 108(2), 171–190.

Joyce, J. (1999). The Foundations of Causal Decision Theory. Cambridge: Cambridge University Press.

Joyce, J. (2005). How probabilities reflect evidence. Philosophical Perspectives, 19(1), 153–178.

Joyce, J. (2010). A defense of imprecise credences in inference and decision making. Philosophical Perspectives, 24(1), 281–323.

Karni, E. (1985). Decision Making under Uncertainty: The Case of State-Dependent Preferences. Cambridge, MA: Harvard University Press.

Karni, E. and Schmeidler, D. (1980). An expected utility theory for state-dependent preferences. The Foerder Institute of Economic Research, Tel Aviv University, Working Paper 48-80.

Karni, E. and Schmeidler, D. (2016). An expected utility theory for state-dependent preferences. Theory and Decision, 81(4), 467–478.

Keynes, J. M. (1921). A Treatise on Probability. London: Macmillan.

Kolodny, N. and MacFarlane, J. (ms). Ought: Between subjective and objective. Manuscript.

Koplin, J. and Wilkinson, D. (2019). Moral uncertainty and the farming of human-pig chimeras. Journal of Medical Ethics, 45(7), 440–446.

Korsgaard, C. (1996). The Sources of Normativity. Cambridge: Cambridge University Press.

Kvanvig, J. (1989). Conservatism and its virtues. Synthese, 79(1), 143–163.

Lazar, S. (2018). In dubious battle: Uncertainty and the ethics of killing. Philosophical Studies, 175(4), 859–883.

Lewis, D. (1980). A subjectivist's guide to objective chance. In R. Jeffrey (Ed.), Studies in Inductive Logic and Probability, Vol. 2, Berkeley: University of Berkeley Press.

List, C. (2003). Are interpersonal comparisons of utility indeterminate? Erkenntnis, 58(2), 229–260.

Lockhart, T. (2000). Moral Uncertainty and its Consequences. Oxford: Oxford University Press.

Lovett, A. and Riedener, S. (2019). On keeping things in proportion. Journal of Ethics and Social Philosophy, 16(3), 229–258.

MacAskill, W. (2014). Decision-Making under Normative Uncertainty. PhD thesis, University of Oxford.

MacAskill, W. (2016a). Normative uncertainty as a voting problem. Mind, 125(500), 967–1004.

MacAskill, W. (2016b). Smokers, psychos, and decision-theoretic uncertainty. Journal of Philosophy, 113(9), 425–445.

MacAskill, W. (2019). Practical ethics given moral uncertainty. Utilitas, 31(3), 231–245.

MacAskill, W., Bykvist, K. and Ord, T. (2020a). Moral Uncertainty. Oxford: Oxford University Press.

MacAskill, W., Cotton-Barratt, O. and Ord, T. (2020b). Statistical normalization methods in interpersonal and intertheoretic comparisons. Journal of Philosophy, 117(2), 61–95.

MacAskill, W. and Ord, T. (2020). Why maximize expected choiceworthiness? Noûs, 54(2), 327–353.

Maher, P. (1993). Betting on Theories. New York: Cambridge University Press.

McCain, K. (2008). The virtues of epistemic conservatism. Synthese, 164(2), 185–200.

McClennen, E. F. (2009). The normative status of the independence principle. In P. Anand, P. Pattanaik and C. Puppe (Eds.), The Handbook of Rational and Social Choice, Oxford: Oxford University Press.

McMahan, J. (2010). The meat eaters. The New York Times, September 19, 2010.

McShane, K. (2017). Is biodiversity intrinsically valuable? (And what might that mean?). In J. Garson, A. Plutynski and S. Sarkar (Eds.), Routledge Handbook of Philosophy of Biodiversity, Abingdon: Routledge.

Meacham, C. J. G. and Weisberg, J. (2011). Representation theorems and the foundations of decision theory. Australasian Journal of Philosophy, 89(4), 641–663.

Mill, J. S. (1998 [1861]). Utilitarianism. R. Crisp (Ed.). New York: Oxford University Press.

Moller, D. (2011). Abortion and moral risk. Philosophy, 86(337), 425–443.

Mongin, P. and D'Aspremont, C. (1998). Utility theory and ethics. In S. Barbera, P. Hammond and C. Seidl (Eds.), Handbook of Utility Theory, Volume 1: Principles, Dordrecht: Kluwer.

Nagel, T. (1979). The fragmentation of value. In Mortal Questions, Cambridge: Cambridge University Press.

Nau, R. (2006). The shape of incomplete preferences. The Annals of Statistics, 34(5), 2430–2448.

Ng, Y.-K. (1997). A case for happiness, cardinalism, and interpersonal comparability. The Economic Journal, 107(445), 1848–1858.

Nissan-Rozen, I. (2015). Against moral hedging. Economics and Philosophy, 31(3), 349–369.

Nover, H. and Hájek, A. (2004). Vexing expectations. Mind, 113(450), 237–249.

Nozick, R. (1974). Anarchy, State, and Utopia. New York: Basic Books.

Oddie, G. (1994). Moral uncertainty and human embryo experimentation. In K. W. M. Fulford, G. Gillet and J. M. Soskice (Eds.), Medicine and Moral Reasoning, Cambridge: Cambridge University Press.

Ok, E. A., Ortoleva, P. and Riella, G. (2012). Incomplete preferences under uncertainty: Indecisiveness in beliefs vs. tastes. Econometrica, 80(4), 1791–1808.

Parfit, D. (1984). Reasons and Persons. Oxford: Oxford University Press.

Parfit, D. (1997). Equality and priority. Ratio, 10(3), 202–221.

Parfit, D. (ms). How we can avoid the repugnant conclusion. Manuscript.

Pfeiffer, R. S. (1985). Abortion policy and the argument from uncertainty. Social Theory and Practice, 11(3), 371–386.

Pyke, S. (1993). Philosophers. Manchester: Cornerhouse Publications.

Rachels, S. (1998). Counterexamples to the transitivity of better than. Australasian Journal of Philosophy, 76(1), 71–83.

Raiffa, H. (1968). Decision Analysis: Introductory Lectures on Choices under Uncertainty. Reading, MA: Addison-Wesley.

Ramsey, F. P. (1990 [1926]). Truth and probability. In D. Mellor (Ed.), F. P. Ramsey: Philosophical Papers, Cambridge: Cambridge University Press.

Rawls, J. (1980). Kantian constructivism in moral theory. Journal of Philosophy, 77(9), 515–572.

Raz, J. (1986). The Morality of Freedom. Oxford: Clarendon.

Richardson, H. (1994). Practical Reasoning about Final Ends. Cambridge: Cambridge University Press.

Ridge, M. (2020). Normative certitude for expressivists. Synthese, 197(8), 3325–3347.

Roberts, M. (2003). Is the person-affecting intuition paradoxical? Theory and Decision, 55(1), 1–44.

Robichaud, P. and Wieland, J. W. (2017). Responsibility: The Epistemic Condition. Oxford: Oxford University Press.

Rosen, G. (2003). Culpability and ignorance. Proceedings of the Aristotelian Society, 103(1), 61–84.

Rosen, G. (2004). Skepticism about moral responsibility. Philosophical Perspectives, 18(1), 295–313.

Ross, J. (2006). Rejecting ethical deflationism. Ethics, 116(4), 742–768.

Savage, L. (1954). The Foundations of Statistics. New York: Dover.

Scanlon, T. M. (1998). What We Owe to Each Other. Cambridge, MA: Harvard University Press.

Schulz, M. (2020). Uncertain preferences in rational decision. Inquiry: An Interdisciplinary Journal of Philosophy, 63(6), 605–627.

Schwitzgebel, E. (2010). Acting contrary to our professed beliefs or the gulf between occurrent judgment and dispositional belief. Pacific Philosophical Quarterly, 91(4), 531–553.

Schwitzgebel, E. (2014). The moral behavior of ethicists and the role of the philosopher. In C. Luetge, H. Rusch and M. Uhl (Eds.), Experimental Ethics: Toward an Empirical Moral Philosophy, London: Palgrave Macmillan.

Schwitzgebel, E. and Rust, J. (2014). The moral behavior of ethics professors: Relationships among self-reported behavior, expressed normative attitude, and directly observed behavior. Philosophical Psychology, 27(3), 293–327.

Sepielli, A. (2009). What to do when you don't know what to do. In R. Shafer-Landau (Ed.), Oxford Studies in Metaethics, Vol. 4, Oxford: Oxford University Press.

Sepielli, A. (2010). 'Along an Imperfectly Lighted Path': Practical Rationality and Normative Uncertainty. PhD thesis, Rutgers University.

Sepielli, A. (2012). Normative uncertainty for non-cognitivists. Philosophical Studies, 160(2), 191–207.

Sepielli, A. (2013a). Moral uncertainty and the Principle of Equity among Moral Theories. Philosophy and Phenomenological Research, 86(3), 580–589.

Sepielli, A. (2013b). What to do when you don't know what to do when you don't know what to do.... Noûs, 47(1), 521–544.

Sepielli, A. (2014). Should you look before you leap? The Philosophers' Magazine, 66(3), 89–93.

Sepielli, A. (2016). Moral uncertainty and fetishistic motivation. Philosophical Studies, 173(11), 2951–2968.

Sepielli, A. (2018). How moral uncertaintism can be both true and interesting. In M. Timmons (Ed.), Oxford Studies in Normative Ethics, Vol. 7, Oxford: Oxford University Press.

Sidgwick, H. (1907). The Methods of Ethics. London: Macmillan.

Sinnott-Armstrong, W. (1985). Moral dilemmas and incomparability. American Philosophical Quarterly, 22(4), 321–329.

Skyrms, B. (1980). Causal Necessity: A Pragmatic Investigation of the Necessity of Laws. New Haven and London: Yale University Press.

Smith, M. (1994). The Moral Problem. Oxford: Basil Blackwell.

Smith, M. (2002). Evaluation, uncertainty and motivation. Ethical Theory and Moral Practice, 5(3), 305–320.

Strohminger, N., Caldwell, B., Cameron, D., Borg, J. S. and Sinnott-Armstrong, W. (2014). Implicit morality: A methodological survey. In C. Luetge, H. Rusch and M. Uhl (Eds.), Experimental Ethics: Toward an Empirical Moral Philosophy, London: Palgrave Macmillan.

Talbott, W. (2016). Bayesian epistemology. In E. N. Zalta (Ed.), The Stanford Encyclopedia of Philosophy, Metaphysics Research Lab, Stanford University, Winter 2016 Edition.

Tarsney, C. (2017). Rationality and Moral Risk: A Moderate Defense of Hedging. PhD thesis, University of Maryland.

Tarsney, C. (2018a). Intertheoretic value comparison: A modest proposal. Journal of Moral Philosophy, 15(3), 324–344.

Tarsney, C. (2018b). Moral uncertainty for deontologists. Ethical Theory and Moral Practice, 21(3), 505–520.

Tarsney, C. (2019a). Normative uncertainty and social choice. Mind, 128(512), 1285–1308.

Tarsney, C. (2019b). Rejecting supererogationism. Pacific Philosophical Quarterly, 100(2), 599–623.

Tarsney, C. (ms). Metanormative regress: An escape plan. Manuscript.

Taylor, P. W. (1986). Respect for Nature: A Theory of Environmental Ethics. Princeton: Princeton University Press.

Temkin, L. (2012). Rethinking The Good: Moral Ideals and the Nature of Practical Reasoning. Oxford: Oxford University Press.

Tenenbaum, S. (2017). Action, deontology, and risk: Against the multiplicative model. Ethics, 127(3), 674–707.

Thesiger, W. (2008). Arabian Sands. London: Penguin Books.

Trammell, P. (forthcoming). Fixed-point solutions to the regress problem in normative uncertainty. Synthese.

Vahid, H. (2004). Varieties of Epistemic Conservatism. Synthese, 141(1), 97–122.

Vallentyne, P. (1993). The connection between prudential and moral goodness. Journal of Social Philosophy, 24(2), 105–128.

von Kries, J. (1886). Die Principien der Wahrscheinlichkeitsrechnung. Tübingen: Mohr.

von Neumann, J. and Morgenstern, O. (1944). Theory of Games and Economic Behavior. Princeton: Princeton University Press.

Voorhoeve, A. (2013). Vaulting intuition: Temkin's critique of transitivity. Philosophy and Economics, 29(3), 409–425.

Weatherson, B. (2014). Running risks morally. Philosophical Studies, 167(1), 141–163.

Weirich, P. (1986). Expected utility and risk. British Journal for the Philosophy of Science, 37(4), 419–442.

White, R. (2010). Evidential symmetry and mushy credence. In T. S. Gendler and J. Hawthorne (Eds.), Oxford Studies in Epistemology, Vol. 3, Oxford: Oxford University Press.

Wiland, E. (2005). Monkeys, typewriters, and objective consequentialism. Ratio, 18(3), 352–360.

Willenken, T. (2012). Deontic cycling and the structure of commonsense morality. Ethics, 122(3), 545–561.

Williams, E. G. (2011). Ethics Under Moral Neutrality. PhD thesis, Rutgers University.

Williamson, J. (2010). In Defence of Objective Bayesianism. Oxford: Oxford University Press.

Zimmerman, M. (2008). Living with Uncertainty. Cambridge: Cambridge University Press.

Zynda, L. (2000). Representation theorems and realism about degrees of belief. Philosophy of Science, 67(1), 45–69.

Index Rerum

Index Nominum

This index only includes people mentioned in the main text, or discussed at some length in the footnotes. Simple references to authors in footnotes are not included.

www.ingramcontent.com/pod-product-compliance
Lightning Source LLC
Chambersburg PA
CBHW030935090426
42737CB00007B/433